MISADVENTURES
OF A
FLY FISHERMAN

JACK HEMINGWAY

MISADVENTURES
—OF A—
FLY FISHERMAN

My Life With and Without Papa

TAYLOR PUBLISHING COMPANY
DALLAS, TEXAS

Library of Congress Cataloging in Publication Data

Hemingway, Jack. 1923-
  Misadventures of a fly fisherman. Includes Index.

  1. Fly fishing. 2. Hemingway, Jack, 1923- —Biog-
raphy. 3. Hemingway, Ernest, 1899-1961. 4. Fishers—
Biography. 5. Authors, American—20th century—Biography.
I. Title.
SH46.H38 1986   796.5'092'4 [B]   86-1876
ISBN 0-87833-379-7

Printed in the United States of America

0 9 8 7 6 5 4 3 2 1

*This book is for my beloved Puck
and our daughters, Joan, Margot and Mariel*

ACKNOWLEDGMENTS

I would like to acknowledge the sacrifice, encouragement and support of my first editor, Jim Nelson Black, as well as the fine and diplomatic editorial skills of my editor, James A. Bryans. Special thanks are due to Dan Callaghan and Everett Wood, both of whom needled, cajoled, insisted and kept faith over the years, and to all the friends who share my love of nature, of the good life and of the hard life.

Jack Hemingway, Idaho 1986

AUTHOR'S FOREWORD

On October 10, 1923, my father, who later described himself as a writer of hardcover books, hurried from the train station to Toronto General Hospital where his wife, Hadley, had given birth seven hours earlier to a healthy male child, me. After assuring himself that all was well, he checked in at the *Toronto Star* where his boss, Harry Hindmarsh, the city editor, tore into him abusively for not having checked into the editorial offices before going to the hospital to see his wife and newborn son.

Three months later we were sneaking out of our apartment to avoid the landlord—the lease still had time to run—to catch the train to New York where we would board the boat for France and my father and mother's return to Paris. My mother didn't feel safe until the Cunard liner, the *Antonia*, was well at sea after its stop in St. John's, Newfoundland. Until that moment, she was sure the authorities would come aboard to take us off the ship.

Paris welcomed them back. We moved into a noisy but relatively comfortable flat above a sawmill in a courtyard on rue Notre Dame des Champs, a short walk from Gertrude Stein, my godmother, and her friend Alice B. Toklas' handsome digs on rue de Fleurus. The Closerie des Lilas was scarcely a block away, and in those days it was still a simple cafe without frills, and cheap.

We had Marie Cocotte to help, and Papa worked hard and well, often escaping the apartment to get away from the noise of the sawmill and my occasional crying to work at one of the cafe tables. There was a little money coming in from the occasional pieces Papa wrote for the *Star* and a few poorly paid "little magazine" pieces, but the principal source of funds came from a small trust my mother had from her grandfather and an additional small inheritance from a favorite uncle.

We spent quite a lot of time in Gstaad and later in Schruns where both of them worked on their skiing, and eventually I was carried along in Papa's rucksack. We were a happy family until my father got himself into the unfortunate position of loving two women at the same time. While such affairs are not all that uncommon, it was unacceptable to him and to my mother without making a definite choice. After much self-chastisement, he made that choice and that changed life for my mother and me. For Hadley it presented a challenge which she met head on and with amazing grace and equanimity. As for me, I no longer had my Papa as an everyday father but saw him mainly only during vacation times, except during the short period soon after his marriage to Pauline when he and his new wife lived in the same neighborhood in Paris for part of the year.

This book goes into some detail about several of the incidents in those early years because they cast an interesting light on the times and the relationships involved. But the main body of this work deals with my own lot in life and how I dealt with it, especially with the role that fishing, fly fishing in particular, played in the series of incidents, adventures and misadventures which have graphically punctuated my story. I have been fortunate, over the span of sixty years, to have known some of the most fascinating men and women of our century. Those who were fly fishermen will be recalled in greater detail because the relationships will have been closer. Fishing has been a native impulse and an incentive for me as long as I can remember. My own reflections upon the subject, and upon specific experiences in a diversity of places, suggest that, beyond the entertainment they have provided, outdoor sports have a wonderful way of reflecting deeper values and, not surprisingly, values which affect our lives whether or not we fish.

This is not a fishing book except in the sense that fishing has played an important part in my life. It is my fondest hope that each reader will find amusement, entertainment, and perhaps some new insight that will make the reading worthwhile. However, any resemblance between people in this book and actual persons living or dead will be the inadvertent result of the writer's having portrayed them accurately!

John H.N. Hemingway
Sun Valley, Idaho, 1985

ONE

My first experience of fishing—which was to become a lifelong passion—was strictly as a spectator sport. There was always fishing of some sort going on along the quaisides and embankments of the Seine. Whenever I went there with Papa to visit the bookstalls, or with Tonton, my nurse's husband, a retired soldier who worked in the French civil service, we would stop and watch the fishermen of the Seine. They were, and still are, a breed that's unique. These men with weatherbeaten faces and shabby clothes, wielding long bamboo poles with goose-quill bobbers, seemed as rooted in the landscape as the ancient trees.

In the late twenties and early thirties, the great river was perhaps not so polluted as it is now, but it was by no means clean. It ran full of rich, organic sewage. Today, the sources of pollution are far more dangerous, being composed of insoluble inorganic chemical compounds. But the Seine fishermen are unchanging and eternal.

At any rate, the fishermen did seem to catch greater quantities of fish as well as more highly-prized fish for the table then than now. The degree of sophistication in tackle has changed greatly, but essentially a Seine fisherman was and is a skillful and a very patient man who is never without hope no matter how unappealing the weather or the river conditions.

You need to watch longer now to see an angler on the Seine catch a fish than you did in those bygone times. Some in the old days were successful enough to be able to sell their catches of whitebait to the small specialty restaurants which deep-fried them for finger eating. They were a great treat and a great favorite of my father's and mine.

We sometimes took the paper-wrapped fries to a bench on the Henry IV bridge. After our feast, we often tried our skill at spitting from the bridge into the funnels of the *bateaux-mouches* excursion boats that plied the current of the Seine from dawn till dusk every day of the year, except in times of serious flooding. A successful spit into a moving funnel was rare and resulted in the reward of a beer or an aperitif for Papa and a grenadine or an ice for me at one of the nearby cafes. Just watching the fishermen made me want to try to fish someday, but I never dreamed how soon it would become possible.

It was during a long weekend at the Mowrer villa in Crécy-en-Brie that I could restrain myself no longer. Paul Mowrer, a fine newspaperman from Chicago, my mother and some friends had gone for a long walk as was their custom on a Sunday afternoon. I was left alone with fat Madame Fouk, the cook, and Kimi, the fat black cat. Kimi had often followed me down to the lower end of the garden before, where we would slip out of the gate in the high old stucco-covered stone wall to the river bank. The Grand-Morin, a placid little French river with deep weed beds and a nearby mill dam, provided Paul with an ideal spot to swim and to enjoy his beloved sport of canoeing. The canoe was kept upside down on the bank next to the path and against the wall, and locked to the post with a chain and padlock.

There was a small dock extending into the water. From its outer edge I could watch the different kinds of minnows swimming in the current and among the waving strands of water weed. On this particular day I had fashioned a hook from the proverbial bent pin with pliers and a small hammer. Using some of the strong black thread Paul used to perform his marionette tricks for a fishing line, I fastened the line and the hook to a three-foot piece of willow shoot. With some of Madame Fouk's bread—the part inside the crust—I rolled some tiny dough balls and impaled one on the barbless hook. I had a difficult time fastening the thread to the pin, but somehow I managed.

I had no bobber but the water was so clear I could see the minnows attacking my baited hook as it drifted in the current. I tried to imitate the style of the Seine fishermen I had seen. It worked. Not often, but often enough to excite and encourage me. I was able to time a strike *cum* heave and found a shiny minnow flipping and squirming on the dock beside me. Kimi took advantage of me and rounded out his already rotund shape even further with a feast of minnows, but I did manage to get some back to the kitchen in my pockets.

They were well received, and after Madame Fouk had taught me how to snip their bellies with a small pair of sewing scissors to remove the guts, they were eaten as a special treat that night along with the regular dinner—although I was later admonished for using my pockets for a creel. Thereafter, I was provided with a cloth flour sack and my fishing forays became a regular feature of our Crécy weekends. I didn't know it, but a radical change had taken place in my life. I had become a fisherman and would never ever be quite the same again.

*   *   *

The roar of lions and tigers woke me with a start. My mother, Hadley, and I were in our new apartment at 98 Blvd. Auguste Blanqui at the corner of La Glacière in the working class XIIIth Arrondissement. The Metro ran above ground for a way along Auguste Blanqui and our sixth-floor flat was about two levels above the tracks. When I went to sleep I delighted in hearing through the open window the trains screech to their regular stops at the Glacière station, but lions and tigers were an altogether different matter.

I slipped out of my child's bed and sneaked into my mother's room and into her big double bed beside her. She gave me a hug and reassured me that I had only had a dream and that it wouldn't come back. Nevertheless, I stayed with her the rest of the night. My mother was a warm, cuddly person.

The next day Marie Cocotte, our housekeeper-cook and my nurse, nicknamed for her cooking specialty, chicken *en cocotte,* took me along to do the marketing. We walked across the boulevard, under the Metro, and up La Glacière toward the *place* where the street market was operating in our neighborhood that day. The small street was filled with the usual sights of the day, the coalmen with their jute sacks turned wrong-side-out on one end to fit over their heads and the main body of the sack filled with lumps of soft coal hanging over and down their backs. They carried their loads to each building. We watched the horse-drawn Nicolas wagons with their huge loads of wine barrels making deliveries, and countless bicycles and pedal-driven carts making their rounds. I was, as always, fascinated by everything, and what still stands out clearly in my memory is the smell of fresh roasting coffee and fresh-baked loaves of crusty bread which quite literally perfumed the air of what cannot have been the purest collection of scents, what with the garbage and rubbish being thrown into the gutters along the sidewalks and only at the end of the day being swept into the sewer drains.

As we passed by a large, barred gate leading into one of the courtyards, I distinctly heard the deep-throated growl and smelled the pungent odor of cat. I pulled at Marie Cocotte's arm to stop her. I told her about hearing the lions and tigers the night before. With some doubt, she spoke to the man inside the gate who, with a wink, opened the bars and let us in as a special treat. We discovered that part of a traveling circus had rented the courtyard to house their wild animals temporarily. We actually saw them in their cages from close up. It was a stirring sight that remained fresh in my mind for years. They were only there a few days at most, but I listened for them during the next few nights, which, at age four, seemed a lifetime. This time I enjoyed the sound and stayed in my own bed seeing in my mind the great gaunt beasts pacing their cages.

We had spent the previous summer, after Papa and Mother's divorce, in the States. We visited friends in New York, then went on by train to Chicago and Oak Park to visit my Grandfather and Grandmother Hemingway, for their first sight of their grandson. I was very impressed by the big old house and loved Grandfather's beard. From there we headed south to St. Louis for a visit with my mother's family, Auntie Phon and her husband, Professor Roland Usher, and my cousins who, though older than I, were still my first true American family who at least were my contemporaries.

My English improved by leaps and bounds with them. Up until then I had spoken mainly French, Austrian, and a little baby English with my mother.

We went on from St. Louis to Carmel for the balance of the summer and lived in a small rented cottage a few blocks from the beach. By early autumn I was full of new Americanisms and, beach brown from the California sun and surf, I had almost completely forgotten my French. But on returning to Paris in September, it came back immediately and, though my mother tried to keep up my English, I spent so much of my time with Marie Cocotte and her husband Tonton that the English suffered accordingly. Not until I was about nine years old did both languages remain with me on a permanent basis without constant relearning on each trip back and forth across the Atlantic.

Mother and I moved into the apartment on Auguste Blanqui because an American architect friend, Paul Nelson, had a studio penthouse there where he drew his plans for the famous Lille Hospital, one of the first in the modern style in France.

He was just one of many friends who helped us out during that period of change. Manuel Komroff, who later became well-known as an author and a regular with *Esquire* magazine, was another friend. Sometimes when Mother wanted to go out in the evenings, she would ask Komroff to stay with me and tell me stories.

Mother never lived anywhere without a piano and spent long hours practicing and playing. I think I loved her keyboard exercises as much as her playing, and they were part of my life. Whenever I hear one of her favorites, such as "Greensleeves" or Bach's "Jesu, Joy of Man's Desiring," I think of her.

Before Papa and Pauline, his new wife, moved to Key West, I spent a lot of time with both of them and met many of their friends including writers, poets, artists, musicians, and not a few scoundrels. Often on afternoons or weekends I accompanied Papa to Sylvia Beach's bookstore on Rue de l'Odeon where he would become involved in long conversations with James Joyce, Ezra Pound, John Dos Passos, Ford Madox Ford, Archie MacLeish, or any of a dozen others. I was left pretty much to myself in the bookstore and I usually played in a sort of half-loft overhead. I remember how sweet-faced Adrienne Monnier was, who had the bookshop across the street, and how plump and soft she was compared to Sylvia, with her bony face and figure.

In the first edition of *The Sun Also Rises,* which Papa dedicated to Hadley and me in 1926; he cited Gertrude Stein's remark that "You are all a lost generation." The label, which eventually stuck to that circle of friends, seems to offer a convenient handle for what appeared to be a movement, but Papa never liked the term and did not mind ridiculing anyone who took too much stock in it. Papa wrote with the conviction that an artist had to conquer his own devils. This eventually prompted some disagreements with his early friends, Gertrude Stein and Sherwood Anderson. He invariably seemed to prefer the company of those other artists and writers in Paris who shared the reality of hard work.

I especially liked going to the Right Bank when Papa or Mother would have to go to the Guaranty Trust Company to cash a check, since we would inevitably stop for a treat at the Cafe de la Paix near the Opera. The cafe was the site of a famous story about Pauline (whom I called Paulinose as a child because the answer to any question I had was always

"Pauline knows") which I am not certain whether I witnessed or heard about later. At any rate, they were seated at a table close to the street when a friend stopped to say hello to Papa. Pauline was introduced to him and had a frightening reaction to the man; she told him, "You're not alive! You're dead!" She said it completely seriously and everyone laughed, but it turned out that they heard later that the man had indeed been killed that day in an auto accident. She had an incredible clairvoyance, and she could also read palms and was very conscious of the mystic side of her ancestry from her Irish mother.

Aside from the Albee brothers and Paul Sheeline, whom I met later, most of my playmates before I started school were girls. It just happened that most of Mother's friends had daughters. The ones I knew best were Julie Bowen, Stella and Ford Madox Ford's daughter, at whose house I often played because it was close by, and Betsy Drake, whose mother was from the Drake Hotel family in Chicago and who was also related to Sam Insull, "The Man Without a Country." Betsy was already very pretty and very close to my age. She stayed pretty and at one time was married to Cary Grant.

I was exposed to poetry early on and my first feeble attempt at rhyming on my own was the name of Ada MacLeish, Archie's wife, whom I admired very much and always referred to as *"La belle chemise de Madame MacLise."*

One of the exciting parks in Paris for a little boy was the Parc Montsouris because it had one of those water slides ending up in a pond and I wanted in the worst way to ride on it but was happy just to watch. Mother took me there fairly often because John Gunther and his wife lived in a bright, modern apartment with a sun deck on one side of the park. Mrs. Gunther was one of those ladies who sunburn easily but can never get enough sun anyway and was always covered with lotions and medications for her burn.

I'm sure I must have known the Fitzgeralds, and their daughter Scottie, but I cannot remember them, although I have fond remembrances of the Murphys and their children from our holidays in Juan-les-Pins and from Paris as well as of occasions years later in New York.

In those early years in Paris, the men who most influenced me, apart from Papa, were Tonton and Paul Mowrer. Paul was already very close to my mother and would eventually become my stepfather, but there were unresolved matters to be settled with his first wife before that could happen. I remember clearly that it was understood by all of us, including Winifred Mowrer, that Paul and Hadley would be married, but our relationship was friendly and we still visited with her and the Mowrers' two sons, who were some years older than I, when the boys were home in France from school in the States.

The Mowrers rented a villa one summer on the shore of Lake Annecy in Haute-Savoie and Mother and I spent some pleasant weeks there before I was sent packing to visit Papa in Key West. Richard and Dave Mowrer had air rifles and used to build battleships from boards pointed at one end, and with a tin can nailed to the top, to resemble the *Monitor.* The boats were floated out on the lake and provided targets for their air-rifle coast artillery.

Tonton Rohrbach had already instilled in me a fondness for all things military. He was a devoted Bonapartist; truth to tell, I believe he lived and breathed the times of the French empire. The only book in his tiny seventh-floor flat at 10 bis Avenue des Gobelins, near the tapestry works, was *Le Livre de Napoleon,* an enormous book in two volumes of history, fully illustrated in color, with all the uniforms of the great regiments of the *Grande Armée.* When he referred to Napoleon in our conversations, he called him *L'Empereur* in such deep-timbred tones of respect that the room fairly reverberated.

At the Mowrers' villa I climbed, with my mother, my first mountain, which I remember as gigantic, but which, in fact, was less than a thousand meters above the Annecy lake level and was called "Le Chapeau de Napoleon." I was proud to be able to tell Tonton that I had climbed Napoleon's hat.

Tonton, who was retired from the *Infanterie Coloniale* because of serious wounds, worked as a civil servant in the subbasement of the Paris *Hotel de Ville* (the city hall) performing marvels of calligraphy, producing the typical documents required of the city bureaucracy of the time. He insisted I memorize all the regiments by their uniforms and would test me on them when we visited the Invalides Museum or the Grevin Waxworks Museum.

The *Musée Grevin* was one of my favorites. Some of the scenes depicting various periods of French history were so grim I would dream about them, or certain aspects would show up in my dreams. The scene of the royal family being held in prison awaiting their execution, with rats on the floor just about to nibble at the dauphin's feet; the guillotine scene with the head newly dropped into the basket; and the one of Marat in his bathtub having just been stabbed by Charlotte Corday, were the most spellbinding.

The guillotine scene was brought home to me one day when I was seven and walking to school. I had taken my usual route along La Glacière past the main entrance of the La Santé prison. I always stared to see if any prisoners were in the courtyard or up at the high, barred windows (expecting them to be garbed in stripes, convict style), then I proceeded all the way to Blvd. Arago where I turned left, still skirting the edges of the high, grim stone walls for another block. As with most Paris boulevards, there was a broad walkway of raked gravel next to the prison wall and an unplanted but tamped-down belt of dirt with a line of fine horse chestnut trees between the sidewalk and the cobblestone boulevard. Halfway up the block there was a crew of workmen in blue coveralls dismantling a large wooden structure and putting the parts away into crates. I asked one of them what was going on but the overseer shooed me away, though not before one of the workmen leaned over and muttered to me that it was *"La Guillotine,"* and that it had performed its grisly duty at dawn that very morning. Indeed, I had a tale to tell in school that day.

Tonton heard my tale as well and told me further stories my mother and Marie Cocotte would not have found amusing at all. When, for whatever reason, Marie Cocotte would burst into tears, Tonton would impart to me the wisdom of French manhood condensed into one short sentence. *"Bambi, tu sais, les femmes pleurent comme les enfants pissent."* (Bumby, you know, women cry like children piss.)

Boulevard Arago had another attraction for me, then as now. Beyond the La Santé prison but still on the left side was an iron grill gate in another stone wall. Through it I could see the erratically laid out, dark red clay tennis courts where my mother sometimes took me, and where Papa used to play with Ezra Pound and other friends. They are still exactly as they were then, save for a few newer buildings in the background.

I usually went up Arago as far as the Lion of Belfort and there crossed the maze of intersecting avenues and boulevards to the corner of Montparnasse where the Closerie des Lilas was already serving *croissants, petits pains,* and a shot of cognac to the early workingmen. Our favorite waiter waved me hello as

I headed down the rue Notre Dame des Champs where we had lived with Papa in the apartment over the little sawmill. What we called the "sawmill" was, in reality, a master carpenter's *atelier* where finished flooring, cabinets, doors, and window frames were made and stored in several large workrooms immediately below our flat.

Just down the street from our former lodgings was the back entrance to the *École Alsacienne,* my first school, where I attended kindergarten and first grade. Except on official visits with my mother to the principal, who was called *Monsieur le President,* when we would enter on the rue d'Assass side along the edge of the Luxembourg Gardens, we lower school children used the Notre Dame des Champs side where our classrooms were located.

I attended two other schools in or near Paris until I was eleven. All were severe and left their mark of strict discipline and fear of corporal punishment. All were severe as well in their demand for academic excellence. There was no shirking in class at all and very little during recess and play periods. Yet, we were somehow mostly cheerful youngsters and delighted in the manifold charms that Paris extends to children, such as the *Guignol* and the toy boat ponds in the Luxembourg Gardens, though I can't deny I deeply resented being singled out for being American and receiving more than my share of the kicks that European youths tend to use instead of the traditional American fists to settle their grievances. These schools were all demanding yet, withal, rewarding in the results they achieved. The second, the *École du Montcel,* near the small village of Jouey-en-Josas just south of Versailles, was run by Swiss protestant brothers (not in the religious sense) who had taken over a late eighteenth century chateau and converted it into a boys' boarding school. It was rumored among the boys that Napoleon had kept a mistress there.

I attended Montcel for two years, the first starting in the autumn of my eighth birthday. Frankly, it was hard leaving home so early in life. I did get to go home on weekends, but that only seemed to make it more painful when I was taken to the school bus late Sunday afternoons at the Etoile to return to school. I remember that after the first weekend, which we spent out in Crécy with Paul, I wept copious tears on the bus, though I think I managed to control them until my mother was out of sight. This was a critical time for her and I didn't realize at the time that sending me away was really the only practical solution to resolving her relationship with Paul without a little boy underfoot the whole time.

We wore uniforms at Montcel, and organized sports were a big thing. Field hockey, which is played very ferociously by men and boys in France and other parts of the world notwithstanding that it is generally a girls' game in the U.S., was a major sport, as were soccer and track-and-field events in the spring. The grounds were extensive and there was access to a large forest, beyond which lay the Villacoublay Airdrome. We often played war games in the woods and usually managed to spend some time along the edge of the airdrome where we saw French military planes of the period—Farmans and Breguets—take off and land.

Another attraction was a series of tunnels running from the basement of the chateau to various points in the woods. The tunnels were frightening, dark, and damp, but the little pools of water there were exceptional hunting grounds for newts, frogs, and toads which played an important part in the dirty trick department. Such creatures showed up in some hypersensitive boy's desk when he opened it in the morning, or in someone's bed. The school had its own vegetable garden and we younger students were often assigned, with our housemother, to pick and shell peas. It was a good school and I was sorry to leave it after two years.

Next I went to an English boarding school in St. Cloud. This was the Denny School and was even stricter and, for me, more difficult because everything was conducted in English. By the time I was there, I spoke English fairly well because of annual visits to the States. But I hadn't yet the vaguest idea of written English nor of the rules of grammar or syntax. The Denny School did its best to remedy these defects.

I had thought the French schools tough. English schools accomplish their discipline in a much more subtle and effective manner by using the students, themselves, to enforce the rules and traditions. The older boys were, or at least could be, absolute tyrants. They were permitted to inflict corporal punishment and did so all too frequently. The headmaster, however, was the only one permitted to administer caning. I was caned only once but I'll never forget it. Though there remain some fearsome memories of the Denny School, there are aspects of my time there that I remember fondly and with gratitude.

The first was that we were introduced to English poetry by a marvelous teacher who helped make it come alive, despite having to ingrain in us the disciplines of form in verse. The other was my first headlong immersion into table tennis, which was played at the school with an intensity unimaginable to me at the time. By dint of constant exposure and endless defeats, I came to be among the best players in the whole school; and while I suffered much envy from my school chums, I also finally gained the respect of my peers and found it extremely satisfying. Even then, though, I sensed that, satisfying as racquet sports can be, they cannot match the endless mystery of those expeditions into another element which we call fishing.

TWO

In the years following my parents' divorce until my mother and Paul Mowrer were married, when we moved back to the States permanently, I had practically become a trans-Atlantic commuter. I spent the greater part of every summer with Papa and Pauline, and though they kept an apartment in Paris and used it periodically, their principal residence was in Key West, at the very tip of the Florida Keys.

Sometimes I traveled alone under the supervision of ship's personnel, but usually I went with a friend or relative who would deliver me into Papa's safekeeping at the docks in New York.

The first of these expeditions to New York stands out especially because the memory was heightened by an unusual incident. After leaving the docks and the cab ride to Scribner's on Fifth Avenue, there was a pleasant visit with Max Perkins followed by a restaurant lunch where I listened with fascination to Papa and Perkins' men's talk. Next to Papa's burly figure, Mr. Perkins seemed a reed of a man, with a schoolmasterish bearing and a total lack of egotism. I remember his calm, low voice—quite a contrast to Papa's—as they talked of books and writers, though what they said was beyond my understanding.

Afterward, I took a bus ride on the open top of a double-decker Fifth Avenue bus to within a couple blocks of the Perkins' brownstone where I was left for the rest of a very pleasant afternoon with Mrs. Perkins and had the run of the garden while the sun still shone, then took my customary nap.

That evening Perkins accompanied us down to the train at Penn Station where we boarded the Pullman bound for Miami and the Florida Keys. At Trenton, a bit before Philadelphia, the conductor delivered a telegram to Papa. Papa explained to me that Grandfather Hemingway was dead and that he must go to the funeral and take care of things for the family. I had nothing to worry about since I would be left in the care of the Pullman porter who would see that I got my meals and went to bed on time, and would see me safely to Key West where Pauline would be waiting. I was, as yet, unacquainted with death, and these events didn't seem to me, an experienced world traveler of five, at all unusual. Papa did not tell me then that Grandfather had shot himself in the head with his old Civil War pistol.

After a few months in Key West, we all returned to France via Havana and Spain; but when summer came, off I went again to Key West: this time for what was to be the first of many car trips west with Papa. After traveling via Piggott, Arkansas to visit Pauline's family, the Pfeiffers, where I was taken in with great kindness, love, and affection, we took the Model A Ford Coupe, with its running boards and rumble seat, west through the center of the country into the Rocky Mountains and on to the L-T Ranch near Cooke City, Montana. These trips west were always great adventures. From Grandfather Paul Pfeiffer I learned that being a step-grandson of the bank president and owner of the cotton gin, as well as the largest landowner thereabouts, was a privileged position which entitled one to the luxury of "charging" sodas and sundaes, and any number of wondrous goodies that had not existed in France, at the local drugstore. And there were other spectacles and adventures on every hand as we headed west.

It was the Depression and hard times were upon the land most of those years until the outbreak of World War II. Papa was becoming a successful writer during a period when a great majority of people felt a deep financial crunch. The parts of the Deep South through which we drove seemed to be populated only by undernourished-looking black families in run-down shanties, and I don't remember ever seeing much change in that regard until well after the war.

Papa was naturally generous and friendly, especially when he was away from the intellectual coterie of his writing life. Whenever there was room, we would squeeze in some riders along the way who couldn't afford the price of a train ticket. They weren't called hitchhikers yet. Papa would always talk freely with them and get their story out of them. There were hard luck stories of every ilk and most with the ring of truth. For me it was learning that couldn't be duplicated elsewhere. There seemed always to be some humor and hope though, no matter how depressing the tale.

One year we had a nearly very serious accident. We had left the Gulf Coast after a night's stay in New Orleans where we'd paid our usual visit to the oyster bar and the shooting gallery near the Monteleone Hotel where we always stayed. We were

on the way to Baton Rouge when a smallish hog suddenly started across the road in front of the car. Papa always drove fast in
those days and it was a close call but he managed to hit the hog
with only a glancing blow and caused only the most superficial
damage to the car while inflicting sudden death on the hapless
hog. Now, that hog was no fat, prime specimen of its kind. It
was in about as poor shape as a hog can be and still qualify for
the title of hog.

Its owner rushed out of the roadside woods yelling, "That's
my prize hog you just done kilt, mister, and he's going to cost
you twenty bucks!"

Papa parried back, "You deliberately pushed that hog out
onto the road when you saw the car coming, and it's the most
worthless-looking hog I ever saw."

Papa and the man settled for five dollars and then Papa
instructed me to be on the lookout from then on, whenever
there was cover along the road, for what we called "hog launch-
ers." We decided it was an honorable profession during hard
times and that you just had to be wary of them when traveling
through prime hog-launching country.

It became a tradition on these journeys that, in order to
avoid getting in the habit of using bad language and cussing
and telling dirty jokes, there was an established time in the latter part of every evening when, for an hour, we were permitted
full license in all these respects. When my younger brother,
Patrick, was old enough to come along this became especially
important because we would tend to get pretty wild. The situation was even more extreme when Patrick and I rode in the
rumble seat and Papa and Pauline were up front. It may not
have been pure coincidence that this period of condoned ver-
bal misbehavior took place when it was time for Papa's first
drink of the day, which I was trained early on to mix for him
with just the right measure of two big fingers of scotch and little
enough water not to drown it. Ice was used when available.

Among the more ludicrous, but never to be forgotten, cre-
ations of these sessions was "The Famous Bathroom." This
was scatology carried to its ultimate extreme. "TFB" was a
museum which we would create for the preservation of fecal
specimens not only of all the various species of living creatures, but of famous historical characters as well. Our imagina-
tions knew no bounds in this project, and during the time when
such talk was forbidden, we often spent time planning for the

dirty hour. It was not an unhealthy activity and it actually opened the doors to questions it is sometimes difficult to approach one's own parents about, although Papa never condoned or liked conventional dirty jokes.

The first real Western mountains we crossed on that first drive were the Bighorns in Wyoming. The road then was just a thin dirt ribbon and much of it passed between sheer cliff on one side and pure precipice on the other. On one stretch we met a rarity in those days, another car coming up the grade toward us. It took some serious maneuvering on the edge of the precipice while the other car squeezed between us and the cliff. I remember being nearly paralyzed with fear sitting next to the window on the outside. The next day, going through Yellowstone from the south entrance, we were held up for hours by repair work on the winter-ravaged road. The worst, however, was the fourteen miles of mostly corduroy road from just outside Cooke City to the ranch. We lost our oil pan and finally had to be pulled out by a team of horses. In later years, after the construction of the Cooke City/Red Lodge Highway, getting to the ranch was a snap, although the new highway excavation near Cooke City triggered land and mud slides which adversely affected the clarity and fishing quality of the Clark's Fork River for many years thereafter.

Lawrence Nordquist's L-T Ranch was situated on the south side of the valley of the Clark's Fork. Now it is reached by crossing a wooden bridge after coming off the Cooke City/Red Lodge Highway and then crossing a series of broad meadow pastures and fields of oats to the ranch house, with its cluster of log cabins scattered through the grove of lodgepole pine.

That first year we arrived via the "old" road which crossed the stream by a ford in its shallow headwaters close to Cooke City and skirted myriad swamps, rock falls, and finally ended crossing the sagebrush flat beyond One Mile Creek near the ranch. The main building was typical Western guest ranch—very simple but clean and piney, with a big living room with lots of chairs, and books left by former guests. The lodge had a couch or two and a big dining room where overabundant but delicious meals were served. I was alone, that trip, with Papa and Pauline and had a little room of my own in their cabin. The Franklin stove was in their room, and my first job in the morning was to put some of the kerosene-soaked sawdust and a few small logs on the fire to get the cabin warmed up.

After breakfast at the main lodge, Papa and Pauline would get their fishing tackle ready and, after getting the horses saddled, they would take off with a pack lunch to some point on the river, usually several miles downstream. I was left pretty much to my own devices and the ranch was well organized for kids.

There must have been three or four other children there, though I think I was the youngest. Ivan Skinner, the top wrangler, saw to it that we all had proper-fitting saddles, and within a few days we had all learned to saddle up by ourselves and knew our horses pretty well. I was blessed with a white horse speckled in fine-grained liver. He was called Pinky. He was hard to saddle because he would bloat up his stomach when I tried to cinch him up tight. Consequently, I had numerous accidents when I would end up beneath him; but I eventually learned to give him a slap or a good knock just before the cinching so he'd let out the air long enough to get the job done right.

Learning to ride was fun and, at first, consisted mainly of long rides in line following one of the wranglers to some nearby lake or stream, or up the squaw trail to get over the rimrock and up into the Hurricane Mesa country where Billy Sidley's grandfather had his monument plaque and where they had scattered his ashes. I thought it was a beautiful place to have your ashes scattered and thought about having the same thing done for myself someday.

Billy was my best friend at the ranch and helped initiate me to the tricks of being a proper horse wrangler, as we liked to think of ourselves. He was only a couple of years older than I, but he'd been coming out to the ranch from Chicago for several summers already and knew all the ropes. His family had been coming for years, and the ash-scattered grandfather had built a fine log cabin for their family down across the meadow on a small sagebrush promontory overlooking a beautiful riffle of the Clark's Fork. In later years the Sidleys stopped coming out and Papa was able to rent their cabin, which was much better suited to his writing since it was situated well away from the many distractions and noises of the main corral and ranch buildings.

Another job I had that year was to gather wild strawberries which grew in abundance, rare for the species, in the woods around our cabin. In the cabins, we had those old-fashioned heavy glass tumblers, and I had to fill two of these as first priority. Pauline would then crush the strawberries into the bottom of the tumbler and add gin for their first-of-the-day "ranch cocktails." I took my strawberries straight. They were so sweet they needed not the least sprinkle of sugar.

One day Pinky done me wrong. We kids had been playing horseback tag in the irrigated pasture down by the river. The horses were tired and when we came into the corral everyone but me unsaddled and brushed off their mounts. I made the unfortunate mistake of deciding to ride Pinky to the cabin to fetch something or other and he decided to revolt. At first he refused to move, and then when I gave him a good whack of the leather quirt, he took off like a scalded cat right through the compound of cabins. That would have been all right, since he'd have just run himself out in a little time, but he headed for the place where Mrs. Nordquist hung out the laundry on wires strung between the pines. I managed to duck the first wire, but the second caught me right across the chest and took me right out of the saddle. The scar is gone now, but I can understand why everyone was so concerned. That wire could just as easily have taken my head off, and that would have been the end of this tale.

On the days that Papa worked, Pauline would sometimes go on the trail rides. This was my cue to stay home. Not because I didn't want to be with Pauline, but because I knew that Papa would go fishing near the ranch by himself when he was through work. I knew he really wanted to be alone, but, on the other hand, I really wanted to learn about trout fishing. He knew I was just hanging around waiting to be asked to join him so he could teach me how to cast and all the other great mysteries. He didn't, so I tried sneaking up to the river where he would be wading in his chest-waders in the fast, clear, green-tinged water.

He spotted me right off and came over to the bank.

"You know, Schatz, trout spook awfully easily—"

"I'm sorry Papa, I only wanted—"

"If you really want to watch just stay back a little from the bank. You mustn't move around until I go further down. Then move very slowly and stay low."

"Yes Papa!"

"That way the trout won't spook."

I tried to become a part of the shadows along the stream side.

I had to settle for this role for the rest of our stay that year, except for the last few days when I was rewarded with an opportunity to fish with Pauline's already set-up outfit with a single hook which was an old, worn fly that Papa trimmed the dressing off of so I could impale a grasshopper and fish it in the swirling back eddies that Papa pretty much ignored while he was fishing his two- or three-fly wet-fly rig through the riffles.

My purported patience during the endless periods of being a watcher had been a sham. I had darn near died of impatience to have a real go at it myself, and the trout that Papa caught were so beautiful compared to my Grand Morin minnows that my desire to capture one became an obsession.

Nevertheless, I learned a lot about casting and about playing fish once they were hooked. Papa was a pretty straightforward wet-fly fisherman. He used Hardy tackle and his leaders were already made up with three flies. His favorites were a McGinty for the top, a *cock-y-bondhu* for the middle, and a woodcock green and yellow for the tail fly. He sometimes fished with single-eyed flies and added a dropper. At the ranch, for these, he preferred Hardy's worm fly and the shrimp fly.

Ninety percent of the time, Papa was an across and downstream caster whose team of flies swam or skittered across the current so that a taking fish pretty much hooked himself. He played the fish gently and well and with the necessary calm that eliminates hurrying a fish too fast or playing it too long, which is just as great a sin.

He seldom failed to land his trout except for the rare double-header when one or both fish were often lost. He taught me how to clean them and insisted that the part along the backbone which looks like coagulated blood, which ought to be the aorta but is in reality the trout's kidney, be left if the fish weren't to be kept too long before eating. He said this improved the flavor.

He used a woven grass basket rather like a shopping bag from Hardy's for a creel and laid the trout in it on fresh leaves of grass or branches of fern. The creel was dampened in the river and the evaporation kept the fish cool. "Never waste fish, Schatz, it's criminal to kill anything you aren't going to eat," Papa told me. Then he impressed on me how important it was never to waste fish or game by not taking proper care of it.

The trout Papa caught were seldom cooked in the ranch

house kitchen. He preferred to cook them himself, usually for breakfast, on top of the stove in the cabin in a frying pan with lots of butter and lemon and salt and pepper. He always added the lemon while the fish were frying, claiming this gave them a better taste.

My immediate problem, now that I was rod in hand with a six-foot leader and the hopper impaled on the fly hook, was that the grasshopper wouldn't sink, because of its natural buoyancy. I had no idea then about floating flies, nor did I know about lead split shot used for sinking a bait or a fly. With just the leader and hardly any line extending beyond the rod tip, I flipped the hopper out toward the center of the whirlpool, and then it was pulled under into the vortex and I immediately saw my line twitch, and I gave a powerful yank and, unlike the minnows which had flown out of the water in the same circumstances, I found myself with a bent rod tip and a very active, strong, living creature doing its best to get to the middle of the stream.

I tried to emulate what I had watched Papa do, and with luck on my side, I finally landed the most beautiful fish I had ever seen. It was a rainbow cutthroat hybrid about eleven inches long and looked enormous to me as I pounced on it on the sandy backwater shore.

It's hard to imagine what a miracle that first trout seemed to me. Everything about it was perfect, and after the long weeks of watching in frustration as my father fished, it truly seemed the ultimate reward. That trout was consumed in its entirety by me at the ranch house that night, amidst much ado. It was the first of many from that lovely river, although the next few days were filled with various frustrations, some of which were overcome.

I just continued to fish places exactly like the one where I had had my initial success. Experiments in different types of water were unsuccessful, but the seed had been well-planted and it had grown into an overwhelming desire to fish for trout—a desire which remains just as strong to this day.

I sometimes wonder if I'd have retained my enthusiasm to such a degree, or at all, if my father had followed the usual path of providing me with all the necessaries and plying me with detailed instructions and supervision. I know he wanted me to love fishing and hunting, and I believe that he deliberately set about to make me really want to do it on my own initiative.

Tennis parents and stage mothers should take note. The kid has got to want to do it, not just to please the parent, but for himself.

The winter following the first summer at the ranch was filled with dreams of trout streams, but the next summer was not to bring a return to Wyoming. That summer was unusual nonetheless.

The first part of the summer was with Marie Cocotte and Tonton in the Côtes-du-Nord department of Brittany. Though he hadn't yet quite reached retirement age, Tonton had bought a small plot of ground on the outskirts of Mur-de-Bretagne. Marie Cocotte's family lived in a nearby village only about three kilometers away. The village consisted of four or five houses and their outbuildings and was surrounded by small pastures and fields that had been subdivided since earliest times until few of them could supply the needs of any one family. These tiny villages worked out agreements among themselves to achieve some sort of efficiency in farming their plots.

For me it was a shock to find yet another language. In Marie Cocotte's home village, none of the older people, including her parents, aunts and uncles, spoke a word of French. The French call Breton a French patois, but it is Old Gaelic and is highly flavored and difficult. Despite the barrier, with Marie Cocotte's help, and that of the cousins and nephews and nieces, I got along pretty well. While I was struggling with "patois" and being stuffed with such local goodies as *crêpes au blé noir* with unsalted butter over which was sprinkled coarse sea salt—then rolled up and eaten by hand—Tonton was negotiating with craftsmen to help him with the building of his retirement home.

They already had some chickens which were left in the charge of relatives after vacation time, and he showed me how properly to kill and bleed them by slitting their throats from the inside with the very sharp blade of a pen knife and then hanging them by their feet in preparation for Marie Cocotte's special roasting with herbs.

One weekend we attended a pagan rite in which all the people surrounded a special haystack which was burned in an ancient sacrificial ceremony to the gods of the Druids. Since this sort of pagan ritual couldn't be wiped out, the Church went along with it and the local priest gave it his blessing by attending. There were first communions which were a sight to behold, with the starched lace peasant dress of all attending as well as the pretty white communion dresses of the communicants.

Dragées, candy-coated almonds, were handed out liberally and I remember their taste and the scuddy, white clouds, and the joviality as if it were yesterday.

When Tonton's vacation was over, we had to return to Paris where I was taken over by Papa and Pauline, and off we went to Spain. It was the mid-thirties by then, and we saw bullfights in many small and large places, mostly in Central Spain. The first place, though, was Pamplona, and while those memories of the first visit are very dim, I do remember liking the bullfights despite the blood and gore because Papa took the trouble to explain them well to me and to see that I knew the reason these various bloody stages were necessary in the progression of the ancient ritual sacrifice these fights truly represented.

Papa was always surrounded by friends and admirers and it was a special excitement for a little boy to sit at the cafe table with him and listen to them all talk about the day's events, and whether the wind would affect the style of some particular matador, and all the special trivia that followers of tauromachia indulge themselves in discussing endlessly. Because of their enthusiasm, one couldn't help being swept up in it.

The gypsy encampment just outside the ancient walls of Pamplona was especially intriguing. We went there often to fill the *botas* we carried everywhere. In those pre-plastic days, a *bota* had to be cured, and the process involved several changes of wine to help remove the strong pitch flavor the lining gave to the contents. Naturally, good wines weren't wasted in this curing process and we bought the cheap gypsy wines for the purpose.

I was always allowed a little wine as a child and today the taste of the bota wine and the spicy Pamplona sausage, a kind of *chorizo* eaten raw, still evokes the gypsy camp with the horse trading and the little, colorfully-decorated carts. On my next trip to Spain, at the ripe old age of ten, I'm told I became insufferable when discussing the bullfights with my brother, Patrick, or anyone else who would listen. We had spent part of the summer in Hendaye with Patrick and his nurse, Henriette, living in a small rented cottage down toward the Bidassoa River not far from the large hotel lodge where Papa and Pauline and several visitors, including his attorney, Maurice Speiser, and Speiser's wife, were staying.

We got together with the grown-ups on most days for swimming in the surf and playing on the fine, sandy beach. The Bidassoa is the border with Spain for the last several kilometers of its course and flows into a broad bay bordered by rugged foothills of the Pyrenees on the south and the sandy swales of the French Basque country and the Landes on the north.

On the point across the bay to the southwest we could see the moorish tower of Fuentearrabia. We took the electric train on several occasions, crossing the border at Irun and on to San Sebastian. It was there, I am told, that I declaimed to all who would listen that, *"Quand j'etais jeune, les courses de taureau n'etaient comme ça."* (When I was young, the bullfights weren't like this.)

That summer in France and Spain was to be my last in Europe for many years. Paul and my mother were married and he was recalled to Chicago by the *Daily News* to become its managing editor, and eventually its editor-in-chief. He was a two-time Pulitzer Prize winner for journalism. Despite his great abilities as a newsman, Paul had the temperament of a poet and a sweet, calm disposition, though he could be tough when the occasion warranted. My mother was very fortunate to have found such a fine man with whom to share her life.

I was fortunate in my childhood that neither of my parents ever expressed any rancor toward the other. It was only years later that my mother confided in me that, once the initial trauma of her separation from Papa was over, it was actually "like the lifting of a great weight" from her shoulders.

Papa was a complete contrast to Paul. Papa was excitement and unbounded enthusiasm interspersed by dark moods. He opened up the possibilities of life for my mother and through him she gained strength and independence, as well as the confidence she had so desperately lacked in her family situation in St. Louis where she had been made to feel helpless and useless and a physical inferior because of a fall suffered in her youth.

Through Papa she learned her own worth and that she could get along and make her own friends, even learn another language, become athletic, and make a happy home in another land, alone. She was eight years older than Papa, and my personal opinion is that in the long run the breakup of her marriage to Papa was a blessing. It took place while she was still an attractive and desirable woman, and it surely would have come to an ill-fated end once her looks were gone. Although Papa aged very rapidly and visibly, because of the fast-paced life he led, he was not a man who could accept gracefully the oncoming of old age. For me, that is the true tragedy of his life.

The move to Chicago was made in stages. Paul, of course, went there and took over his new job. Mother took me to St. Louis and left me in the care of Auntie Phon while she went up to Chicago to help Paul find a suitable apartment. When I finally joined them, coming up on the Wabash Railroad, I found that we were ensconced in a fine, large apartment at 1320 North State Street, just a few blocks from the lake and a short walk to my new school, the Chicago Latin School for Boys, on Dearborn Street, with Lincoln Park one block north of the school. The apartment had an elevator with an elevator man, and a real doorman in uniform. We had taken an economic and social step up in the world.

Some things weren't all that different, though. At school, I was still the new boy, and what a weird one at that! I couldn't throw, except like a girl, but I could kick like hell, and Papa had taught me the rudiments of boxing, but not of fighting. I learned soon enough, and though I was naturally disinclined to violence and particularly hated the idea of being hit in the face, since a blow to the nose invariably made me cry, I didn't have to fight much because I was starting to grow big and strong for my age. I hated football, as I couldn't understand it, and the same went for baseball because of the throwing, which is learned so naturally by kids brought up here but was foreign to me.

As a result, I avoided organized sports to the fullest extent possible and started to become a bookworm. I devoured everything in Paul and my mother's beautiful collection of books. I had always read a lot in France, but mostly stuck to children's reading while visiting my family in Key West. Now, everything from *The Republic* and the *Dialogues* of Plato to Marcus Aurelius, and lists of novels my father recommended, were grist for my mill, including the adventure tales of Howard Pyle.

I remember that my father once recommended an Irish novelist named Maurice Walsh who he said, although essentially a romantic, was one of the finest storytellers he had read. He especially liked *Blackcock's Feather,* a novel of early times in

English-occupied Ireland. Along with Howard Pyle's *Robin Hood,* that book became one of my favorite re-readables.

I learned more history, albeit with a British viewpoint, from the endless series of novels for boys churned out by G.A. Henty. It was also my good fortune to have a Latin teacher who was a serious birder, and under his influence bird watching and sketching became a serious avocation. Mother and Paul were already inveterate bird watchers.

I had trouble with math at Latin School, and Papa came up with the solution of having me spend the balance of the first Chicago winter down in Key West where his poet friend Evan Shipman would tutor me in math.

Evan was a kindly, thin, pale man, the seeming epitome of a poet. It was hard to equate his passionate love of trotting horses and the betting on them that made him such a good math tutor. Even less likely was his later role as a Loyalist machine gunner badly wounded on a Spanish battlefield.

I went for three hours every day to his room at the Colonial Hotel, and he taught me basic principles he'd acquired by being an odds-maker—principles which served me well most of the way through school.

I also learned a lot more about fishing that winter. The years at Chicago Latin School went by swiftly with the usual summer formula of visiting Key West for a month, followed by the drive out West to the ranch, with the exception of two summers we spent in Bimini and the Bahamas where I was exposed to a lot of saltwater fishing, which I hated because I became seasick every time we went out.

Nevertheless, I learned a lot about fishing the flats by going out with the local boys—all black except for the commissioner's son—and fishing for whatever came along. We'd dive for conchs and eat them raw with limes instead of taking a sandwich along. We'd see and stalk bonefish but had no tackle to catch them, but we did get one with a bait-casting outfit and a piece of shrimp while fishing for snappers.

The nights were the best. Papa would let me take one of the old, light saltwater rods and a medium-sized reel with a woven wire leader and a big 12/0 hook. We'd take a barracuda and cut him into big chunks for bait and chum. Then we'd fish right from the beach where everyone swam in the daytime. It sometimes took a little while, but usually not more than twenty minutes at the most before we'd feel a pull at the bait, and then it would be dropped and a little while later there would be another pick-up and, finally, one of the sharks would swallow the bait and head out for the blue of the Gulf Stream. That was real excitement!

Sometimes it took up to an hour to land one of the big ones and we'd leave it there until the next morning when one of the locals would come around in his skiff and take whatever they wanted of the shark and then haul the rest out into the current to be eaten, presumably, by its brethren.

The boys also introduced me to sex. There was quite a bit of promiscuity among the young blacks, and quite often girls would come down with us for fishing and to build a fire, and maybe sneak some beer and try smoking if someone had cigarettes. I was crazy about the hotel keeper's daughter, who was a year older than I. Naturally, she would have nothing to do with me, so I gave in to the temptations on the beach with the sister of one of my black pals who encouraged me to do so. All I can say about it was that I liked it immensely and the experiment was repeated a number of times.

During these years, the gap in ages between my two younger brothers and me seemed a gigantic gulf and, while I was fond of them and we shared many interests in common, I always felt a separateness which was abetted by Ada Stcarns, Gregory's nurse, who also served us all as surrogate mother and housekeeper much of the time. After she departed the scene much later on I came to know both boys much more closely and to appreciate the qualities each had. Greg was the natural athlete with a flair for the handling of money which won him the nickname of "The Irish Jew" from Papa. Patrick was always viewed as the intellectual and Papa sometimes joked of a time when the three of us would be put to work to support him in his old age. Patrick would write the books, Gig would handle the money and I was to act in the subsequent screenplays.

Apparently, my lack of interest in the deep-sea trolling which so captivated my father was a disappointment to him, but I caught the largest amberjack of the year in Key West, and when I was ten I was the youngest ever to catch a marlin on rod and reel off Havana. I think that first summer of fishing in Cuba is what put me off. There was an epidemic of polio and I had to stay on the boat the whole time in the harbor so as to avoid exposure. The harbor stank at night in the heat of the summer and with no breeze at our mooring. The greasy food and the long days out on the water, and my adolescent stomach which wasn't catching up to the quick growth of the rest of me, made for seasickness almost every day, and even my love of reading could not dispel it. In fact, whenever I tried to read for long, the motion sickened me even more. Not until I was full-grown did I stop being seasick, and now I can enjoy fishing from a boat on the ocean. Nonetheless, I think I shall always have a strong preference for the fishing of rivers and lakes by wading with both feet firmly planted on solid bottom.

I like the feeling of being fixed in one place and having the water move by me, pressing in against my legs, either wet against my skin or through the thick fabric of chest-high waders. It is only one but an important element in what makes fishing important to me.

THREE

Many changes took place in those years before the outbreak of World War II in Europe. The second visit to Bimini was the last summer vacation time spent with Papa for a long time. Aside from fishing, there were plenty of exciting distractions. Papa drank a lot after coming in from fishing and had several fistfights with other visiting sportsmen either on the dock or in such high-grade bars as "Bethel's Fountain of Youth." This led to his putting up a hundred-dollar prize for anyone who could stay in the ring with him for three rounds.

There were some fine boxing matches, but the two best were with a ringer from Gun Cay called the "Rubber Man," whose specialty was bouncing back up after every knockdown—he didn't make it through the three rounds—and with the older of the two Butler brothers. Papa had a fine match with Louis Butler, but his brother, Hermie, was one big, black dude, and very strong. He had Papa looking pretty well whipped until the latter part of the third round when Papa caught him with a good left hook and then a combination of left hooks and straight rights that put him down. The round ended before the end of the count so Papa paid him the prize money and called a halt to the open challenge. The locals began singing a song about him called, "The big, fat slob's in the harbor; this the night we hab fun!"

Tom Heeney came over from Miami Beach, where he had retired, to spar with Papa. He was a former British Empire heavyweight champion and had fought Gene Tunney for the world championship. He and Papa were staying in Mike Lerner's big house overlooking the beach and the Gulf Stream from the highest point on the island, where Mike had lured Papa with tales of enormous bluefin tuna.

I saw Papa and Tom go down to the beach one morning to work out with the sixteen-ounce gloves. It started to become a bit of a donnybrook and Tom told Papa they should quit unless they were being paid a lot of money. What I'm trying to say is that—some biographers to the contrary—Papa was a hell of a fighter. He was not a polished boxer, as his footwork was impaired by the old knee injury from World War I, but he was very knowledgeable, tricky, and could throw a real punch with either hand. Morley Callaghan's derisive criticism of his boxing abilities doesn't take into account that any fast-handed, pretty boxer can make a big heavyweight look bad; but it only takes one punch from the bigger man to finish the whole business. Callaghan was "shocked by the spitting of blood into his face." He would have been considerably more shocked by the eventual left hook which inevitably would have set him down for keeps.

That fall, while Papa went off to Spain, Paul and Mother were building a new house on six acres in the woods overlooking Lake Michigan, inside the Shore Acres Club just north of Lake Bluff. The nearest high school was in Lake Forest and I boarded with a local merchant family until about Christmas when we all moved into the new house.

Lake Forest High was the first school I had attended with girls since kindergarten, and to say that I found it distracting would be a gross understatement. My grades took a tumble, and the following year, after a wonderful summer at Holm Lodge (also called the Crossed Sabers Ranch) on the Shoshoni River, where my fishing improved remarkably, I was sent off to boarding school back East.

Storm King School was on a spur of Storm King Mountain in the Hudson Highlands just north of West Point. The Albee family, who had been artist friends of my mother's in Paris, had sent their sons there and the two youngest, Jack, who was my age, and his youngest brother, Ed, were students there when I arrived. The Albees had strongly recommended the school to Mother and Paul and I was delighted to know the boys would be there. I was even more pleased to find two natural new friends in the Sanchez brothers, Bernabe and Fernando, who were the nephews of Papa's old Cuban pals, Thorwald and Julio Sanchez.

It was an ideal school for an outdoor-loving boy. Set on the edge of the Black Rock Forest, which was a fourteen-mile square right in the middle of the best and the wildest of the Highlands, the land was owned by a member of the Stillman family, who was also a trustee of the school, which gave us access to small lakes and ponds scattered throughout this paradise. Most of the ponds had small streams entering and leaving them, and each led to larger streams down in the populated valleys outside the forest. The ponds boasted eastern-chain pickerel, small-mouth bass, long-eared sunfish, and perch. A few of them held brook trout, and all the streams had brookies in the upper stretches and brown trout in the lower parts. Several had rainbows, which had recently been introduced. Needless to say, when I began to learn these secrets during my three years there, I spent more and more time exploring and fishing.

Storm King was a small school with a student body which never exceeded sixty students during my stay there, from the fall of 1938 through the spring of 1941. Because we had to field teams in a number of major and minor sports, and because there were so few students, everyone was forced to participate, and I was finally trapped into organized team activities.

I went out for football and was a substitute end and running guard my first year. I finally made first string as a senior, playing fullback on offense and tackle on defense. Nowhere but at Storm King could I have made the team. Talent was in such short supply that in my senior year I earned five letters and even made the starting five as a guard on the basketball team. We did not, however, win very often.

The headmaster, Anson Barker, very generously agreed to let us start a fencing program my first winter there and obtained the services of Warrant Officer Bonomo, the assistant coach of the West Point team. He took six of us in hand and soon had us performing well enough to take on the West Point "plebe" team, which we, surprisingly, defeated.

Another boy, Bob Fay, and I took the fencing very seriously and, since he lived in New York City, we spent several weekends at his parents' apartment and were able to go down to Washington Square where Jojo Santelli, the great coach for the perennial champions at NYU, had his *salle d'armes*. Bob preferred saber while I preferred foil and épée, and we both fenced all three weapons and showed rapid progress and a real aptitude for the sport. We both ended up as runners-up in the National Interscholastic Championship—Bob in saber and I in the other two weapons—in our junior year, and only our second year of fencing. Unfortunately, during our senior year the program was dropped because we were needed for the basketball team, though Bob and I kept it up as best we could on the side and without official sanction.

During the Storm King years, Papa came to New York on numerous occasions, and I had several opportunities to spend weekends with him. He started me taking boxing lessons from George Brown and we often went to the fights together. Once he even arranged through *Esquire* magazine for me to fly from Chicago to New York to see the second Louis/Schmeling fight. I was with David Smart—Arnold Gingrich's co-publisher—in the best possible ringside seats and, since we arrived too late to see the prelims, I had the great treat of seeing the great Schmeling completely demolished by an unsmiling Louis in two minutes and eighteen seconds of the first round! That night, returning to the hotel through Harlem was a frightening experience, with blacks climbing all over the stranded cars and taxis in the snarled traffic. Had Schmeling won, it might have proved tragic.

On one occasion, after attending the Lee Savold/Billy Conn fight, a real stand-up boxing classic between two great light heavies, won by Conn on a close decision, we all went to the Stork Club where Sherman Billingsley led us to my father's favorite table, where we met Donald Friede who gave Papa a check for $100,000. It was the first color, imprinted check I had ever seen, and Papa, who was soon feeling very little pain, called Sherman over to the table and asked if he could cash the check. Of course, all banks were closed, but Sherman made every effort to cash the check, calling all over town to every connection he had, since it would be a real coup to be able to come up with $100,000 in cash at that time of night. The Stork Club was, as usual, full of gossip columnists who would have made a big thing of it; unfortunately, he was unable to do it. But I, for one, will never forget that check which Papa called the "Technicolor check" and was from Paramount for the movie rights to *For Whom the Bell Tolls*. Nor will I forget that celebration at the Stork Club. By the way, my father's official biography has a vastly different account of this incident, which I can assure you is inaccurate.

It was during one of those weekends from school with Papa that I first met Martha Gellhorn. The occasion was the opening of the documentary movie, "The Spanish Earth," which Papa had been responsible for producing and which he narrated. I was to meet him at the theater and came directly from the Weehawken Ferry terminal by cab to the theater, off Broadway, where the film was being shown to the critics. When I alighted under the marquee, a gorgeous blonde lady rushed up to me and said, "You must be Bumby; I'm Marty."

Of course, I knew about her but had no idea what a beauty she was, and I did not know for sure that Papa was going to leave Pauline to first live with Marty, then marry her. After seeing her, I was overwhelmed by this marvelous creature who could say the "F" word so naturally that it didn't sound dirty and, otherwise, talk like a trooper or a high-born lady, whichever suited the circumstances.

I was her immediate captive and just accepted Papa's behavior as completely natural. After all, they had been together for many months on end in the Spanish Civil War, under combat conditions at times (I had wanted more than anything to go there with Papa but was too young).

We went inside the theater together where Papa introduced me to some of the heroes of the International Brigade who had been seriously wounded and were there to help promote the film, which was being used for fund-raising for ambulances to be sent to Spain for the Loyalist side. A lot of the people I met that night would be in serious trouble with the FBI in later years because they had fought for the Loyalists in Spain. That was a real shame since many of them were completely naive politically and were good Americans who had just gone either for the excitement or because they thought the Spanish people were getting a raw deal at the hands of the Fascists.

It shouldn't have been such a difficult job to separate the sheep from the wolves and use some of the invaluable knowledge of the new forms of combat that were being experimented with in Spain by the Germans and Italians. Some of these men had been major unit commanders in battles where modern tank warfare had been developed. They could have been used to good purpose in positions of responsibility in the U.S. military. Instead, they were marked for life as security risks and were never given responsible positions. Some of them, in their bitterness, might be excused for not being enthusiastic supporters of our bureaucratic approach to their situations. There were also, of course, some real Communists, some idealistic, and some not so idealistic, who simply followed the party line. The problem was, the FBI apparently made no distinctions.

The film was dramatic because of the great combat footage, but, although the commentary was great in content, it was handicapped by my father's voice which did not really lend itself to that sort of job. His voice came through as nasal and pitched somewhat higher than one would imagine, though it had good timbre.

During that period, I now saw Marty often, and she and Papa were sharing quarters in hotels; while I was pleased with Papa's choice, I knew that the day of reckoning with Pauline had not really been faced yet.

The summer of 1939 was a key one for me. I was allowed by Paul and Mother to drive alone out to Wyoming to meet them at Holm Lodge. I enjoyed the long drive alone, and to give myself time for exploring, I drove straight through without sleep and spent time in Yellowstone Park fishing places I had never had the chance to try before. It was the beginning of a long love affair with the area.

I was particularly entranced by the Madison drainage and spent most of my time right around the big Madison meadows below the junction of the Firehole and the Gibbon. I was starting to get a feel for dry-fly fishing, though I had very little savvy about insect types and recognition of species that might be hatching. The fish, while relatively sophisticated in comparison with the Shoshone River trout, were reasonably catchable, and I managed to land a fair number, though few over a pound.

At that time, my largest trout had been a four-pound rainbow caught on a worm in the Muskegon River, on a float trip in Michigan from Hardy Dam to Newaygo. I had caught no outsized fish on the fly as yet and considered anything above twelve inches very special and was delighted with a one-pound trout.

To add to the information I had gleaned about Yellowstone from chapters on the area in Bergman's *Trout*, I bought a small book at the park by Howard Back called *Waters of Yellowstone*. It was very well written and detailed, with stories of trout much bigger than those I had managed to connect with to date. One of the places it mentioned that intrigued me was Grebe Lake.

To get to the lake, you had to go to the end of a fire trail by car then hike in about two miles. There was a large population of grayling, a lovely troutlike species with a beautifully spotted dorsal fin that smells like wild thyme when first taken from the water. The clincher for me was that around the lily pads at the opposite side of the round lake from where the trail approached, there were supposed to be some very large cutthroat rainbow hybrid trout which could be enticed with flies on rare occasions.

That first time on Grebe Lake I worked my way around the right side of the lake, first crossing the little inlet stream that had the vestiges of an old fish trap where the Park Service presumably took eggs from grayling to distribute in other waters. Nice grayling were to be caught on wet flies and nymphs all the way around the lake, but when I arrived at the sandy point where a second small feeder entered the lake, just a little way from the outlet bay where the lily pads grew in profusion, I started to connect with more trout than grayling, and I started catching some very fine rainbows up to about two pounds.

In my lexicon of fish at that time these were pretty spectacular fish, and they fought magnificently, and I was lucky to be able to land any of them on the light gut leaders I was using in those days. They were willing takers, but my skills were limited and I lost most of them.

As I worked my way around the point and almost reached the edge of the lily pads, I saw a cruising fish that had me shaking with the awesome size of him. To my untrained eye he looked three feet long. In retrospect, he was probably a little over twenty inches and would have weighed close to four pounds if he were in equal condition to the fish I'd taken so far. I crouched low and waited until he was headed across and away from me before getting out a good cast well in front of his nose. The fly settled slowly in the water and I waited until the fish was within five or six feet of it and started a slow hand twist retrieve. That lumbering trout turned slightly and came right for the fly. I saw its mouth open and show white and I set the hook.

The fish panicked and came right out of the water, looking even bigger in the air, and fell back with an enormous splash, heading directly for the lily pads and was off within two seconds, escaping with my fly. He jumped again, twice, and I saw the fly. He looked so big I damned near cried. That was not the last time for me at Grebe Lake, it goes without saying.

Later in the summer when Paul and Mother were at the Lodge, we all took a fine pack trip together with Diana Jane Mowrer, Paul's niece. We went over the range bounding the south side of the upper Shoshone Valley, following Fishhawk Creek and crossing into Timber Creek, which we followed down to the upper edge of Yellowstone Lake, far from any roads. From there, we followed the shoreline south to the inlet of the upper Yellowstone River and up its valley to a beautiful lake just a stone's throw from the river called Bridger, after the famous early scout and explorer, Jim Bridger.

We made our second night's camp there and enjoyed some of the finest and, I must say, easiest fishing for trout I had ever encountered. You could see them cruising around easily, and no matter what fly you put anywhere near them, they would take without hesitation.

Compared to rainbows, the fight was disappointing, though it still felt good to have such hefty fish on the end of your outfit. Some of these fish would go 2½ pounds, but most of them were about 1¾, and almost none were smaller than a pound and a half. They were fat and healthy, and marvelous eating.

Diana Jane was only a year, possibly two, older than I, but she was easily ten times as smart. She was not only better read than I, but she was erudite in German, French, and Italian. She was also very competitive, and it was the first time I allowed fishing to become competitive, as I felt I had to be better at something to protect my masculine ego. But that was a mistake. She took to the fishing very well and quickly, indeed, and it was always a pretty close thing, though the old ego managed to survive somehow. Fortunately, she decided the constant pursuit of fish with a fly rod was not to be the main interest in her life and we went on to become good, close friends for many years.

I was scheduled to go to the L-T Ranch to spend the last days of the summer with Papa and my younger brothers. Pauline had gone to Europe with a friend. From the L-T I would be put on the train to return to school.

Before I left, I wanted to show Mother and Paul Grebe Lake. Neither had ever caught grayling and they both loved to hike. We stopped for a quick go at Yellowstone Lake on the way, but mother got a fly hook caught in her eyelid when a sudden gust of wind caught her line. Paul saved the day by slicing the hook out and Mother never flinched, so great was her trust in him. We continued the hike to Grebe Lake and both of them caught grayling and a few rainbows, then we headed back along the trail toward the car while I went through my usual routine of "just one more cast" which would sometimes last a half-hour or more, though I was confident I would be able to catch up with them.

When I did, I was delighted by the sight of Papa, Paul and Mother sitting on the edge of the trail talking animatedly. Papa had phoned the lodge and was told where we would be. He parked at the end of the fire trail, where we had left the car, and headed in after listening to the news on the radio. It was September 1 and the news was about the invasion of Poland by Germany and the consequent, imminent declarations of war by Britain and France.

By the time I arrived, they had finished their discussions of my progress in school, and any plans relating to me, and were deeply involved in discussing the probable events and calamities which would most likely follow in the wake of the day's events.

Both my father and Paul felt that there would be a long period of war and that we Americans would inevitably be drawn into it, despite the strength of the isolationists in both houses of Congress. It was wonderful for me to see my mother, my father, and Paul all together talking like that. They had maintained a regular correspondence, of course, because of the details of managing my education and travels back and forth, but this was the first time since the Paris days that they had been together, and, as it turned out, it was the last time ever.

Paul and Mother took their leave at the car to drive back to Holm Lodge to pack for their return to Chicago. Papa and I drove around the north end of the park and out the northeast entrance through Cooke City to the ranch. Papa was pleased to see how well my mother looked and how happy she obviously was with Paul. Though I never saw it in that light, it may have helped relieve his conscience.

On the way we stopped to talk to two bears, one a cinnamon and the other black-with-a-white blaze on its chest. Papa liked talking to bears, and it did appear that they reacted to the tone of his voice, either appearing cheerful and alert when he spoke kindly to them, ("Hey Bear, you're looking awful damn fat. Must've had a good summer, eh?") or seeming to cower and look aside in embarrassment when he chided them. ("Bear, you dumb son of a bitch, aren't you ashamed of yourself begging when other bears are out making an honest living, working? Bear, you're just no damn good.") I tried it, but my voice was ignored by the bears who seemed to know which of us in the car was the figure of authority and, possibly, a fellow bear.

When we got to the ranch, there was word that Pauline would be arriving shortly, and I saw her for a bit before I had to leave for school. She had a bad cold, so the boys and I spent our time shooting ground squirrels, fishing, and riding to near-by lakes and streams. After I left that year, Papa didn't stay for his usual fall hunt. Pauline took the boys back to Key West, and shortly thereafter Papa left to rendezvous with Marty and head over to Idaho and their first look at Sun Valley.

I guess this was the definitive rift with Pauline, for after the fall in Idaho, Papa and she were definitely separated and she was living in her apartment in New York while he went to Key West and moved out to the new home he and Marty had bought near Havana, on a hill overlooking the city and the sea. Marty had gone directly from Sun Valley on an assignment for *Collier's* magazine to cover the Russo-Finnish War. When she returned, there remained only the divorce proceedings to keep her and Papa from marrying right away.

That summer I received a tantalizing letter from Papa along with several glossy 8x10 photos which whetted my appetite for a visit to Idaho and, particularly, Sun Valley. The letter described their fine reception there, the great bird shooting, and Papa told about floating down Silver Creek in a canoe. "You'll love it here Schatz . . . there's a stream called Silver Creek where we shoot ducks from canoe . . . Saw more big trout rising than have ever seen . . . Just like English chalk streams . . . We'll fish it together next year . . . ," he wrote, "if money OK we'll spend the whole fall." He sent some photos including some of parties at Trail Creek. I was already hooked by the mention of English chalk streams. These were the ultimate in crystal clear meandering spring-fed rivers flowing through the Chalk Downs of Hampshire where dry fly fishing had got its start.

The photos included one of him with several beautiful, fat rainbows he'd caught in the lower Cottonwoods stretch of the Big Wood River where, he wrote, "The part fished was hundred feet wide, and shallow, and only hundred yards downstream flowed into narrow lava gorge three feet wide and hundred feet deep!"

The spot still exists, by the way, but the gorge has mostly filled in with gravel, and that stretch of the river runs dry during most of the irrigation season. In agricultural Idaho, crops take precedence over nature, which remains in the local ethic as something to be conquered and used and not to be "wasted" by "preservation."

Another photo found a prominent place on my dresser at school, as it featured a bar top in Slavey's Saloon in Ketchum, Idaho. Behind the bar was a comely lass, the bartendress, and lying in state in front of her was a gigantic trout, which the caption said weighed eighteen and a half pounds. To one side of the fish stood the angler, whom I later came to know well. He was Austin Lightfoot, a well-known guide who could, and would, use any means, not necessarily the most sporting, to catch his prey. Austin was, however, highly respected and, along with Taylor Williams, Sun Valley's head guide, had as wide-ranging and diversified a knowledge of the hunting and fishing within reach of Sun Valley as anyone I have ever known. The comely lass, alas, I never got to know. However, she was a true indicator of the great possibilities inherent in the beautiful women of Idaho. In a sense, I was looking at my distant future.

FOUR

My junior year at Storm King, I took my first course with Dean Malcolm Dyer. I had always held him in great awe. He was second in command to the Head; he'd already outlasted several of them, and when serious crises in the life of the school, such as the inevitable homosexual scandal between a teacher and a pupil, occurred, we all sensed his quiet authority, straightening things out and squelching the rumor factory, while the principals in the tawdry affair silently disappeared from our lives without so much as a ripple.

Dean Dyer hardly ever raised his voice, and he didn't have to. The few times that he did so were unforgettable and a strong recommendation for avoiding, at any cost, a recurrence thereof.

He taught Spanish and Latin. I'd had my fill of Latin at Chicago Latin School, but I decided I should add Spanish, since my father was going to be living permanently in Cuba and I was to spend spring vacation that year with him rather than in Chicago. I was to spend the Christmas holidays with Mother and Paul, and attend the Fortnightly Club's annual Christmas ball where the young pre-deb beauties of Chicago's Northside were looking better and better each year.

Dean Dyer was a good teacher and, because of the frequent exposure I'd had to spoken Spanish, I actually hungered for the formal knowledge which would put it all together. He never killed that hunger, and I had the miraculous feeling of having a language suddenly become, more or less, mine in a ridiculously short period of time. When I arrived in Havana, Papa met me at Rancho Boyeros Airport, and on the way home to the Finca I was already conducting a fairly comfortable conversation with Juan, the chauffeur, and secretly thanking Dean Dyer.

*   *   *

The Finca was really lovely, though the way there led through some of the worst slums I had ever seen, and the stench when we passed the tannery was not to be believed. Marty had done a superb job of renovation and the big house was a delight on its hilltop site with the view toward old Havana and the harbor, and inland, to the low range of hills toward Cotorro where the *Carretera Central* turned east toward Matanzas.

The pool had been made functional and was impressive with its two Grecian bath houses and the trellis-covered terrace at the western end where the steps led into the water. Below the pool, and next to it, was the tennis court which was of crushed coral limestone, pale pink, but glary in the hot sun. The backdrop behind the wire fence was a stand of bamboo. There was a guest house on the right of the entrance driveway just before arriving at the broad stone front steps which led up to the front door and the wide terrace on the left where vine arbors provided shade for eating outside. There was a view down the drive to the stand of mango trees, and down to the gardens where papayas and an assortment of vegetables were grown for our use. Behind the front steps, and in front of the east end of the house, was an enormously old ceiba tree which resembled nothing so much as a baobab tree with its large, high-reaching roots extending from the bulbous trunk like sinuous flying buttresses of smooth, grey bark. Many orchid plants lived on its trunk and among its broad branches, but spring was past their blooming season, which was, in fact, at about Christmas time.

All the rooms of the Finca were large and airy with high ceilings and a lot of light which showed off the fine collection of paintings to great effect. The Roberto Domingo original oils of some of his most famous bullfight posters were especially striking because their tall poster shape fitted in perfectly with the high walls. The dining room which gave off the living room formed the base of an L directly in front of you as you entered the living room; it extended to the left and was really more like a banquet hall but on a smaller scale.

Apart from the impressive African trophies, I was most struck by the familiar sight of Miro's *Farm* over the buffet on the left. It was a painting I had loved from earliest childhood, when my father bought it for my mother's birthday. She and I had had it throughout the years in Paris and then, when Mother and Paul were living in Chicago, Papa wrote to ask if he could borrow it for five years. My mother never saw it again.

The routine at the Finca during my visits was fairly regular in nature. Being on vacation, I usually slept in, as did Marty. Papa was always an early riser, whether or not he was working.

When all of us were visiting on vacations, he generally arranged to slow down whatever project he was working on and usually took care of correspondence very early in the morning. Since I slept in the "little house," his typing didn't waken me in any case.

He had a workroom with a big desk and a large double bed and bookcases, and his own bathroom at the west end of the house off the living room. Marty's realm was a beautiful large bedroom off the east end of the living room. She had her desk, and the conjugal giant double bed was in there. Her room suffered the slight inconvenience of overlooking a small courtyard on the north rather than having a view, and that courtyard separated the kitchen and servants' quarters from her room. Also, there was a dovecote overlooking the courtyard and Marty had the full benefit of the perpetual coo-cooing of the white pouter pigeons which inhabited it.

If we didn't drive to Havana harbor or Cojimar to take the *Pilar* out fishing in the Gulf Stream, which flows east to west along the North Coast, we would usually go to the *Club de Cazadores* to shoot live pigeons or play tennis and swim. During hunting season, we'd often go dove shooting over in Matanzas province where there were magnificent shoots with each gun averaging from 150 to 200 birds a day. We would take what birds we wanted for our own use, or for friends, and the rest would be sold and the proceeds given to the local kids and farmers who acted as our "*secretarios*," carrying ammunition and picking up birds as well as spotting the incoming targets for the less experienced hunters.

Papa invariably acted as the general and chief organizer, and I must say he had a real gift for getting people to function efficiently in activities with which they were often totally unfamiliar. He was, however, none too patient with fools, who, along with phonies, he would not suffer. I believe more than one friendship was ended by the incapacity of an otherwise intelligent person to follow simple instructions regarding some outdoor activity, when not following those instructions caused either an unpleasant or dangerous situation for others involved. I have noticed that many persons of notable intellect seem to have difficulty adjusting to situations requiring the subjugation of their view of themselves for cooperative purposes. But Papa gave no other choice.

Evenings, often as not, were spent around the table at the

Finca, but otherwise we would all go to the fronton for the *jai alai,* preceded by drinks at the Floridita. Sometimes it would be the fights, where Kid Gavilan was just getting to be known; Kid Tunero, a former Spanish European champion, was a good friend. Afterwards, there would be dinner at the El Pacifico, a rooftop Chinese restaurant where most of the vices were available on the other floors we'd pass on the rickety elevator to the roof garden. Or dinner might be at the Centro Vasco where many of the *pelotari* (the jai alai players) from the fronton would show up, and more than a few were there because Papa had helped ease their way óut of Spain after the Civil War.

They were fantastic athletes, though their taste for serious training was questionable. Sometimes they would come out to the Finca to play tennis. Their strokes were a joke but they retrieved absolutely everything. It was literally impossible to put away a shot on them. They were also jolly, cheerful, and great fun to have around, provided you weren't planning to be serious about anything.

Seldom did Papa consent to go out to nightclubs, or even movies, though I remember him taking me one time to see the first version of "The Island of Doctor Moreau." He detested formal parties and functions of any kind unless it were a Basque party for one of his friends where he could show up in his usual shorts and polo shirt, or slacks with a big belt worn outside the loops and a shirt and jacket but never a tie.

When at the Centro Vasco, we invariably spent some time before dining in the bar where there was usually an outburst of singing. Usually these were the old favorites which we all knew and in which we could participate but, occasionally, there would be some of the current Cuban popular songs which were particularly catchy. It was always great fun, and I believe Marty enjoyed it as well. Her tales of the Russo-Finnish War, from which she had just returned, were fascinating and, being a person of great responsibility and conscience, she was already showing signs of wanting to be off again to where the world was obviously starting to erupt.

This was the time when Papa was getting in his best licks on *For Whom the Bell Tolls,* and it was also almost the end of the phony war when the German invasion of France brought the world to a well-perceived state of very real crisis with the complete fall of France, the threatened invasion of Britain, and even more serious rumblings in the Far East where the Japanese were close to a complete control of China and were already hawking their Greater East Asia co-prosperity sphere.

*   *   *

I returned to school to complete my next-to-last year. Mr. Borg, our English teacher, made *Time* magazine required reading and, as a result, we were probably better informed than the average kids our age in the country. I found I had to soft-pedal my father's pro-Loyalist sympathies in the Spanish Civil War, since most American thought at the time regarded his point of view as revolutionary and anti-establishment.

On the whole, we Americans were a pretty smug people and quite satisfied to let the rest of the world go to hell, so long as it didn't cut us directly.

All of the years at Storm King were satisfying from an educational point of view. There were no girls, so my grades came back up to their old high standard which had faltered badly during the year at Lake Forest High. As I remember it, there were two or three dances a year at the school, and there was much planning in advance and great letter writing. Since most of the boys were from the greater New York area, most of them had girlfriends who could attend these affairs. Most of us from farther away formed a stag line and, very occasionally, acquired some juicy tidbits as the result of a fight between some guy and his gal. We learned to be optimists of the highest order in this regard, and I remember establishing a pleasant relationship with a girl who came as someone else's date for spring house party.

I got together with her several times in New York, but she was a part-time teen model for catalogs, and her tastes in entertainment were too sophisticated for my movie-and-a-snack allowance. I foolishly took her to a nightclub with dinner show and thought I had enough to cover the tab but ended up having to borrow ten dollars from her, which I repaid over a two month period. That was the end of that friendship. I couldn't afford it.

Since the early sexual experiences in Bimini, there had been no recurrences of that happy phenomenon. I was quite shy and seldom got past an occasional kiss, and that usually only at the end of the evening as my reward for having been entertaining or whatever.

The summer of 1940 witnessed my entry into some rather serious groping, which still led to nothing more than frustration. I spent the early part of the summer around home and up in what we then called "The North Woods," fishing in Wisconsin with Paul and my mother before finally driving out West in mid-July by myself for a spell at the Crossed Sabers Ranch, and then for further exploring in Yellowstone before driving across Idaho to meet Papa and Marty in Sun Valley. A nice girl from Chicago got me into the groping. Her parents had left her at Crossed Sabers for a couple of weeks (after they'd been obliged to return) because she loved it so much there and was a horse nut. We came awfully close but no good, or harm, depending on the point of view, came of it.

Sun Valley was like paradise found. Papa's letter of the previous fall had in no way exaggerated. Papa and Marty stayed in a suite at the Lodge while my brothers and I had adjoining rooms sharing a bathroom at the Inn. We could charge by using our room number anywhere within the confines of Sun Valley proper. This new temptation was the ruin of my youngest brother, Gregory. He went completely berserk and charged unbelievable quantities of any and everything from the drugstore, restaurants, bowling alleys, stables, ice-skating rink, the photo shop, tackle shop, and the trap and skeet ranges. The figure on the room bill would have been enough with our legitimate charges, but the number with Greg's signature was nothing short of astronomical, and Papa was furious. Thanks to Sun Valley's publicity department, run by Steve Hannagan, which had invited Papa and Marty the year before, the rooms were complimentary, but they didn't pick up the tab for extraneous expenses. By the time the smoke cleared, needless to say, Gigi had gained a whole new respect for the idea of credit.

Comping our rooms was not a bad deal at all for Sun Valley since it was no secret that Papa was just finishing work on the galleys for *For Whom the Bell Tolls,* and that there would be a lot of publicity forthcoming and, with any luck, Sun Valley would be prominently mentioned. Later that fall it was, of course.

I had gone back to school and Bob Capa, Papa's *Life* photographer friend from the Spanish Civil War, was assigned to do a feature story on "Hemingway in Sun Valley" with some great shots of Papa with Gary Cooper and my kid brothers hunting as well as partying at the Lodge and at Trail Creek Cabin. It was a cover story because *FWTBT* was starting to break records in sales and it was then that Donald Friede first came out to discuss movie rights for Myron Selznick of Paramount. It was later that fall, when I went to New York for a weekend from school, that the aforementioned Technicolor check incident took place.

Quite apart from the glamorous side of Sun Valley itself, for me the exploration of the fishing possibilities was the primary consideration. I would not be able to stay long enough to take part in that fall's hunting, but there were about two weeks in which to check the Big Wood River and Silver Creek. Both had received some publicity in *Field & Stream* in an article by Ray and Dan Holland concerning the making of a film on dry-fly fishing called "Silver Rainbows." It was apparently every bit as difficult and demanding as the greatest English chalk streams on the Hampshire Downs.

Clayton Stuart took me down to Silver Creek for my first try at it. We drove the thirty-odd miles with me peppering Stu, who was in his early twenties, very little older than I, with every question imaginable about the potential size of the fish, which flies to use, leader length, and tippet size. He was in his first year as a guide for Taylor Williams and he had the natural fine manners of a real Westerner, which was ideal for dealing with anxious city sportsmen who really needed to be put at their ease so as to avoid becoming competitive in their fishing, so they could settle down, relax, and enjoy the pure magnificence of it.

What puzzled me was that the entire trout population of Silver Creek was composed of rainbows. There were no brown trout, and yet I had read time and again that the truly difficult fish are browns, and that rainbows are relatively easy to deceive. I was to learn over the years just how difficult big rainbow trout can be, especially in the right circumstances. These were the circumstances on Silver Creek.

Located in a broad, pastoral valley with little incline, but surrounded by high, humpbacked, sagebrush-covered hills on both north and south, with the north hills backed by great mountain ranges, Silver Creek is formed by the confluence of a number of small tributary spring feeders into three prime tributary creeks, all of which join together on a property which belonged to the Union Pacific Railroad—owners, at the time, of Sun Valley. It was called the Sun Valley Ranch and was composed of about 780 acres.

In those days, the tributaries were all closed to fishing and there was no farming of any importance in the whole valley. The valley was devoted almost entirely to grazing, and even that was relatively light. There was no agricultural activity on the ranch at all. As a consequence, the creek was almost crystal clear at all times. There was a luxuriant growth of a wide diversity of aquatic plants, all of which made for ideal conditions for a great profusion of aquatic insects, scuds, shrimp, and snails. Such, then, was Silver Creek when Stu took me down that first time.

We crossed the sagebrush flat in our waders toward the inside bank of an acute horseshoe bend. At the top of the downstream leg of the horseshoe, a wooden stake was impaled in the creekbed, and it had trapped a line of weeds which streamed for ten feet below it. Stu cautioned me to stay low and then we sat on the bank with our legs in the water about thirty feet below the post and waited for the hatch, which he said was due to start at any time now.

It was a perfect day with a few scattered high clouds, and soon I saw the first rise. It was slow and deliberate, showing the head and then the dorsal fin of the fish as the pale-colored mayfly disappeared in the swirl. Stu suggested I put on a #16 ginger quill, one of the patterns we had stocked up on at Lane's shop at the Valley. I had on a 4X gut leader of nine feet.

Repeated casts—which seemed perfect to me—to that fish and to others which started rising regularly in two lines along either side of the weed line and ahead of the post, produced absolutely nothing, though I did manage to avoid putting them off their feeding by frightening them. We tried other patterns to no avail until, finally, a very small rainbow of about seven inches engulfed a Woodruff and was promptly released because it was too small. When we left, after two hours of frustration, I was thoroughly humbled, and Stu kindly assured me that it was that way quite a lot of the time, and that there were times when the fish seemed to be easier and would take more freely. I was certain there was a solution to the problem but I sure as hell didn't know enough to solve it yet. As we drove back, I was determined to figure it out and learn to succeed regularly when the fish were so obviously feeding.

I returned to Silver Creek alone several times but only improved my success very modestly, using the small, more delicate patterns I had had some success with in Yellowstone. I suspected there was something going on that I simply didn't understand, and it wasn't until many years later that I would gain a real understanding of the great variety of things going on under my very eyes that, at that moment, I hadn't the knowledge, capacity, or understanding to recognize and differentiate.

I had my best success when there was really no particular hatch taking place, and the only fish of any respectable size I caught were those waiting for targets of opportunity, such as insects blown into the stream from the banks. Such fish were not so particular so long as I didn't scare them by a careless approach or a sloppy cast.

Wood River was altogether another matter. I had no trouble catching decent fish in the stretches of the river close to Ketchum and Hailey. After Silver Creek, it was duck soup. When they were feeding, the fish rose freely to my flies, and when there was no surface activity, I simply fished wet flies and continued to catch the occasional fish.

But what I really wanted a go at was the place where that monster in the picture with the comely bartendress was caught. Austin Lightfoot wasn't around because he was guiding some fishermen up by Sunbeam Dam on the Salmon River, so Taylor Williams arranged for one of the finest big-fish fishermen in South Idaho at the time, Art Wood, to take me down to the Big Wood, down below Magic Dam in a narrow basalt canyon only three miles long, before the diversion dam siphoned off a considerable portion for a big irrigation canal.

Art was a big man in every sense. He looked to be about six-foot-four and he had the meat on his bones to go with it. It was said he could wade any river in the state. At sixteen, I was already five-eleven and heavy-boned and long in the legs, so I was a pretty good wader, or thought so until that day.

After an hour's drive across the desert country to the south, we arrived at the edge of the canyon above the very pool where Austin had caught the monster the year before. It was called the Wagon Wheel Hole, and we put on our waders and set out rods with line and leader but without putting them together so we could go through the maze of wild rose thickets and willows along the sides of the canyon.

We climbed carefully down a short stretch of black basalt cliff, being exceedingly careful about where we stepped or put our hands since two shed rattlesnake skins on the rocks were proof enough that we were in snake country. The rest of the way down was over a steep slope of fallen, black boulders to the bottom where we tried to stay along a scarcely visible path through the heavy brush until we had progressed, sweating through the oppressive heat of the bake-oven canyon, about 200 yards upstream.

We broke out into the open on a small, sandy shelf above a heavy current that looked about a foot deep but proved to be more like 2½ feet deep when we were standing in it. We put the rods together and I had an ungreased silk line on with a nine-foot leader to OX, and I put on one of the big, heavily-dressed wet renegades that Art handed me.

He rigged up a six-foot leader and an Andy Reeker flasher spoon with a 2/0 siwash single hook. He didn't bother to fish at first but spent his time showing me where to wade and which currents the fish were likely to be lying in. It wasn't fast and furious fishing, but every few yards as we worked our way along an unseen path down the middle of the river—a path which Art seemed to have perfectly mapped—there would be a jolting strike usually just as the big wet fly started to come off its natural downstream drift and headed cross-current toward a point directly below me.

The fish were fat and active and very strong in the heavy current, and most were 12 to 14 inches, with one or two up to 16 inches. Their condition factor was excellent and they were deep and heavy with the small heads of young fish that have grown disproportionately fast. The bottom was of coarse gravel, all covered with a dark, brownish-green moss, like algae, which was an indicator of the tremendous food-producing capacity of the water. There were parts where Art literally had to hold me down to keep the current from sweeping me away, and my felt-soled waders were no great advantage. Art was wearing old, hobnailed brogues which seemed to cut through the algae to the rock and hold better, which was another lesson for me.

The fishing tapered off as we came to the middle, deepest part of the pool, and we wended our way back toward the shore behind us. At this point, Art started fishing his Reeker, just letting it out on a medium long line and letting it work its wobbly action in the deep cut that was gaining strength toward the tail-out of the pool on our side. He directed me out onto the shallowing wide apron of the tail-out and told me to fish it all carefully and work my way all the way down through the shallow riffle leading into the top of the Wagon Wheel.

Art hooked several nice fish which were all bigger than mine, and he lost a fine fish of over three pounds which threw the Reeker as it cartwheeled in the air. The sun was below the canyon rim, and while my fly was traveling through what appeared to be the shallowest part of the riffle, there was a huge boil behind my fly and then a torpedo line toward it and I was suddenly hooked up to the biggest trout of my lifetime. It jumped clear of the water before tearing the hook free as it surged toward the shelter of the deep pool below.

Art yelled, "That was a real 'ne, Jack. Mebbe six pounds. If you hook another like him, let him get on the reel so's he can run. You can't hold fish like that!"

"I guess not," I returned, sadly, though I don't think he heard me above the rush of the water around our legs.

I finished out the riffle and the head of the pool where the tongue of heavy current dipped over the lip into the deep water, but no further action was forthcoming. Art came over to where I'd ended up and practically hauled me up through the riffle and through the heavy cut where he'd hooked his fish, and we clambered out and carefully climbed out of the canyon to the car. Going home that evening, Art, who wasn't known for gushing off at the mouth, finally said:

"Jack, you cast like hell, and if you keep fishing that stretch of water you're gonna end up with one hell of a fish someday." A gracious compliment.

"Art," I answered, "if I could wade that water like you, I'd be down there every day 'til I have to leave."

"Son, you just keep eatin' heavy and don't worry. You'll make 'er one of these days."

It was hard to leave Sun Valley to return to Chicago for a few days before my return to Storm King. Papa had been in good form and we'd had great times with Rocky and Gary Cooper, Howard and Slim Hawks, and our new local friends. I got to know Howard and Slim from sessions at the skeet range. He was a skillful and enthusiastic shotgunner, then on the top of his directing career. Both he and Slim were fit sporting types on the lean side. Slim was a great beauty, though despite my liking her open manner she didn't have the sort of beauty which at that time appealed to me. They were the sort of looks which endure, however, and to this day she is a knockout. We shot together later again for doves in Cuba, and I was somewhat surprised when Slim later went on to become Mrs. Leland Hayward.

Rocky Cooper liked shotgun shooting as well and was a friendly, easy person to get to know despite her tough veneer. It was a long time before I felt comfortable around Coop; my own fault I suppose. I was simply too shy around his fame. I didn't yet know how shy he himself was.

What was especially difficult, though, was having to leave Sun Valley while Pat and Greg, known then as Mouse and Gigi, got to stay on through the hunting season. Still, since then I've more than made up for it.

*　　　*　　　*

It was an exciting school year. Suddenly it was important being a senior. Aside from the diversions of weekends in New York with Papa and Marty, more boxing lessons with George Brown at his gym where Papa worked out, and meeting Marty's friend H.G. Wells, who was in no way condescending to me, there was the excitement of planning for college, although it was decided that I was to have a job for a year before going on to college. However, this was sweetened by the prospect of spending the whole fall of 1941 in Sun Valley before going off to work on one of the construction crews building U.S. defense bases in the Pacific. Actually, this prospect came up later on when Papa and Marty returned from an extended trip to China and the Burma Road, from January until May 1941.

My longtime ambition to go to Oxford was now out of the question because of the war. My headmaster, Anson Barker, an old Amherst grad, suggested I try Brown. I was also attracted by the well-known fisheries research at Cornell, and we'd had the Cornell football team stay at our school for a few days before playing West Point—we were awed by the enormous and friendly gridiron heroes. Howard Stiles, my French teacher and football coach, suggested his *alma mater* in Maine, Bowdoin, or possibly Dartmouth, because both had all the outdoor amenities that I was known for loving so much.

At any rate, I had plenty of time to decide, with the prospect of a year and a summer between graduation and going to college, whichever school I chose. In those days, if your grades were respectable and you could afford it, you could choose any college you wanted, and, chances were, you would get it.

It was an exciting year all around. Paul's oldest son, Rich, was a foreign correspondent and had been captured by both sides the previous year during the fighting between the Germans and the Russians in Poland and had just got out by the skin of his teeth, by a long escape route south, and ended up in Turkey just in time for one of the most disastrous earthquakes in their long history of quakes. He got the story and went on to Israel where he was in the Hotel St. George when the Stern Gang blew it up, and he was lucky to get out with only a serious leg break. While in hospital there he met a local nurse and fell in love, which is, apparently, not an uncommon phenomenon. They married and, after a home visit when we all met the bride, they went on to Alexandria, Egypt where he became the local correspondent and had some hair-raising experiences during the early days of the desert war. His younger brother, Dave Mowrer, was an aeronautical engineer for Boeing in Seattle involved in the design of a very advanced new bomber which would, just a few years later, make all the difference in the air war all over the world. It wasn't yet called the B-17.

Paul's younger brother, Edgar, who was Diana Jane's father, and his wife, Lillian, had a sticky time of it getting out of France during the German siege and barely made it out through Portugal. They settled in Washington, D.C. where he became a syndicated columnist specializing in foreign affairs.

Though I was more aware of the imminence of war than most, because of these family connections, it still seemed a distant thing, and graduation, followed by an exciting summer, was foremost in my mind. That spring of 1941 I broke new ground for me by catching two brown trout over 16 inches in the small brook that ran down from Stuart Pond through the Black Rock Forest behind the school. The importance was that I located the fish and saw that they were nymphing and actually used an upstream nymph for the first time successfully. I was starting to develop a bit more breadth to my flyfishing repertoire.

FIVE

Graduation was full of excitement. Paul and Mother drove all the way from Chicago in their new Pontiac and planned to take the train back from New York City, leaving me to drive the car back to Chicago along with a couple of friends, Bernabe Sanchez and Hilary Maher—Hilary was the younger brother of my old pal, Boolie, who was graduating from Milton Academy.

It was to be our first drive across the eastern states into the Midwest, and when we got to Lake Bluff we had about a week to kill before two other friends, Al Millet and the elder Maher, would be ready to leave. Mrs. Maher, who had been divorced from her architect husband a couple of years, had a good friend who owned the Hines Lumber Company with a big mill out in Oregon, just outside Burns in just about the geographic center of the state. She was able to arrange for Boolie, Al, and me to get jobs in the mill starting the latter part of July as "lumber students." This was a sort of industry training program which allowed us to work in the mill without having to be union members, as it was supposed to be the preliminary stage of an executive training program.

We decided to drive my old '37 Pontiac sedan, which had replaced the '35 coupe, up to the Upper Peninsula of Michigan.

*　　　*　　　*

On June 15 Al Millet, Bernabe Sanchez and I took off from Chicago headed north with the objective a new one for all of us—the Big Two-Hearted River in the Upper Peninsula of Michigan. Al had been closest to it since he had spent many summers with his family at the Huron Mountain Club. He assured us it would not be good because it held only a spring run of lake dwelling rainbows, but I insisted that it must have fish in the swampy section my father had described in his short story, "Big Two-Hearted River," that we had all read in school.

We passed a lot of likely-looking water on the way north but remained firm in our objective. The road across the U.P. was not promising and the country looked less trouty by the mile. It was alternately rolling, flat, dusty, and sparsely wooded and I was starting to lose faith in my conviction. On the way to Newberry we did cross one fine looking stream, the Fox.

When we finally arrived at our destination it was hard not to give in to abject disappointment. The place where we hit the river, which was really a pretty small stream on that hot June day, was disenchanting, to say the least. We were prepared for the tea-colored water, but the pure sand bottom, the marginally warm temperature, and the featureless straight-away from the edge of the sand dunes where the stream made its long shot parallel to the shore before finally emptying into Superior, were not calculated to raise our hopes of catching trout.

Where it wound in sharp bends through the dunes, things appeared to be somewhat better. There was at least some kind of cover in the form of snags, stunted trees of varied kinds, and most of all there were blueberries. We set up camp—just our sleeping bags, a tarp and cooking gear—and then put up our rods. We took the car and followed a track which looked well-worn and then left it to be closer to the stream. That was our fatal error, though we weren't to find out about it until the next day.

We fished different stretches of the river. I headed up, skipping a long stretch, to try to find the swamp. I found an approximation of a swamp where, to no avail, I fished blind to every indication of possible cover or depression in the sandy bottom. I never saw a single rise form nor any sudden movement across the light covered bottom and, hoping for better things with the cooling advent of evening, I gave in to the berries. The picking, hoarding, and eating of blueberries can be a fascinating pastime when nothing else is going on. I loaded up and then fished my way down toward our camp where I arrived at dusk with not even a pull on the wet flies I had used. I found my friends in the same straits. Not a sign of a fish seen or felt by either of them. We decided after a heated canned dinner that we would get the hell out of there first thing in the morning and find us a real trout stream.

The next morning reality struck with a vengeance in the form of our inability to get the car through the seemingly short hundred or so feet back to the track without sinking up to the hubs in sand. We had no shovel and didn't want to sacrifice our new sleeping bags as mats as we had saved all winter for them. Hell, we were just plain stuck. I was elected to walk out and somehow get to the nearest town for help. Help was much closer than I expected in the form of a berry picking camp about two miles along the track. I asked the man in charge if he could help us and he replied that he could and it would cost us ten dollars. I knew we barely had that among us and it would have to go for gas to get us home. I told him we were close to broke and he said we could work for it by picking berries. If we stayed at it all day we could make it in two days. He said if we were regular pickers we could do it a lot faster; but since we were new, it would take two days for sure.

I got the boys and we went to work. Ever since then I've sympathized with the Chicanos who bend over all day picking fruit and vegetables. Man, it's a killer, especially if you have been stuffing yourself with berries and have to hit the bushes every two hours.

Well, we finally made the two days and the boss got his rig into where our car was and got us out. We decided we were short on time and low on money and headed back to Chicago. But I still love blueberries and I still love trout fishing. I have not, however, set foot in upper Michigan since.

Years later I told my father about the trip and he said the Big Two-Hearted never was much of a year-round trout stream after the logging and the fires. He had loved the name but fished another place. I could have used the information a lot sooner.

*　　　*　　　*

The trip to the U.P. taught us, at least, that we could all four fit into the old Pontiac with all our gear, after eliminating a few unnecessary items. It had been a proper shake-down cruise, even if a little hard on our morale, but we were, if anything, resilient and looking forward to our great adventure in the West.

I was the only one who had been before; Bernabe had never even set foot west of the Hudson. Phil and I had taken a week's bicycle trip up in Wisconsin once when we were thirteen. At the beginning of the trip we had been on the best of terms, but by the end of it, when we were staying at a fishing lodge on Ghost Lake and got cabin fever from too much of each other's company, we were hardly speaking. In the meantime, we'd gotten over those difficulties and become fast friends again.

Phil knew Al Millet better than I did, but Al's mother was a close friend of my mother's and of Paul's and I could vouch for his deep enthusiasm for fly fishing. Phil had fished with him at the Huron Mountain Club and they both knew what they were doing. Bernabe loved fishing and, after I had introduced him to fly fishing in the Black Rock Forest, he experimented with it, fishing for bass on his family's cattle ranch in Camagüey province in Cuba. He had read all the fishing books that I had with me at school and was dying to have a really serious go at trout. You might say we were, all of us, trout crazy and that fly fishing for these fish was the real enthusiasm of our young lives—taking precedence even over chasing young ladies.

We had each been given enough money by our parents to handle our bare necessities and no one had more than anyone else. We'd planned the trip very carefully and there wasn't much room for extras. We could have telegraphed for money in case of emergency, but I think our pride would have prevented our doing so except under the gravest of circumstances. We pooled our resources and ate the same, or at least the same-priced, food when we were on the road and, of course, when we were cooking in camp. On the road there wasn't much of a problem since we all had hamburgers, french fries, and milk shake appetites. After the routine of school food, these were true luxuries and we seldom tired of them. Also, it was our common opinion that the quality of these American basics varied greatly, and, moreover, they improved the further west we traveled. This was apparently true up to a point, but more about that later.

We all took turns driving and, since there was room enough to sit three-abreast in the front seat, one of us could always be napping on the back seat. We were so impatient to reach the Yellowstone country that we just kept driving right through, stopping only for meals and to relieve ourselves and freshen up at gas stations. It was a wonder the old Pontiac put up with such a grueling ordeal. It never did get a rest until we'd reached the east entrance of Yellowstone Park. We avoided the temptation of stopping in the beautiful Bighorns of East Central Wyoming even though Ten Sleep Creek, coming down the west slope of the range, looked fishable, though still a little bit high from a late runoff. We were all of one mind: get to Yellowstone.

The weather being good, we camped in our sleeping bags one night outside the park entrance, at Pahaska, and the next morning proceeded into the park. We couldn't resist Sylvan Lake, the first one we came to, which was small and which I had tried once before with some success. It was surrounded by trees right to the bank, so it was necessary to wade out into dead trees that had fallen into the quickly deepening water to be able to cast properly. All of us managed to get into at least one or two of the many small cutthroat trout in the lake by fishing ungreased silk lines and letting our nymphs sink slowly to the bottom before starting a slow hand twist retrieve. The boys were delighted but I hurried them away from there since I felt that we wanted to get to some of the areas where we would have a chance of bigger and more difficult fish.

We had decided to use the Madison Junction campground as base headquarters for our extended stay in the park, but, first I wanted them to have a look at the park as a whole so they'd have a better idea of the topography and the possible choices. All of us had read Howard Back's *Waters of Yellowstone* and Ray Bergman's *Trout,* so even the first-timers had preconceived ideas about where they wanted to concentrate their activities.

Actually seeing what you've read about in a book or magazine article can be quite a shock, since we tend to construct our own image of what we expect to see from the author's words. I thought both Howard Back and Ray Bergman had done splendid jobs of describing the places they fished and particularly enjoyed, but I was a poor judge, since I had already seen most of the places they described before reading their work. My friends had built images from the writing without having seen any of it and I was anxious to see if they would be surprised, disappointed, or pleased by the actuality.

After leaving the little lake, we descended toward Yellowstone Lake and followed its shore north and west to Lake Junction where we started north on the upper loop of the figure-eight road which delimits travel within the park.

It's always a pleasure to take an appreciative audience through a magnificent piece of country such as Yellowstone. We made the whole inner circuit that first day and there was enthusiasm about everything from the geyser basins to the magnificent Yellowstone River, its Grand Canyon and its Great Falls, and farther down river, Tower Falls. We had no cameras with us but some of these sights remain indelibly in the memory and require no camera to bring them back.

We made the high ridge to Norris Junction and then down the Gibbon drainage to Madison Junction where we established our semi-permanent campsite. Even though Madison Junction campground was relatively uncrowded in those days, it was, nonetheless, crowded from our point of view. With our primitive arrangements, and just a tarp instead of a tent, it was unpleasant having people's dogs, which were supposed to be muzzled and leashed in the park at all times, come around sniffing us in our sleeping bags, or, as sometimes happened, chasing a bear through the camp when the bear was only doing its regular rounds of the garbage cans.

A lot of people stayed in that campground most of the summer and they had fancy tents or trailers, which were just starting to come into vogue. They were mostly retirees and they would go into West Yellowstone to buy supplies periodically, and most of them didn't even fish but just lazed around and gossipped among one another. They were friendly to us and gave us helpful hints about where to stop and what foodstuffs would last without going bad too fast. It was dangerous to keep food even in your car, let alone in the camp, because of the bears who could, and sometimes actually did, open up a locked car if the aromas emanating from it were sufficiently tantalizing. They could open it with a swipe of their paws just like a can opener and it was awesome to see a car they'd broken into. It gave you, so to speak, food for thought.

We found that West Yellowstone had the best tackle stores and, at that time, both Pat Barnes and Don Martinez had the fly business all sewed up between them. We were inclined to overspend our budgets when we went into their shops. The problem was that they had really well-tied flies which were successful patterns in the area and, though we brought tying equipment with us, our materials were limited in scope.

I had learned tying from the son of the British Consul in Chicago, Peter Bernays, and then, through a connection of Paul's on the Chicago *Daily News,* I had the opportunity to spend a couple of days at Paul Stroud's operation in Arlington Heights, just outside Chicago, where he had a bevy of ladies tying for him. He was a good commercial tyer and took the trouble to teach me lots of shortcuts and tricks of the trade, including tying his standard hair wing patterns very sparse so they could be fished upstream and would sink quickly. The tendency in those days was for commercial tyers to overdo the materials because people thought they were getting more for their money, while, in fact, they were receiving inferior goods which didn't become effective until they were half worn out. Most importantly, watching the ladies tie was an eye-opener in the art of neatness and organization, and it was there that I learned to make small neat heads on my flies.

Paul Stroud kindly gave me some sample nylon leaders and tippet material which he had dyed brown with silver nitrate. The brown was useful for the Wisconsin and Michigan streams where he and his customers did most of their fishing, and where the water was, often as not, of varying shades of brown due to the acidy bogs through which they flowed. Several streams in the Madison drainage, including the Madison itself, have the same tint to a lesser degree, but for different reasons, I believe.

The nylon leaders were a huge success but it was hard to share them equitably. I must admit, there is a fine feeling in having a bit of an edge over the other guys in the matter of tackle. The leaders made it possible to land larger fish on lighter tippets and, while they tended to float, unlike their soaked-gut counterparts, it didn't seem to make much difference, though all the authorities used to insist that the fly in dry-fly fishing should float but that the leader should be completely submerged while the line floated. It was not often that even a highly-skilled angler managed to get it all together, and it usually didn't last long when he did. So it was a real pleasure just to forget about trying to sink the leader altogether and to have the results better than they had been heretofore.

The month in Yellowstone was a memorable one for all of us. We each had our favorite places and we moved around a lot, but because of its convenience and the transportation problems, we concentrated heavily on the Madison drainage, which includes the Gibbon and Firehole Rivers, and the Madison itself, which is formed by the juncture of the other two. This was, by all odds, the most challenging fishing and it enabled us to be easily distributed at various points in a relatively small area, to be picked up later by whoever took the car.

Each of us had our particular high points, and I had three that stand out still as bench marks of that trip, and milestones in my fishing progress.

The first was an incident late in the evening after a long and frustrating day on the Madison where I had frightened each and every big fish I had tried to approach. We were all tired and it was someone else's turn to cook. I decided to walk up across Firehole Road and fish for the last half-hour of light in the grass meadow of the last quarter mile of the Gibbon just before it flowed under the bridge to join the Firehole a few hundred yards downstream. I had an English Hardy Brothers tied #16 blue-winged olive with double-duck quill wings dyed dark slate blue and a quill body dyed olive with dark olive hackle and tail. As I approached the stream across the meadow, I heard the *plunk* rise of a big fish and could only guess at the exact location next to the overhanging grass along the opposite bank. I knew I could not get a long drag-free drift and just hoped I had guessed right about the location.

I had, and I heard the slurp of the fish taking my fly and tightened carefully into a fine fish that didn't fight spectacularly at all but was my biggest brown trout to date when he came to the net and I could admire all nineteen inches of him and his beautiful red spots and butter yellow lower flanks.

I didn't then realize the importance of not killing a fine fish such as this one and I quickly dispatched him and took him back into camp where he was admired and quickly cooked and consumed. He was the first one we'd had to cut in half in order to fit into our large frying pan. I cleaned the dishes willingly that night and slept soundly through any bear invasions that may have occurred.

The second highlight was also on the Gibbon but way up at the top end of Gibbon Meadows, above the falls and some ten miles from camp where Phil and Al had remained to fish the Madison while Bernabe and I explored the upper Gibbon. It was afternoon and Bernabe started at the lower end of the big meadow while I went into it some 200 yards above, where it wound around out of the lodgepole pine woods and where its meanders were a nightmare filled with deadfalls all the way from the foot of the Virginia Cascades.

The first two hundred yards in the open meadow yielded only tiny brook trout, though a few torpedo-like wakes appeared from unlikely spots in the slick water side of undercut bends as large trout were surprised in their hunting of smaller trout and minnows in the shallows when I approached from below, directing my casts to the more obvious deep currents running against the undercuts. It was starting to get late, and that strange time when there seems to be very little activity if any was upon us. I had almost reached the edge of the woods and there was a log lying in the stream with its root system upstream and about twenty feet of tree extending downstream alongside the edge of the bank close to the road, and invisible from the road.

The tangle of roots was at the top end of a straightaway just below a sharp bend, and the current above the bend flowed almost directly into the top of the roots where it was then deflected to the right and down along the edge of the log. It was a natural place for a big trout because the current had gouged out a deep spot under the log and just ahead of it. The current was slow and there was no rushing water by the log but just an easy flow with an occasional bubble.

I saw no rises along the log but couldn't resist it anyway, so I worked my casts up very carefully and gradually, each cast landing just a bit farther upstream than the one before. I was using the same blue-winged olive from Hardy's that had done the damage with the 19-inch brown on the lower meadow in the evening. I had changed from the lighter-colored flies I'd used lower in the meadow, as the small brookies had demolished them. I was totally unprepared for what happened next.

I was so certain there was a big fish along that log that when the fly disappeared in a tiny bubble I didn't even bother to strike, as I was sure a small fish had taken it again and I didn't want to frighten the big one by having a baby thrashing around as I pulled it out to free the hook. Unfortunately, my fly had apparently been snagged on an underwater protrusion or a weed when the small fish took it under and I applied pressure to release it as carefully as possible.

That's when the "fit hit the shan," as Dr. Spooner was wont to say. It hadn't been a small trout at all but a very large rainbow who'd simply sipped the tiny morsel from the surface making hardly any disturbance at all, save for the single bubble. He'd held the fly in his mouth totally undisturbed or frightened until I set the hook thinking I was releasing from a snag. He came right out of the water and I was lucky he didn't reenter on the other side of the log or in the tangle of roots. He then headed out across the current and rushed down past me and tore line from the reel before jumping again, two or three more times. After that it was just a dogged resistance with a couple of short runs and finally he lay on his side in the shallows about twenty-five yards downstream where I shakily tried to get him into my net, which was too small except when I got him bent almost in half.

He was the most beautiful rainbow I'd ever seen and was in excellent condition. He measured 22 inches, exactly. I laid him out on the grassy bank after dispatching him and just sat there admiring him for about ten minutes until Bernabe came slogging up in his water-filled waders. He had taken a dunking farther downstream but had stung a good fish, and otherwise, had had the same experience of tiny brook trout that I had. He was as ecstatic over the big rainbow as I was and suggested that we get it to West Yellowstone the next morning first thing and have it shipped with dry ice to my mother and Paul in Lake Bluff.

He came into town with me the next day and we got it off all right, but what was received at home was quite another matter. There had been some delays in the train schedules and the delivery to the house, and that notable fish arrived a rotting mess, though we didn't find out about it until much later.

I was very lucky with that fish and it taught me several important lessons which I try not to forget. A quiet bubble rise is very often the rise of a truly large trout in slow water. Art Wood's advice about fighting the fish directly on the reel, instead of hand-lining him, if he's big, is the only sound way to proceed if you're to avoid trouble. And, finally, luck is important.

The last week of our time in the park we decided to do a real backpack-type hike into an area totally unknown to us, where we would be completely away from it all for a couple of days. It was to be our grand finale as a complete group because Bernabe had to leave us to go back to Cuba for the balance of the summer where he would be working on the Camagüey ranch. Our proposed destination was Heart Lake, one of the sources of the South Fork of the Snake River, which runs out of the south end of Yellowstone through Jackson Lake and Teton National Park to its eventual destination in Southeast Idaho.

The trek to Heart Lake is a grinding eight-mile hike over a hump lined with geysers and hot springs on the downhill side, dropping down to the lake. We did not, in fact, have any backpacks but simply rolled what we needed into our sleeping bags which we rigged as horseshoe rolls and slung over our shoulders with pots and pans jangling from our belts and rods and reels in our hands. We left our waders behind in the locked car at the trail head. The weather was unusually warm and we were hot, sweaty, tired, and hungry when we got to the lake shore. We didn't bother making camp properly because our first action was to take off all our clothes and run and dive into the lake for a bracing swim. Then, of course, instead of getting things organized, we all decided to have a go at the fishing around the stream mouth where the flow of many small, cold streams and the hot springs we had passed made an alluvial fan out into the lake, which otherwise appeared to be quite deep around its shores.

The fan should have been a natural feeding place for big trout, since it was a gathering place for minnows, and big fish can corner and catch minnows more easily in shallow water where the schools panic when they are chased against the shore, falling easy prey to the attackers. Such was not the case in this instance and we kept doggedly fishing until it was pitch dark and not one of us had had a strike.

As it turned out, we should have fished all night, even if we caught nothing. When we quit and went back to the pile of sleeping bags and organized some food, we ate quickly and, being bone tired, just left the cooking mess, the dirty tin plates, and the frying pan with its thick film of grease to clean in the morning. We would never have been so sloppy around our permanent camp at Madison Junction because of the bears, but we had been led to believe that all the bears in the park were concentrated near the roads, campgrounds, and garbage dumps where the pickings were easy.

Our sleeping bags were rolled out in a line, each about two feet away from the next. Mine was on one end near the doused-out campfire. We all fell into a deep sleep with no difficulty at all, and we were glad we'd left the big tarp we'd used for rain shelter back at the car, since the weather was so fine and warm.

I awakened to a distinctly unpleasant odor and the sound of rattling metal very close. I didn't want to open my eyes but I did, and looking straight up could see nothing at all of the clear night sky. There was a heavy grunt right above me and, instinctively, I tried to shrink into the smallest possible form I could, which provoked an instant reflex action from our visitor who swiped at the offending form under it and then went on calmly licking away at the greasy frying pan and the leavings of our meal, not to mention the rest of the food we had planned for the next day.

I had distinctly felt a sharp blow at the moment of the swipe and I was frozen with fear. The bear, for such it was, moved over a few yards to get better purchase, I presume, on one of our cans and I finally ventured an arm out of the bag to touch Phil who was on my right. He groaned and I pushed insistently until he rolled over and asked what was up.

"Look behind me," I said. "What do you see?"

He got up on an elbow and immediately scrunched back into his bag muttering, "Oh, God!"

I heard the bear scrounging around for what seemed forever before it finally left. I didn't get out of the bag to check it out, I can assure you, and finally went back to sleep, though how, I don't know.

The following morning, bright and early, we had damage assessment. Phil just thought he had had a bad dream until I showed him the rip in the top of my sleeping bag and the very faint scratch marks across my chest. Our eating and cooking utensils were a mess, and the other two wanted to know why we didn't wake them. We readily admitted that we were too damned scared. I know I was, and the tear in the bag, and the scratches, faint as they were, demonstrated what a truly close call I'd had. We all kidded about it on the hike back out, which we started right away since the next two days of fishing had to be aborted, but I can assure you that I never slept completely without some foreboding in the Western wilds ever again, even if only subconscious. Also, I think all of us learned never to leave food around a campsite, whatever the circumstances.

We decided to try the famous Widow's Preserve for our last expedition together with Bernabe. Its real name is Culver Springs, but in those days it was still the property of the two sons of the widow who had established her home on a knoll overlooking the head of the long spring pond. The greatest volume of spring flow came into the pond right there at the head in a beautiful shallow pool with a light-colored bottom punctuated by patches of bright green water weeds. The spring was about an hour's drive out of West Yellowstone over a summit into Idaho and around Henry's Lake to another small dirt road over a small divide into the upper end of the Centennial Valley.

We followed the directions in Howard Back's book and found the brothers' cabin without difficulty, and there was no one else fishing there. The brother we talked to said that we could go ahead and fish but that we would have to come by the house afterward and have the fish weighed and pay forty cents a pound for them cleaned. With our slim budget, we agreed among ourselves that we would only keep a couple of fish each to eat, and release the others.

We went right down to the spring head to start fishing, distributing ourselves around it. We were considerate of each other and could all fish a small area like this in a cooperative fashion without causing too much of a ruckus and frightening fish. Over the course of the trip, we'd learned not to tear our fly lines out of the water to start the next cast, but to finish out the retrieve and lift out lines as gently as conditions permitted, avoiding false casting as much as possible when we were fishing wet, and learning to shoot line accurately.

From a mechanical point of view, we had become accomplished fly fishermen, all of us. We acquired a lot of know-how, but mostly, we made up in enthusiasm and energy for what we lacked in knowledge. The latter would come only with the passage of time spent on streams, ponds, and lakes over a lifetime. I know that at this juncture we thought of ourselves as being pretty hot stuff, and, of course, we were headed for our come-uppance. We all caught very nice brook trout from a pound to three pounds fishing nymphs crawled very slowly along the bottom. They were gorgeous fish with their glorious color array at its brightest in the perfect water of the springhead.

We had heard that there were giant rainbow in the pond farther down and that there were some unusually big brook trout as well. Reputedly, rainbows had been caught weighing close to twenty pounds and brookies of six to eight pounds were supposed to be a distinct possibility. Whether or not this was true, one thing was certain. This secret hideaway contained some of the biggest fish we had encountered so far and they seemed to be lacking in sophistication to an extent that would enable us to come away from there with the fish of our lifetimes.

No one had mentioned to us that there were a lot of very large grayling in the long pond as well as rainbow and brook trout. As we worked our ways separately around the pond, the first surprise for all of us was seeing rising fish that seemed fairly large and, from the look of it, were apparently feeding on emerging and adult damsel flies—the long-bodied kind we often called "darning needles." We didn't then know that the nymphs would probably be the most effective for the larger fish, and besides, we didn't know what damsel fly nymphs looked like.

We all found our own solutions, and mine was to find the largest spent-winged dry flies I had in my box, which happened to be spent mayflies that Paul Stroud's ladies had tied to imitate the Michigan mayfly, or *hexagenia*. It filled the bill and I started catching very large grayling that were twice the size of anything I'd run across in Grebe Lake. I kept one that was unusually large, measuring twenty-three inches. Farther down the lake I saw some more rising going on in a small bay where I had to wade out through a tangle of water moss of the water buttercup family of *ranunculus*. By the time I reached a point where I was at the edge of the weed bed and could reach relatively open and clear water, I had waded almost to the top of my waders which reached about halfway between my belt and arm pits. It was awkward casting, but from the heavy look of the rises which were now within reach, it would be more than worth it.

I thoroughly dried the big spent mayfly and soaked it in the floatant we used in those days, which was a mix of cleaning fluid and candle wax which dissolved if we kept the bottle in a pocket against our body, and left a light film of wax on the fly. When we shook the fly in the capped open-mouthed bottle, the solution cleaned off the slime from any fish it had caught previously. It had the slight disadvantage of changing the color of the fly to some extent, but we didn't let that bother us, and it apparently didn't bother the fish.

It did seem important, however, to flick the excess fluid off thoroughly by casting and completely drying the fly before casting to a fish. Otherwise, the fluid left an ugly coating on the surface of the water like oil or gasoline. The fish would consistently refuse such a fly almost as if it were a repellent. This certainly wasn't the case in the little moss-filled bay. The very first cast when the fly alighted on the surface brought a vigorous rise and solid take. I didn't even have to strike or tighten up. The fish simply took the fly and dove for the bottom, which was apparently lined with more of the moss, because I was suddenly tangled in some kind of growth and, naturally, lost the fly trying to retrieve it.

I had about a half dozen of the big spent-wing hexes. Before putting on another, I retrieved everything and shortened the leader from nine feet to 3X by removing the last eighteen inches of tippet and fastening the fly directly to the heavier 2X. After the full procedure of dressing with floatant and drying, I cast out again and once again had a firm take in a big boil of a rise and the fish dove once more into the moss and was lost.

I'm fairly sure they were big brook trout. I never really did find out, though, because I never managed to land one of the damned things, even when I was down to three feet of butt section which must have tested about ten pounds, at least. At that point I was determined to hold the fish out of the moss at any cost. I cast little more than six feet of line and the short leader and fly, and when the inevitable take came, I held on as hard as I could, and I'm no weakling. The fish dove like an irresistible force and the hook straightened out and came free. I was thoroughly beaten.

I left the little bay and had a hell of a time getting out, as I'd been sinking in deeper and deeper the longer I stood on the mucky bottom. When I reached shore, I'd been over the wader tops and was soaked to the skin and in a foul mood. I couldn't take the beating I'd been given by a bunch of dumb fish. They had to be dumb or they wouldn't have been fooled by the fly on such a short, heavy leader.

They beat me, anyway, and I shudder to think what would have happened if I'd hooked one of the big rainbows. These brook trout must have been well over five pounds to exert so much power, though I can't swear to it. It's still nice to think about, though, and to wonder how I'd solve the problem now if I had it to do over again in the same place.

My companions had had similar experiences, but all different in their own way. One of them did have a hookup with a big rainbow that took off on a power run and jumped off. Bernabe showed the good sense to stick with the springhead pool and its edges and caught many more fine brook trout and some of the big grayling. We had all kept our two fish; each of us had one grayling and one brookie.

When we checked out at the cabin, we had just over twenty pounds of fish between us and it cost us a little over eight dollars—a lot more than we'd expected. On the other hand, each of us had broken his personal best on brook trout, including Al who had fished for coasters (the big brook trout of the Great

Lakes) in the river mouth at the Huron Mountain Club.

I returned to Culver Springs many years after the war and found it was government property and part of a federal migratory waterfowl refuge. If the big brookies are still there, they are not in evidence and there are no longer any grayling. There was a large feed-storage tank for the waterfowl and the tracks of many anglers as well as trash. I've never bothered to go back again.

SIX

Now that the first part of our summer's idyll was over, with the departure of Bernabe Sanchez, the three of us remaining had to start facing up to paying the piper for all the great fun and fishing we'd enjoyed. We had a few days before we had to report to the Hines Lumber mill, so we headed off the Yellowstone plateau toward Idaho. Besides occasional rest stops along the way, we stopped for a milk shake in the small town of Sugar City which turned out to be, in our highly-educated opinions, the zenith of milk shakes we had encountered in our travels. From there west, the milk shakes steadily deteriorated until they were almost as insipid as East Coast shakes.

I wanted my companions to have at least a quick go at Silver Creek, so we headed north to Blackfoot and across the desert to Arco. From there we skirted the south flank of the mountains with the great lava desert to our left until we came to Picabo, only a few miles from the Sun Valley Ranch on Silver Creek. It was hot, dry, and dusty, and we stretched out in our sleeping bags by the fence line and, after a canned meal, slept, dreaming of big rainbows rising to the dry fly.

While we suffered some frustration, we did much better as a whole than I had the previous year, and it was attributable to better and finer tackle and a better understanding of fly types and their presentation. We all had good hookups with respectable-sized fish, though the fine gut we were using made landing them difficult because of the proliferation of weed in the creek. We had a lot of action with small and medium-sized rainbows and, all in all, Silver Creek lived up to the expectations I had built up for it.

It was hard to leave after only one day, but we headed west through Boise and Ontario, Oregon along US 20. The route followed the winding canyon of the Malheur River through Eastern Oregon and then climbed through higher country and over two passes before descending into a vast plateau which we later learned was an ancient lake bed called Lake Harney. Except during spring runoff, the lake is dry. Malheur Lake, at the center of the bowl, has since become a refuge for waterfowl. We followed the northern edge of the lake bed on an absolutely straight road, watching a long plume of dark smoke in the distance. The smoke was coming from the area which was to be our new home, thirty miles away.

The little city of Burns, Oregon was a typical cattle-country town. The only difference was that it was also populated by a considerable number of lumber mill workers and served as the entertainment and shopping center for a vast geographic area with one of the lowest population densities in the country.

On Saturday night, Burns played host to loggers from the mountainous areas, cowmen from the meadows of the Harney basin, and mill workers from the nearby settlement at Hines. The town had a small movie theater, a number of bars, several eateries of doubtful character, and a place where all the action was then, called the Pine Tavern. We were able to check all this out with a single pass through town on the way to the mill office a mile away.

We checked in at the mill. Though it was Saturday, we found the paymaster/bookkeeper hard at work in his office. He'd been expecting us to check in Monday but was glad to get us organized and out of his hair ahead of time. We had to fill out forms attesting to our ages and that we were not subject to having to join the union because we were to be "lumber students."

We were shown to quarters, which were not in the bunkhouse but in a long, unfinished attic above the administrative offices. Two others were already lodged there, young men out of college forestry programs doing their stint in the home office learning the ropes before going to the field. They were, in fact, what we were supposed to be. They were a little puzzled by what our status might be and we shied clear of the fact that one of us, Phil, had close connections to the chairman of the board.

We were supposed to supply our own cots but decided to save the money and continue sleeping in our bags on the floor. Unfortunately, Central Oregon is one of the more dusty places I've encountered. There's a lot of wind and the fine silt from the dry lake bottom and the volcanic ash from the surrounding high ground find their way into the air and seem to have the capacity to penetrate any orifice. It was a never-ending battle to keep the floors swept and the dust out of our sleeping bags, eyes, ears, noses, and throats.

There was a bathroom with sit-down john and washbasin, but the shower was in another building beyond the chow hall, and was available to the men in the bunkhouse as well as to us. The chow hall had the usual long tables with long benches on either side. The cook was a large, cheerful lady who made us feel welcome immediately and assured us that only good manners would be tolerated, but that reaching across or down the table for anything was permissible so long as we didn't stick our arms or elbows into someone else's plate, or get our hand stabbed along the way. We would, she insisted, be required to clean up before coming to chow, and she would check us out, herself. The food turned out to be hearty and plentiful, and in view of the number of calories we expended every day in the mill, every bit was needed.

Monday morning we reported to Mr. Haggerty, the paymaster we had met, who took us to the mill and put us in the charge of our foreman, Leo, who turned out to be one of the nicest men I've ever had the good fortune to work for.

The mill was awesome in size, and we were told it was the largest completely covered mill in the world. All the lumber cut in the forests, twenty to fifty miles to the north, was shipped in on a private rail line and kiln-dried there. It was all ponderosa pine, Leo told us, generally of high quality and in great demand in the Midwest where the Hines company had its principal distribution area.

Leo separated us from each other for good tactical reasons. He put each of us with an experienced man on the lumber chain and we were introduced to the art of "pulling lumber." Following Haggerty's instructions on Saturday, we had gone into town and bought heavy leather work gloves and leather aprons. These, we learned quickly, were the key to successful lumber pulling. The secret was to use leverage and slide the boards off the chain into a balanced position on the apron and, again with leverage, heave and slide it onto the correct pile. Leo and one other old-timer did the actual grading by marking the boards as they came onto the chain from the milling section with a code indicating the grade.

Each of us along the chain had from two to five different grades to pull as the lumber came by. We had to keep each in distinct piles, perfectly aligned, and when the stacks reached a certain number of layers, cross pieces were put in to start a new stack. We built each stack to the maximum height a forklift could carry, then they were moved out to storage or shipping areas and we started a new stack.

The first few days were real back-breakers. At first we were using nothing but muscle-power and were, of course, totally exhausted and sore the entire first week. As we got the hang of it we expended less and less energy. Leo allowed as how he was proud of us and asked if we would like to go to a movie with him Saturday night. I can't remember the name of the film, but I knew it wasn't the one showing at the local theater. Leo proceeded to drive us all the way to the town of Bend, over 120 miles away, to see the movie, have a few beers, then head back to Hines—a two-hundred-forty-mile round-trip for an evening's entertainment. These Oregonians seemed to have no sense of distance.

When we passed the two-man town of Brothers, where there was a slight bend in the otherwise straight road, Leo told us, "Those two guys make a living off'n the drunks that don't make'er through the bend and drive off through the sagebrush. They got car repair all locked up for miles around!"

Our five weeks at the mill were a combination nightmare and circus. It was the hardest any of us had ever worked, and after our easy-going pace on the fishing trip, the change was especially startling to our physical and nervous systems. There was also another problem: a certain resentment from some of the crew members who viewed us as spoiled brats with our Eastern accents and privileged assignments. They were always on the lookout for opportunities to pick a fight. Leo did a pretty good job of keeping us out of trouble, but we managed to get into some of our own, after hours at the aforementioned Pine Tavern.

Phil, Al, and I managed to get beered up one night at the tavern and, on the way out, we were accosted by a couple of thoroughly drunk crew members who thought we needed taking down a notch or two. As it turned out, the three of us were a match for the two of them, though we quickly found out there were no rules. We settled it outside and, with only a few marks to show for it, wound up drinking with our opponents until we were almost as inebriated as they were. I ended up getting my first-ever ticket, for driving without any lights on the way back to the mill. I was lucky the deputy didn't haul me in for drunken driving.

Another incident took place while we were there which was a shock to all of our sensibilities. In the central area of our part of the mill there was a large pit called, appropriately enough, the pit. At various times during the day, usually between shift changes, there was a general sweeping-up of all the areas, and the sweepings, composed mainly of sawdust, were dumped into the pit, which was some ten or twelve feet deep and about fifteen feet wide. One man worked in the pit and his job was to shovel the sawdust and other debris into several large pipe mouths which sucked the material to a large burner some distance away.

Needless to say, this wasn't the most popular job in the mill. As it turned out, the poor unfortunate who held the job when we were there was a known sexual deviate called by one and all "The Queer." He was being made to pay for his nonconformity by working this worst of all jobs, but the worst of it was that occasionally one of the good, normal types in the mill would shout, "Hey, let's all go piss on the Queer!" and the shout would be taken up, and everyone going off shift would convene at the pit and urinate into it and all over the queer.

There was no escape for the victim of this barbarity. I'm ashamed to say that we all were drawn into it and participated in this morbid exercise of vicious cruelty which, unfortunately, I remember enjoying thoroughly at the time.

One Sunday Leo, who was also a fisherman, offered to take us to see the best trout stream in those parts. It turned out to be two streams, the Donner and the Blitzen, which joined together where they came out of their respective canyons to form a single stream called, oddly enough, the Donner and Blitzen, then continued, after being robbed of a considerable part of its flow by pasture irrigation, across the flat bottom of the Harney basin to Malheur Lake, the swampy remnant of the once great lake which now serves as a duck-breeding area.

Like the ride to the movies, it turned out to be much farther than it appeared, and the lower part of the stream was disappointing. Over what passed for a road, we went as far as the forks, and my friends stayed and fished down the main stream, which was reasonably trouty-looking, while I headed up the right canyon, fishing my way along with a grasshopper imitation. I picked up the occasional fish and missed some impressive takes from the surprise of seeing large fish boil to my fly in such a relatively small stream. I was in the stream the whole time and had moved well up into the canyon. I had finally hooked and landed one of the larger fish that came to my fly. It was a brightly-colored rainbow with some cutthroat markings and I later learned that it may have been a distinctive species native to the area, known as the red-banded trout, which is now near extinction.

I was delighted by this twenty-two-inch specimen that put up a fight worthy of any rainbow. Needing to relieve myself, I stepped up on the bank and proceeded to do so. Suddenly I heard a rattling buzz like a rapidly shaken gourd full of seeds. I stared at the coiled rattler and heard another to one side, then another. The whole area was absolutely infested with rattlesnakes and I could see them everywhere along the banks. I had been so taken with the fishing that I never noticed them. Now that I had, it was hard to keep from total panic. As it was, I felt real fear and, finally gathering my energies, I made a near-record standing broad jump into the water and made my way downstream without so much as another cast.

As I came out of the canyon I saw snake after snake along the bank, and I couldn't believe I hadn't noticed. I also understood why there were so many large fish in that stream. Only a fool would fish there.

Leo was the first to notice me when I arrived back at the pickup. "See any snakes?" he asked.

"Too goddamned many!" I yelped.

He was surprised that I had gone in so far and fished for so long. "Most guys go in there and head right back out when they see all the rattlers."

I showed him my big fish and told him it was almost worth it, but that I didn't think I'd go back in there, even for a twenty-four-incher.

Leo said he thought there were fish that large in the stream but they were pretty safe from most fishermen. I couldn't have agreed more.

I regret that we didn't get to know any of the ranchers in the area. We did, however, meet some very nice local people. We struck up a conversation with the manager of the movie theater who turned out to be something of an intellectual, and through him we met a few of the local luminaries. That's when I first learned to appreciate the true Western style which accepts strangers as being all right until proven otherwise—the complete opposite of the Eastern city, or even small town, where outsiders are looked on with suspicion until proven okay. It's only when you mess up in a Western town—then you're in deep trouble!

Those five weeks seemed like six months. Though we had some fine experiences, including a couple of wild night jackrabbit chases across the sagebrush shooting rabbits in the car headlights at full speed using .22 pistols, plus getting acquainted with a couple of the town's ladies of the night, we were all three relieved when it was over and we'd signed off and waved our last goodbye.

When we headed West again, there was just a week left before Phil and Al had to return home to prepare for their first terms at college. We agreed that the word "lumber," or the name of any other wood product, would no longer be a part of our vocabulary. But before the last hurrah, I persuaded the others that we should have a one-day shot at fishing the famous North Umpqua River we had read about in Ray Bergman's book, *Trout.*

The drive to Diamond Lake wasn't bad, but from there on down the "unimproved track" was truly something else. We left the volcanic barrens and the high ponderosa forest on the eastern slope and wound down a narrow, twisting road through dense forests of rhododendrons, vine maple, and enormous towering Douglas firs. It was very steep and, suddenly, we came to a stretch where no track could be seen at all. There was simply a large expanse of bare, black rock. There were no tracks on the rock, so we got out and crossed to the other side where the forest started once again, and the track picked up, wandering through the trees even more steeply downward into the canyon where we could just hear the first roaring sounds of the new river far below in the gorge.

Altogether, from Diamond Lake to Steamboat, our destination, there were six hours of driving. (Today it's a forty-minute drive at moderately high speed.) When we finally came within sight of the river we stopped and looked down from high above and saw two large fish lying in the tail-out of the big, deep pool below. They were larger than anything we'd ever seen in fresh water and, in retrospect, they may have been salmon rather than steelhead, as we thought then. In any case, we put together our rods and clambered down the cliff to the head of the pool.

Phil drew the big pool, so Al went one pool up and I went to the next one downstream. We spent about an hour and I tried a wet royal coachman because it was the only big wet fly I had that was bright enough. I had on a gut leader, since we had long since run out of Paul Stroud's miracle dyed nylon. The heaviest gut leader I possessed was a 3X and, soaked, it probably didn't test more than a pound and a half, if that.

The pool I was fishing had not been visible from above because of a large outcrop overhanging the head of the pool, and where I set up looked deep and strong and limpid, though I couldn't see the bottom due to the turbulence. Because of the overhang, I had to use the steeple cast I had learned so long ago from Leander McCormick. This enabled me to direct my back-cast perpendicularly behind me before extending it forward to its target. With it I was able to do a creditable job of covering the pool with my casts, but nothing happened until I reached the lower end with a full extension of the line.

The fly skimmed across the water just in front of the tail-out where it sped into a chute that dropped to the rapids below then entered another pool out of view. As the fly sped across the lip, there was a giant bulge in the water just behind it and a splash, and I saw, for a frozen instant in time, the maw of an enormous fish reach for the fly and miss. Anyway, I thought it missed, for I felt nothing and my rod didn't double up, as they say in the big fish stories; nor did my reel scream. I just stood there aghast, and started to try a cast to the same spot again as soon as I stopped trembling. Then I realized there was no longer a fly on the end of my leader. As it turned out, the last section of the leader was also missing and, doubtless, trailing from the jaw of the steelhead. Even though we hadn't done battle, and had barely touched gloves, I felt in no way cheated. There was pure exhilaration in the sure knowledge that I had found something entirely new to me, and which was going to stimulate endless interest, anticipation, and excitement from then on.

Phil and Al had each fished out their respective pools without result and were yelling at me to get back to the car. The thought of the river down below in the famous stretches we had read about was compelling enough to get me up the cliff to the narrow ledge, and off we went, with me spouting off about "the one that got away," about which there was a lot of playful kidding.

It was nearly dark by the time we arrived at the junction of Steamboat Creek and the main river and, though the road was an improvement over the high parts, it was still narrow and winding and dangerous because of the constant temptation to look at the river. We passed the Mott Bridge a couple of hundred yards before the Steamboat Creek Bridge and decided to camp on the point just upstream where we found some fine, soft fir needles beneath the majestic trees. It was as soft and comfortable a spot as we had found to sleep on our whole trip, and we slept soundly with the perfume of pine and ripening blackberries in the air.

The next morning, after a quick breakfast, we did a bit of arranging with whatever leaders we had, and each of us ended up with a nine-foot gut leader to 1X, and our biggest squirrel tails on #8 hooks from Paul Stroud's. First we walked up to the Mott Bridge where we could see what the river really looked like from above, but the light was not right yet to have a clear view of the long pool below, so we split up, with Al on the right side going down and me on the left, fishing it a little above the bridge downstream, foot by foot. Phil opted for the junction, which we later learned was called the station pool, though Bergman referred to it as the plank pool, as there was a plank set up from the bank to a rocky reef where the middle and lower parts could be covered easily by even the most inadequate caster.

I was fishing faster than Al and reached the lower part of the pool, which is called the Upper Sawtooth, where two distinct reefs project up into the pool and cause the first turbulence in the 200-yard length of water. The reef point closest to my side lay a bit downstream of the one on Al's side, and the near side of his reef was the obvious target of choice for a thorough working-over. That looked like the ideal holding spot for any big fish that might have just moved into the pool from below.

I remembered that Bergman had fished this pool from the opposite side and wrote of having hooked a fish just above the reef. This time I was somewhat prepared for what might happen, but when it did, I was just as shocked and excited as the first time. The only improvement was my immediate reaction of letting go of the line in my left hand. I would eventually learn not to hold it at all when fishing for steelhead or Atlantic salmon because of the great possibility of their breaking away immediately if they can't take line directly off the reel.

The Sawtooth fish took the fly and, as I let go, he turned sharply and ran down into the chute on my side, which was pure luck, then the leader snapped. Once again I was left with nothing, though I did see the fish jump in the run below. Shakily, I retrieved my line and leader. My reel had made a funny noise and seized. It was dry and should have been oiled but, beside that, if the fish had kept on going he'd have broken away anyway because none of us had any backing on our small trout reels—just the thirty yards of fly line which we had always thought would be adequate for any situation.

We had all been taught the usual homily that a fly reel was just a place for storing one's line out of the way. We had at least progressed to the point of recognizing that a smooth click on a reel not only stopped overrunning, but also served as a means of slowing down a stronger-than-usual fish. We were not, however, prepared for what fish the size of steelhead could do, and do so quickly.

I sat on the bank and waited for Al to fish out the pool on the other side. Just as he was about to reach the hot spot, from which he would be able to cover the front tip of the reef, I heard a voice behind me and looked around to see a state trooper.

"Hello," he said politely, then asked to see my license. I took it from my shirt pocket and showed it to him. After looking it over he asked, "Is the young fellow fishing up on Steamboat Creek with you?"

I said that he was, and so was the other fellow across the river. He motioned for Al to join us at the bridge, and as we walked up the road to where his pickup was parked he told me he'd issued Phil a citation for fishing without a proper license.

Since we'd never been checked before, Phil thought it was worth the risk to purchase a local license instead of the more expensive non-resident license. As much as we would have liked to, we couldn't lie for him, and we were all together in a car with Illinois plates. Phil was sitting dejectedly at the Steamboat Bridge; his rod and reel had been confiscated by the patrolman. The only way to get it back would be to appear in court and pay the fine. When asked, the patrolman opined that since Phil was from out-of-state, this particular judge was likely to impose a stiff fine and that it might be better to give up the rod. After we'd gone back to the Mott Bridge to check Al's license, we were free to go, but without Phil's precious rod. It was a hard lesson but one that made a permanent impression on all of us. The temptation to lie about our place of residence had been great because of the disparity in price between the two licenses; in retrospect, not so great a price after all.

That pretty well wrapped up the summer for us. That was the last fishing stop, and we couldn't very well go on fishing with Phil just looking on. He was unhappy enough as it was. We decided to get on our way down to Roseburg and to the main highway south to San Francisco where Pauline would put us up for a couple of days before Phil and Al caught their train back to Chicago.

Pauline had taken a large apartment on Telegraph Hill. The couple of days we spent there were great fun, even though we were camping on the floor of the guest room. Al, who was a true jazz devotee, found out through whatever grapevine exists for music nuts that there was a really hot combo playing in the back room of a small restaurant at 1935 Sutter Street, in the Fillmore District. The leader was a hot tenor sax player, named Saunders King, who was supposed to be right in the same league with the great Coleman Hawkins.

When we arrived, we received some hard stares from patrons of the all-black establishment, but we were led into the back room and our obvious enthusiasm for both the food and the music quickly dispelled the suspicions and we were welcomed and treated as friends. Phil and I just shut up and listened while Al carried on with the local gentry about the relative merits of this or that musician. We all got a little high and, some time later, crept back into the apartment so as not to disturb Pauline and have her see us in our cups.

After my two friends left, Patrick and Gregory arrived from summer camp in Northern California near Mt. Shasta, and after a week in the city, where we met Pauline's cousins, the Merners, and her good friends, the McEvoys, we toured the sights. I was entrusted with the care of Pat and Gig, as they were now called, and we all drove up to Sun Valley where Papa and Marty had just arrived from Cuba. Toby Bruce, Papa's man Friday and general factotum, had driven the car up with Papa, and Marty came on by train after visiting her mother in St. Louis. It was already later in the season than I'd ever been able to stay, because of the exigencies of school. Dove hunting season was over and, in the shooting department, there was nothing open to shooting except sage grouse and rabbits until pheasants some time in October.

Gary and Rocky Cooper were there and, through the fall, a parade of notables made their appearances. I became involved in tennis on the clay courts between the Lodge and the Inn.

There were many fine players on hand, and the pro, Roland Bloomstrand, had been a Swedish collegiate champion. As a junior, he had been a ball boy for King Gustav. He was now working with some talented young players from Utah State, where he coached when there was no tennis at Sun Valley. It was good fun and sometimes Rocky and Gary Cooper would play doubles against Papa and me. When Marty was there, she and I would team up against the Coopers, or she would team with Papa.

I had been somewhat awed the year before by Coop. He was the first real star I had ever met and he was just like he appeared in films. This time I had the chance to spend enough time with him and Rocky to feel natural with them. While Rocky was from a society background, she had worked as an actress and flaunted a veneer of tough aggressiveness from which she derived her nickname. It made a startling contrast with Cooper's very shy and gentle manner and natural westerner's way. I would find them both to be good friends and outdoor companions.

Most of the time I just went over to the courts and got up a game with Fred Iselin or Sigi Engl. They were great fun to hit with; they were hard ball-hitters and I've always had an easier time hitting off pace than generating it off slow, high-bounding balls.

It was a pleasant, relaxing time; practicing on the skeet range and fishing to my heart's content, tennis, and some cutie from California who was there with her skating mother, a teaser who kept me up nights but was, at least, an objective. Thus, the time passed all too quickly.

My fishing highlight that fall was going out with Pop Marks, an old-time guide. Using my old car, we drove down to Bellevue and crossed over what we used to call Muldoon Summit, going high up then descending into the upper Little Wood River above Carey Reservoir. In 1941 the dam was lower than it is now and, consequently, the best part of the valley wasn't flooded by the high water of the reservoir. It wasn't much of a stream and the fishing wasn't much to brag about during most of the season. However, come October there was a fine run of rainbows which, being of hatchery stock, were inclined to come up the river in the autumn rather than in the spring as the wild rainbows do.

It was the day of my birthday, the tenth of October, that Pop showed me the way over there. We stopped some distance away from the stream because it was in a sandy bottom where it would be easy to get stuck and we walked out across the willow flats. Pop had kept this spot pretty much a secret and it didn't get hit much, if at all, even by the local fishermen.

Pop knew I preferred to fish dry fly so he picked a spot about halfway into the good fishing area and I headed upstream while he fished down, with the agreement that we meet back at the car by 3:30 to give us plenty of time to get back over the hill in time to clean up for my birthday party which was scheduled to be held at The Ram.

Pop favored wet flies and didn't mind the old Andy Reeker which his cohort, Art Wood, preferred. He went for the Reeker right away, which was a big surprise to me since the stream couldn't have been over ten feet wide in the broad spots and was seldom over eighteen inches deep. I had already developed a strong penchant for the Adams, especially the version called the Lady Adams, which had a yellow egg sack at the end of the grey fur body and was the latest hot fly from Michigan, according to *Field & Stream*. These, and their variants, were my current favorites, and they had produced well all fall everywhere but on Silver Creek, a place where there were seldom any easy solutions.

So I put on a Lady Adams and went to work within talking distance of Pop for a little while. The main flat of the long, narrow pool, between the gravel banks and willow thickets, was shallow and featureless and the water was just a little off-color from a rain shower the night before. I got no action until I arrived within range of the faster and deeper current at the head of the pool where there was a snag of willow roots in the water. Very much like the log pool on the Gibbon, the first fish that took did so so quietly that all I detected was the disappearance of my fly under water just as if I had forgotten to put the floatant on it and it had sunk. There was, however, a slight dimpling of the water and I tightened gently into a good fish of some seventeen inches with a fine deep belly. The fish jumped immediately and came tearing back down the creek toward me and went on past. Pop turned around when I yelled and saw the second and third spectacular leaps. I played the fish carefully then brought it in and put it into the grass creel where it would soon be joined by half a dozen others nearly the same size, plus one gorgeous fish of twenty-three inches. Pop was delighted by the success of the dry fly, whose effectiveness he had admittedly doubted and was especially surprised that our largest fish came to a dry and not to the Andy Reeker spoon.

My birthday party at The Ram that night was a great success and, much to my surprise, Pop Marks had arranged for the trout to be arrayed on a serving tray brought in from the cafeteria to show to the guests. Pappy Arnold, the Sun Valley photographer who accompanied us on many of our hunts and other expeditions in the area, took some photos with his Speed Graphic which still show as pretty a mess of trout as you could want to see. In those days there wasn't, as yet, any ethic about returning fish to be caught another day. As a matter of fact, quite the opposite was true and one took pride in the number and size of fish killed. We had no idea then that one day there would be so many fishermen that the wild resources we cherished so much would be threatened by even small limits, and that it would become praiseworthy to limit killing nearly altogether except in unusual circumstances. Still, turning eighteen had been a splendid occasion in every way.

Before Pat and Greg left for school, accompanied by Toby Bruce, the three of us went with Papa and Marty, and a visiting sport from California, to the Pahsimeroi Valley for a historic antelope hunt. The whole retinue came along with Taylor Williams as head guide, Lloyd Arnold for pictures, some of the horse wranglers, and a camp cook. The drive over Trail Creek Summit, and then the Big Lost Valley and Lost River Range via Double Springs Pass, was spectacular. The valley of the Pahsimeroi, itself, was almost treeless except for a few willows in the bottoms, where the spring-fed creek flowed, and the aspen grew in the rolling foothills. There were evergreens on the high flanks of the valley and there were already whiffs of new snow on the upper ranges. Nights had a bite to them that made leaving the cozy warmth of the sleeping bag difficult in the dawn hours which seem so much a part of the world of hunting.

There is still a photo, somewhere, that shows our hunting party with a group of hanging antelope, all of us in a line and big grins on our faces. There is only one incongruity that becomes apparent on closer inspection. One young man is not wearing jeans, chaps, and boots like the others, but waders. That nonconformist is me; I had been much more intrigued by the idea of an unfished spring creek with giant rainbows than by the idea of pursuing the elusive antelope. As a result, two things happened. In one instance, I missed seeing Papa achieve what Taylor Williams said was one of the finest pieces of rifle shooting he had ever seen, when Papa, after a grueling uphill stalk, made a particularly difficult running shot on an antelope at a considerable distance, using, as he always did, open sights. The incident was written as a short piece called "The Shot" and has been reprinted many times. I will say, though, that I certainly heard the story enough times during the next few days that I don't believe I really missed anything. In the meantime, I had some fine dry-fly fishing for smallish trout in as pretty a weed-and-cress-filled meadow stream as I had ever seen, and I kept the camp larder filled with fresh breakfast trout to accompany the enormous feasts of hot cakes, biscuits, and eggs that our cook provided every dawn. My younger brothers were both hunters by inclination and spent the long days afield in the everlasting antelope chase as well as hunting deer which were open then and plentiful in the area.

My curiosity about the outlet of the river into the always-turbid waters of the Salmon River overcame me. The mouth of the Pahsimeroi was only a few miles away from our camp and I had brought my own car, so I drove down the dirt road to Ellis where there was a small post office serving the area. I started wading the creek upstream a few hundred yards, with a small streamer, and I took some fish very much the size of those I had been catching all along—in the seven- to twelve-inch range. There was a solid willow cover on both sides and I could hardly get out even though I would have preferred to walk along the bank. I hadn't learned my lesson well enough on the North Umpqua that summer because I didn't think to change to a heavy leader when I got close to the mouth. I was fishing 3X which would have been strong enough to hold a fish up to two or three pounds, but the last thing in the world I was thinking of was the possibility of a steelhead. Their presence in the Middle Fork was well-known, but they were thought to have been nearly wiped out by the mining pollution in the main Salmon. The fact of the matter is that there simply weren't that many people fishing the wilds of Idaho in those days and no one really knew what was there and what wasn't.

My sense of anticipation was keen when I arrived at the

junction of the two currents. I extended my casts gradually and covered the clear water tongue as it extended into the main river. I had a relatively short line out, maybe thirty feet plus leader, when the little light-winged streamer coursed across the slick of clear water with my eyes glued to it. My memory of that sight is as clear today as it was then and what comes up is the ultimate monster of the deep rising deliberately under that fly and suddenly opening its jaws to engulf the fly, then returning back down into the depths. Fortunately, I was too paralyzed to strike and the enormous fish was on—one should never strike when the line is extended below, the fish will break the leader—though I doubt if the fish knew it. I exerted a little pressure and it turned and headed for the Pacific Ocean some six hundred river miles away.

My reel was properly oiled and nothing went wrong except that when the end of the line was reached there was a pop and the whole line went sliding out the guides on the rod and I watched as the silver and pink crescent arched out of the water almost out of sight with my whole outfit still fastened to it. I'm certain they parted company at that instant, but my fishing was over for the day, and for the trip, since I had no replacement fly line.

I had the shakes for a few minutes until I gathered myself together for the climb up the bank and the walk back up the Pahsimeroi Road to the car. At the time, I had thought the fish was a salmon because of its size, but I'm certain now that it was, indeed, a steelhead, and possibly one of the thirty-pounders the river used to be known for before commercial netting of salmon became so concentrated that the truly big steelhead were all too often taken in the nets intended for salmon and sold as such, and called "incidental catch."

That was the day Papa shot his second antelope, and a big mule deer as well, and we decided that we would return to Sun Valley the following day, but not without a celebration in the little "cowboy" *cum* "mining town" of Patterson that night. It was a rough evening with fistfights and a near-stomping, and even guns were pulled in a threatening gesture, but I missed most of the action because, after a couple of beers, I went back to the car and conked out.

I heard the whole story in detail on the way back to camp and then the next day when it was repeated for Pat and Greg's sake. It was repeated again when we got back to Sun Valley and had assumed epic proportions when relayed to Marty. Patterson was a real fighting town in those days. The cowboys, who had a union called "The Turls," came into town Saturday night when the local miners were also in town on a tear. Miners and cowboys don't get along very well after a few drinks—maybe even before—and they went at it every week. Papa had simply walked into the local social event of the week and, because he was tough, became embroiled with a gigantic miner in stomping boots who, fortunately, finally went down under a barrage of Papa's special left hooks to the head.

SEVEN

Soon after our return to Sun Valley, my brothers left to go back to school. Both duck and pheasant season had arrived. We had prepared for the birds by several rabbit drives, one of which would have attracted the attention of a Cleveland Amory, had such a creature existed in those days. Papa was the general who deployed all of us, including any visiting guests of the moment, in a skirmish line along the property line of a farmer whom we knew to be having terrible problems with crop losses to the hordes of jackrabbits that lived in the sage-covered lands surrounding his farm near Dietrich.

John Frieze and his two sons, who were farming this new area, would bring up the rear guard with a pickup truck and gather dead rabbits as we advanced through the sagebrush toward an irrigation canal where the rabbits would be trapped. When the animals tried to escape by coming back through our advancing line, it literally looked as though the earth were moving, so plentiful were the long-eared predators. This was one of the great peaks of their population cycle and the Friezes collected over seventeen hundred rabbits on that one drive.

Meanwhile, we had done a lot of shooting, and Gary Cooper, who preferred rifles to shotguns, sat on a hillock at the edge of the drive and shot rabbits at long range. It was economically unsound. The rabbits were worth less than the bullets Coop fired, which were all hand loaded for his 2200 Lovell. But it was fun for him and good practice for the upcoming bird shoots, and it certainly helped solve the Friezes' rabbit predation problems. When they had skinned the rabbits, the farmers collected about five cents apiece for the skins from dealers, which was a good piece of change at the time.

Our pheasant opener that fall was on Tom Gooding's farm near the town of the same name. It was a fine hunt but was marred by one bad incident when one of the gunners, John Boettiger, who was along with his wife, Ann Roosevelt Boettiger, inadvertently shot one of the Labrador retrievers, through a careless error. He felt very badly about it, but we all took it pretty hard, and Papa was most unforgiving and forever afterward had little good to say about the President's son-in-law.

It was characteristic of Papa in that he did not easily suffer fools or stupid behavior, particularly in those who should know better. Usually, though, he was more forgiving of human frailty, and Boettiger's mistake was one of carelessness and certainly not malicious in any way. Boettiger felt terrible about it and even expressed the thought aloud that anyone who did such a thing ought to be shot. Unfortunately, Papa agreed, which caused an amusing incident the following day when I came up to his room to bring the morning newspapers.

It was about seven o'clock and there was a high, heavy, overcast sky. Papa answered my knock and, while he glanced at the headlines, I walked over to the window and stepped out onto the terrace overlooking what was then a small pond with some ducks and Canada geese with pinioned wings. There had always been six geese, but I noticed there were now ten.

I said, "Papa, there's ten geese out there."

He immediately put his finger to his lips and motioned me back into the room. Marty was still in the bedroom. He took his model 12 pump from its soft case and quickly shucked three shells into it. Then he ran to the window and out onto the terrace overlooking the pond and four of the geese took flight. One was a giant and Papa poured all three shots at it. It was hit, albeit with lighter loads than one would normally use for geese.

At that point Marty called from the bedroom in a startled voice, "My God, Ernest, you didn't shoot John Boettiger did you?"

The big lead bird was obviously in trouble and, instead of gaining altitude as it would have normally, it headed for Sun Valley Lake a quarter mile away. We couldn't see it from the terrace but we knew it had to go down and roughly where it must go down, and there was a good possibility the other three geese had followed it. Papa called Taylor Williams who called Pappy Arnold and others of the troops and we all foregathered in the lobby of the Lodge.

Papa and Taylor assigned the positions for surrounding the lake and retrieving the wounded bird, and possibly taking another for our Thanksgiving feast. I was with Papa and no geese came over us, but the three smaller birds flew over Taylor and his group and they got two of them. The big bird was floating dead on the water where one of the big black Labs Averell Harriman had first brought to SV retrieved it. There was much rejoicing, and the birds were beautifully prepared by the cooks at The Ram for our Thanksgiving dinner. The big goose weighed thirteen pounds dressed, and the smaller ones about eight to ten pounds. We were sure there was no better bird to roast for such a festive occasion.

After some successful pheasant shoots down at the Friezes', and some jump shoots on Silver Creek with Papa and me changing ends of the canoe to take turns shooting, the tail end of fall brushed past and winter took over. On the last canoe shoot with Papa, we had gone farther down the creek than ever before—all the way past the "stutter man's" place. He must have been away, for this once he didn't come out yelling, "Ggg-get offa mmmy ppplace!" threatening to shoot us, as he usually did.

The creek narrowed perceptibly in this last stretch and we weren't prepared for what awaited us around the narrow bend where the willows crowded the banks. Papa was in the stern so I was the first to see the water pipe with its wooden housing stretching across the creek. By the time I reacted it was only a few lengths away and the current was too strong to dodge it or, much less, paddle back upstream. As I reached forward to grab the housing, the rear of the canoe slammed around to the right. Papa reached out to steady his end, but the current's force against the wide beam of the canoe forced the upstream thwart under and we were unceremoniously dumped into the frigid water along with our guns and the birds we'd shot.

The way was clear beyond the pipe so we had no trouble getting out, but we were soaked, cold, and gunless. The canoe had run aground at the next bend, so, after setting it aright, we took off our clothes, wrung them out as best we could, and hiked as fast as we could out to the road and back to Picabo where Chuck Atkinson's store was located, and we recovered from our mishap with the aid of a little bit of the stuff that killed Dr. McWalsey. Taylor and I recovered the guns the next day and, fortunately, there was no damage or rust on them. I learned then, for the first time, that things completely under water rust more slowly than those exposed to air.

I shot fairly consistently with the shotgun for the first time that autumn. Up until then, I had always been the rifle-shooting member of the family. The two tend not to be compatible unless you are careful to separate them completely in your mind, keeping the natural instinctiveness of shotgun shooting, in the one instance, while exercising the precision and carefully controlled breathing of the rifleman, in the other. Except for the skeet lessons Carl Bradshire had given all of us boys, and Marty, the summer of 1940, I really had no idea what I was trying to accomplish with the shotgun, other than to get certain leads at certain angles. By dint of doing more shooting, more often, and cutting down slightly on my fishing, I was starting to do the right thing, instinctively, more often.

But there was little doubt that fishing was my specialty and my first love. I was reminded of it every time Papa and I floated down the creek shooting ducks and occasionally frightened a big trout off a waving weed bed. When it warmed in the mid-afternoon, we'd see the big rainbows rising to small flies drifting on the surface. Just the sight of them sent a shiver through me, and as much as I enjoyed shooting with Papa, I knew I'd rather be casting to those rises and testing my skills on those elegant, canny creatures of the streams.

Considering his increasingly imperfect eyesight, Papa was a first-class wingshot. As long as it was game being shot at and not clay targets, he could outshoot just about anyone around, and he seemed to thrive on competitive situations such as the live pigeon-shooting in Spain and in Cuba. The best shot amongst us, however, was Gigi. He used his little single shot .410 to deadly effect and the following winter would be runner-up in the World Live Pigeon Shooting Championship, which was held in Havana that year because of the war in Europe. He was a natural. At age eleven he did not feel the pressure of the competition as severely as others. Patrick was already a good rifle shot and had made a clean kill of his first mule deer the previous fall after my return to school. It was a near-record head and presaged his later career as a successful white hunter in East Africa.

It had been an altogether fantastic fall, but now with Papa and Marty leaving, and the serious onset of winter, I had to face the soon-forthcoming year of working as a laborer on Wake Island. I stayed in the Valley about a week after Papa and Marty's departure and took advantage of an invitation from Rocky Cooper to join her and Martin Arrougé on top of Baldy, one of the Valley's best ski mountains, where there was just enough snow to practice a few turns down the open slopes of

Christmas Ridge before climbing back up. Marty Arrougé, a
ski instructor who was already courting Norma Shearer, was a
true expert. He had been brought up on the slopes of the Sierra
behind Reno and had a contagious enthusiasm for the sport. I
took advantage of the lessons he was giving Rocky to learn a
few fundamentals of sound ski technique—something I had
done without all the years at Storm King. But, finally, my time
was up and I had to make preparations to return home.

*　　　*　　　*

I took the train back to Chicago from Shoshone where Taylor
Williams had dropped me off. He had arranged to have Sun
Valley pay for my car with the proviso that I could buy it back
at the same three-hundred-dollar price whenever I should
return. Taylor was fond of the old Pontiac because it was stur-
dy, sat high off the road, and could go a lot of places Sun Valley's big station wagons couldn't.

I hated to leave the Valley just when the good snow was getting started, and especially so because the instruction Marty
Arrougé was giving me, via Rocky, was beginning to give me
the self-confidence so necessary to good skiing. But there was
a lot to be done in a short time. I had to get some khakis, jeans,
and work shoes, and make arrangements to get to San Francisco where the contracting firm, Morrison Knudsen, would
arrange my transport to the building project. Of course, the
main reason for rushing home was to bid farewell to Mother
and Paul before going off for a year and, except for letters,
being totally out of contact. Letters were a weak point and I
hated writing them, except to girls who were important to
me—a condition which was to last for many years.

There were the usual parties in Chicago. At one of these I
noticed for the first time the emerging beauty of the youngest
sister of one of my old flames. I had seen Mary McNulty once
before when, with great trepidation, I had gone to their home
for dinner before accompanying Barbara to one of the parties
put on by the Burnique's Dancing School. At that point, Mary
was a scrawny little thing with long dark curls, braces, and gan-
gly legs. It was hard to believe the delectable creature I now
encountered in Chicago could be one and the same. Suddenly,
going off to Wake Island for a year didn't seem like the great

adventure I'd been looking forward to for so long.

As it turned out, I would be seeing a good deal more of Mary in the next few weeks. On my first Sunday back I decided to go into the city and took the Skokie from Lake Bluff down to the loop where I planned to attend an early movie matinee. There was a newsline in lights on a marquee high up on one of the buildings. I was staring at it without really reading when suddenly it lit up with a flash message. "Japs attack Pearl Harbor!" A few more details flashed across the sign and the downtown crowds seemed to be frozen as the words swept through them like a chill wind.

Suddenly there was bedlam in the streets and everyone started talking all at once. I rushed to a toll phone and called home. Paul answered. He had not yet heard the news but he said he would be coming down to the *Daily News* building right away in the car and asked if I would hang around outside the theaters and around the loop and talk to people to get some idea of their reactions before meeting him at the office.

I was delighted, frightened, awed, and excited, and soon I was caught up in the feelings of the crowds. I spoke to a number of people and immediate revenge was the foremost feeling expressed. Almost all were convinced that we would wipe out the Japs within a few short weeks. But as the details of the devastation wreaked on the U.S. fleet by the Japanese task force began to sink in, the spirit of vengeful excitement began to give way to a certain grimness.

I met Paul at the paper where he marshalled most of his senior staff and assigned them emergency duties. After reporting to him on what I'd heard, I sensed that I was in the way and I headed home. We spent the next few days glued to the radio, listening for late bulletins. Paul would bring home loads of wire service bulletins and it was soon apparent that not only was this war to be a long one but that the long-awaited entry of the U.S. into the European conflict was about to take place.

Germany and Italy declared war on us three days later and the business of getting the country onto a war footing was starting to take place. All the news was bad. Within ten days Wake Island was under siege and, after a valiant defense by the Marines and construction workers on the site, it was taken by the Japanese. Years later I met several of the workers back in Idaho. I was thankful I hadn't been there when the war started.

They spent more time in Japanese custody eating fish heads and rice than the survivors of the Bataan Death March in the Philippines.

I wanted to enlist in the Marines right away but, although my mother said she would permit it if Papa agreed, I was unable to get a quick answer out of him, and both Paul and Mother persuaded me that I would be of more value to the cause by at least starting school and preparing myself to become an officer, with the possibility of fighting in Europe where my language skills would be of some value. Ever since the fall of France, I had been deeply moved and felt strongly about doing something to help fight the Nazis and to see the country of my childhood free again. Since I hadn't made a definite choice yet about which college to attend, there was a series of letters sent and it turned out there was a chance for me to enter Dartmouth at the start of the spring term. It was highly irregular, of course, but these were highly irregular times.

I profited by the long holidays in Chicago to try to strengthen my ties to the youngest member of the McNulty clan. The competition was intense and I'm afraid I didn't make much of an impression, except for my tenacity. I was totally overwhelmed, nonetheless, and was to live with various stages of being in love with her for a long time to come.

*   *   *

I arrived at Dartmouth a couple of days before the beginning of the spring term, late in January 1942. Because of the war, my unusual starting date caused fewer ripples than it might have and I settled into the dorm life at North Mass Hall easily, making new friendships and learning the "system" for getting along in college. Although the college was small as colleges go, it was still a lot bigger than any place I'd attended before. Like any institution of higher learning, the freshman class was the largest, to allow for the failures, and there were many more fellows in my class than I would ever get to know even casually. Also, their entry in the fall had been organized for getting acquainted, and mine in mid-winter never would be. As a result, I really only became close to students with whom I shared classes, who lived in my dorm, or whom I met during extracurricular activities. And I had already missed a lot of the required freshman courses.

I did, however, have a choice of a number of electives among which was a new course being offered for the first time by Professor François Denoeu, called Military French. While, in retrospect, it was quite sketchy, it was a considerable help a few short years later when I would be dealing closely with the French Army. Conversely, a course I had to take in the fall of 1942 called Military Math was a total disaster and I was lost three days into the course, which led to my imminent failure as a student.

Those first few months at Dartmouth were quite confusing for me. The new freedom to go or not go to classes was beyond my maturity to handle. I realize now my parents' wisdom in wanting me to spend a year working before starting college. While I enjoyed the experience immensely, I never did get properly organized and certainly did not, in any way, live up to my potential as a scholar. I have excused my failure because of the new feeling that had infused the whole student body as a result of the war, and also because of my abnormal starting time, but in all honesty, these were only a part of the story. Drinking was, without a doubt, one of the more important activities around campus during my time at Dartmouth. I learned a great deal more about it than I should have, and I found that I enjoyed it inordinately much. I seemed to do it "well" and could even down larger quantities of beer faster than my peers with little apparent effect. In certain circles these skills were viewed as being important, and my social success was assured. Since recognition by one's peers is especially important in late adolescence, I went at it with a vengeance.

Unfortunately, the only sport in which I could participate successfully at this time of year was fencing and, though we fielded a good fencing team and did some traveling to matches and meets at other colleges and prep schools, fencing was still considered a pretty esoteric sport and, frankly, nobody but us gave a damn what we did or how well we did it. I did win my numerals and that was satisfying.

The war had caused the cancellation of Winter Carnival, by all odds the biggest social event of the year. Green Key, the spring house-parties weekend, was retained however. It turned out to be a real bash and we vented a lot of pent-up pressure in girl-chasing and horseplay. I vaguely remember ending up in White River Junction very late after the dates had left. There was some kind of kootchy show in a tent and I remember our laughing wildly at the absurd sight of a naked girl waving her pelvis in our faces with a "V for Victory" shaved in her pubic hair. Such was the patriotism of the moment.

Word was already reaching us that many of the recent graduates had been lost in far-off Pacific battles, most in Naval Air units. Somehow this seemed to make studies supremely unimportant. Revelry ruled unabated by any thirst for learning, and malaise and doubt reigned over our moments of calm and thoughtfulness.

Several more big changes came about because of the war. For those who would complete the necessary units, there was early graduation with ceremonies at the end of each semester. Instead of regular summer school, there was a full-semester schedule through all but the first two weeks of the summer. Since I had been home in Lake Bluff for Christmas, I decided to fly down to Miami where I spent the evening and overnighted at the house of a girl I had met during spring houseparties, then took off the next morning for Dinner Key on the Pan Am flight for Havana.

EIGHT

Papa was at Rancho Boyeros Airport to meet me. He had Paco Garay there to speed me through customs, and he gave me a big bear hug with his day-old stubble gritting against my face. He started bringing me up to date on recent happenings at the Finca, including the fact that Marty was back from a visit to her mother's in St. Louis, and Winston Guest was visiting, staying at the Finca. It was hinted that there were big goings-on having to do with the war and that I would be told more about it later.

In addition to Gigi's having been runner-up in the pigeon championships in December, Winston had gotten into town from an international polo match in Mexico where the U.S. had defeated the Mexican team, and he arrived completely exhausted. Winston was a big man and a fine athlete as well as a good friend to Papa. Papa told me he'd taken him to the *Club de Cazadores del Cerro* where the pigeon shoots were held and got him to the finals of a big shoot by priming him with just the right amount of scotch before every trip to the *cancha* for a shot, then resting him in the shade and protecting him from any intrusion or pressure from the partisan crowd. As a consequence of this fine and skilled handling, Winston retained just the right edge and went on to win the event, after which he collapsed completely.

Winston Frederick Churchill Guest was the end product of fine breeding and, with anyone but Papa, would have been the leader. With Papa he was like Little John to Robin Hood or Lancelot to Arthur. He adored Papa and would have done absolutely anything for him. Six feet five inches tall and a natural athlete, he was, though well educated, in no way an intellectual but for some reason was drawn to Papa as much by his ideas as by his personality. I always felt about him as I would have about some enormous older brother. Because of our relationship as followers of Papa it was hard for me to realize that he was a world class polo player with all of the aristocratic graces as well as great good looks. He could do anything well as an athlete. It was an irony of fate that he should covet most those qualities he least possessed.

It was a fine holiday for me with much shooting, tennis with Marty, Winston, and Felix Ermua, one of the Basque *jai alai* players Papa had helped get out of Spain after the Civil War, many parties, and a visit to the *Pilar* which was being specially outfitted for her new secret war duties.

Papa was betting a lot on the *jai alai* and one night we went in without Marty and, after a few drinks and a light dinner at the Floridita, went with Winston to the fronton to see the main doubles *partido*. As usual, we arrived at about the tail end of the *quiniela,* which was the round-robin singles. We took our usual seats fairly high up and near the center in order to have a clear view and to be within throwing range of Don Andres, our priest friend who moonlighted as a bookmaker at the *jai alai* fronton every night. The bets were put in the slit cut in an old tennis ball and thrown between the bettor and the bookie. Don Andres was obliged to supplement his income in this way because he had been given the poorest parish in Cuba as punishment for his participation in the Spanish Civil War, on the losing side.

The doubles *partido* was first rate, but I noticed Papa and Winston, who were both pretty well oiled by this point because they had kept on drinking daiquiris after dinner, whispering whenever they thought I was completely engrossed in the game. At the end of the doubles they both started talking to me and, finally, Papa asked me, somewhat hesitantly,

"Bum, have you ever been laid?"

"No, Papa," I lied.

"Would you like to be?"

"Yes, Papa." I didn't lie.

At that juncture, Winston said, "Papa and I have it all organized. Do you know how to get to my apartment?"

Though I hadn't been there, I knew where it was. In fact, we jokingly called it his "sin house." I replied that I could find it and Winston said, "Here is the key. Papa and I are staying to bet on the second *partido*. Take a taxi." And then he went on to explain how the buzzer worked, and the elevator, and that I was to phone the number he would give me, ask for Olga, and tell her who I was. He said she would come right over, and when the buzzer sounded I was to press the button so she could get in. Then, he said, she would come upstairs and see that the deed was done.

Papa added that I could take a taxi home in the morning for the fifteen mile ride out to San Francisco de Paula, and he gave me some money, adding that I was not to worry about paying Olga. It was all taken care of.

I followed the instructions given me with enthusiasm. When Olga got off the elevator at the second floor landing, we took one look at each other and burst out laughing. Though I hadn't known her name, Olga had been my companion for an hour the previous evening when I met her in a local bar after leaving a particularly dull movie near the Centro Vasco. I had thought she was a hooker, but she said she was out for fun, and since price hadn't come up, it was a freebie.

Now, while removing her clothes, she told me that Papa and Winston had joined forces in recruiting her for the job of introducing me to the "facts of life." She intimated that they had shown considerable verve in the research effort to find out if she were aptly suited for the purpose. Further, she said, part of her duties was to call my father in the morning after I left to give him a full report on my performance.

This was too good an opportunity to pass up. Between us, we made up a set of bedroom athletic accomplishments that would have done credit to *Superhombre,* the famous Cuban star of the exhibition circuit. Just before I left in the morning, she telephoned the Finca, and to quote only the last part of her report,

"Si, señor. Si, como un toro!"

When the taxi drove up the gravel drive to deposit me at the front steps, there sat Papa with a bemused but pleased look on his face. I paid off the cab driver and said, "Good morning, Papa."

"Hi, Schatz. How did it go?"

"Fine, Papa. Thanks." And that was the end of that, except that I felt somehow that Papa accorded me a certain new respect which had previously been absent, except in the fly fishing department. I never disabused him of any ideas he might have acquired.

In my last couple of days at the Finca, Papa told me about the upcoming operation using the *Pilar* as a Q-boat posing as a sport fishing *cum* research vessel. He had enlisted the enthusiastic support of the American Ambassador, Spruille Braden, and consequent logistic support in the form of weapons, communications equipment, and one skilled radio man with combat experience. The rest of the crew would be made up of Spanish Basque expatriates and Winston Guest.

I was promised a cruise, or rather a combat patrol, the next time I came down for a visit. Unfortunately, Marty did not appear to share Papa's enthusiasm for the project and apparently she felt the same about the counter-espionage operation he had become involved with which I learned nothing about until after the war. Quite justifiably, Marty felt the role of a writer in times of great stress was to witness those events and participate in them to the fullest extent possible. On the other hand, Papa felt justified in his own mind that he could, for the present at least, witness and participate in this sideshow of the war both to the benefit of the overall war effort and to the satisfaction of his own whimsy. It was becoming increasingly evident that Marty would not remain long satisfied to sit around the Finca, housewifing, when opportunities to cover the big stories in the European Theater came her way. I was sorry to see the beginning of this strife, but I thought it would all sort itself out with time. I was proved wrong.

I returned to Dartmouth by the same route I had followed down. The window shades on the Pan Am flight were to be kept closed for security reasons but I peeked a couple of times and caught a glimpse of several oil tankers burning off the coast. The threat of German subs, and other espionage, was not an imaginary danger. While Papa's sorties with the *Pilar* were not exactly a front-lines confrontation with the enemy, they were, nonetheless, a significant effort, as would be proved later on.

I was full of my adventures and, though the crush of parties was not so intense that summer in Hanover, the temptations of fishing and lazing around in the warm New England sun were strong. I found some new fishing friends at the college and started learning some of the local rivers and streams. I had gone out with a couple of friends to Newfound Lake the previous spring before my trip to Cuba. Contrary to custom, we fly fished for landlocked salmon casting from a rowboat. We got two strikes then hooked what proved to be a spawned-out cockfish which had not recovered from the spawning, apparently a common occurrence when the spring smelt runs were down. Since the smelt is a primary food source of the landlocks, a reduced smelt population means the salmon are unable to regain the weight lost after spawning and the low metabolism and near-fast of the previous winter. While New-found Lake, near the center of the state, was beautiful and the fishing at least stimulating, the streams around Hanover were a greater delight. Fish of any size were rare, but I came in contact with a few.

My single biggest handicap was having no car, not even a bicycle. I waded in my sneakers and often hiked to the Mascoma which was the closest stream of any interest. The water was dark and mysterious and was reputed to hold some very large brown trout. It was about a six-mile effort to get there, which made the round-trip a chore, especially coming back after a full day's fishing at last light. I caught some smallish browns on dry fly and nymphs, but the big ones eluded me.

With the advent of the summer semester I moved out of the dorm to a less expensive apartment off campus on an alley right in the middle of town. There were more than six of us there, at 23½ South Main Street. Most of us were members of the class of '45. It was crowded and fairly noisy, especially on weekends when there was always a party. Dartmouth policy forbade pledging to fraternities until after two semesters; the policy at 23½ South Main was for its residents to pledge as great a diversity of fraternities as possible so as to give everyone a broad spectrum of facilities to use. A number of my friends were Psi U pledges so I spent a lot of time there, though I wouldn't be able to pledge until the next fall semester.

Tom Ludwig, who lived at 23½, introduced me to two brothers at the Psi U house, one of whom became a lifelong friend: Joe Dryer, a member of the class of '44. The other, Dexter Richards, was a senior who was courting the daughter of Spruille Braden, Papa's friend in Cuba, which made for a common interest. Two other friends whom I met through the hunting and fishing part of the Dartmouth Outing Club, *Bait and Bullet,* were Chan Stein and Pete Bontecou. Each had access to a car on occasion and we took advantage of every opportunity to try some fishing farther afield. On one occasion we drove all the way across Vermont and around the lower end of Lake Champlain to fish the big Ausable below the forks, though it was so high from a summer rainstorm that we ended up fishing Cranberry Brook. That was an experience I'll never forget because it was the first time I spotted a fish taking caddis flies, and I chose the right pattern, a Welshman's button tied by Hardy's, and took a confident fish on the first cast, a nice 14-inch brook trout. Most of the fish in the brook were brookies; however, we had some good sport, though damned little before we had to head back for the long drive to Hanover.

Another time Pete invited me to his home near New York and we drove to the Beaverkill where we had a half day's fishing on some fabled water of one of the old clubs. Having fished the big Beaverkill when I was at Storm King, I was amazed at how small the water was on this famous stream which was reputed to produce some very large fish. The largest fish we saw was at Pete's house where there was a large, spring-fed, covered cistern which was home to a brookie of impressive proportions who enjoyed having worms fed to him and looked to be about eighteen inches long and weighed about 2½ pounds.

And so the summer passed, an unbalanced mix of books, lazing on the float at Occum Pond, some but not enough fishing, and endless rounds of partying. Just before time to go home to Lake Bluff, several of us went down to Boston to take the physical for the Naval Air Force reserve training program, V5. I failed to make it because of an inability to change focus rapidly enough from far to near and vice versa. I was given a set of eye exercises to perform and told to try again in six months. My companions who passed the test were fated for a slim chance of survival, mostly in the South Pacific.

The visit home was crowded with renewing friendships in Chicago; tennis; the great preoccupation of the moment, the war; and future plans. I would be nineteen that October so I didn't have to worry about being drafted for at least another year, possibly two, but the problem was just the opposite. College and studies held no promise for me. There really was no light at the end of the tunnel and all that faced us seemed an endless expanse of years of war with little promise of victory. It was not surprising, then, that most of us found it difficult to concentrate on preparing for a distant peaceful future when the great immediacy was war and our soon-forthcoming role in it.

Paul was helpful in giving me a head start in military thinking by introducing me to a variety of military reading, including von Clausewitz' *On War* and, particularly useful, *Blitzkrieg* by F.O. Miksche, a Czechoslovak military analyst who had attended the German general staff college and clarified the tactical and strategic concept of "lightning" war, from small unit infantry tactics to the exploitation of successful break-through by armored units and military aviation. He also covered aerial envelopment by parachute and other airborne units. Paul also gave me a copy of *The Officer's Guide.* For me, this became a turning point. While it did nothing for me as a student, it helped focus my thinking on a particular objective, that of becoming a good soldier and, eventually perhaps, an officer. College, as far as I was concerned, was over. I was now intent on a military career, the first and most important function of which was to take part in the liberation of France and Continental Europe.

Aside from the infamous course in Military Math, which left me in a daze after three sessions, the only memorable classroom experience was Freshman English with Professor David Lambuth, who seemed a caricature of the professor in "The Man Who Came to Dinner." He had a white beard and laughing eyes; dressed in white suits with white shoes, shirts, and ties; and affected a black beret and black cape. To avoid confusion by his famously absent-minded wife, who was known to put her groceries into any vehicle in sight, he also drove a white Packard. Above all, he was a bloody wonderful teacher of the English language. He would have commented that I should use the active verb to say so, but he taught clear thinking and active expression, and I wish I had completed the course.

My friend, Joe Dryer, demonstrated his innate foresight that last fall. The war had brought with it rationing of various kinds, but most bothersome was the rationing of gasoline. Joe foresaw this early on and did two memorable things about it. He made a deal with a local farmer for the leasing of his silo a mile or two out of town. He purchased vast quantities of gasoline by the fifty-gallon drum and had it delivered to and stored in the silo. The vehicle benefitting from this largesse was a Buick convertible which was the ultimate girl-trap of the time. We all took to cutting classes regularly so as not to miss the racing meet at Rockingham or a weekend at Skidmore or Smith.

Joe had spent some vacations in Germany with friends and relatives and had a wonderful collection of German songs on records, including military music, and one I rather liked, until I heard it again two years later under very different circumstances. I had an album of songs of the International Brigade in the Spanish Civil War. The similarity between the German battalion's song, *Freiheit,* and the *Hitler Jugend Lieder* was a bit spooky. Though they're not the same, they are so similar in style it is easy to confuse them.

It was a time of mixed blessings. There were football weekends, including one in Boston where a number of us were thrown out of the Copley Plaza after merriment, damage, and possible injuries to a passerby exceeded all bounds, and weekends at girls' colleges where their bounds were vastly exceeded.

There were three memorable grouse hunts where I first saw and shot ruffed grouse and woodcock over a friend's English setter in cover which varied from abandoned apple orchards on open hillsides to beechnut groves and alder swamps. But above all, there were parties and heavy drinking. I reached the point where true self-disgust set in and I knew it was time to leave what had become a rat race for me. I was no longer even making a pretense of attending classes. Finally, one incident convinced me that I was fast becoming a moral bankrupt and that it was too late to redeem myself by diligent study or a change of course in my college life.

On this particular occasion, a young lady at a party in one of the fraternity houses was persuaded to leave her date and come over to 23½. There, to our delight, she demonstrated her willingness to share her favors with one and all. She was very attractive, and she told me she had been celebrating her engagement to the date she had left at the fraternity house. This rang a bell and I called Joe. After returning her with no problem, since her "fiancé" was passed out on the sofa, we decided after much soul-searching that the hapless fellow had to be told, and Joe undertook the task. I believe we used the term "nymphomaniac" to describe her. I think it was probably grossly unfair, but it was part of protecting the double standard of behavior which prevailed in those days. That standard dictated that it was perfectly all right for us to cat around all we wanted, but we expected the kind of girls we would marry to hew to the straight and narrow. If a girl enjoyed the use of her body, she was marked out of bounds by so-called gentlemen for any serious purpose.

I ran into her again in Boston a year later and, to my shame and her credit, she bore absolutely no ill will about our having broken up her engagement. Furthermore, since I was then in uniform, she did what she could to improve my morale and did so in the way she knew best.

I said my farewell to Dartmouth in mid-November and,

after writing home to break the news to Paul and Mother, and a note to my draft board to let them know where I could be reached, I headed down to Cuba, taking the bus with a couple of changes to Miami and then on to Havana by Pan Am. No one was overjoyed to hear my news, either in Chicago or Havana, but they put on a good face about it though I had clearly disappointed everyone by my dismal performance in college.

Papa invited me to come on one of the "combat" patrols of the *Pilar* along with Winston Guest, who was now called Wolfie, and the rest of the crew. There was no sighting of any U-boats. We engaged in a practice assault drill to which some zest was added by attracting some sharks with overripe baits while we were hove-to well out in the Gulf Stream. When the sharks, mostly yellowfins, were on the verge of a feeding frenzy, a fragmentation grenade with the pin removed was dropped overboard among the sharks and one swerved to ingest it about ten feet below the surface. The timing was perfect and we could clearly see the sudden stop of forward movement and small white lines streaking away from the shark's body in all directions, like a starburst, followed immediately by reddening of the water in the vicinity of the shark.

In a few moments the other sharks were cutting toward the victim, drawn by the blood, and tearing away great hunks of flesh. It became impossible to see what was going on for the blood staining the water. But it was over quickly and the sharks dispersed, leaving the area as empty as it had been before the jettisoning of the baits, proving again the shark's awesome efficacy in natural waste disposal.

Christmas was quiet at the Finca though I was going to a lot of parties given for the young people of the Cuban social set I had met through my old school friends, the Sanchez brothers. We also attended Embassy functions to which Papa and Marty were invited because of the involvement of the Embassy with the Q-boat business and the counterespionage operation. Ambassador Braden and Papa got along very well, and Ellis Briggs, Braden's number-one man, was a close friend and confidant who came often to the Finca and took part in shooting and fishing and our perpetual social life. I was intrigued by the fact that he was a Dartmouth "graduate," something beyond my reach.

Before I left in early January to return to Chicago, much of

the glamour of the Finca had gone. Somehow, without con-
sciously knowing why, I was becoming aware of the ever-more-
strained relationships and the occasional unwarranted gruff-
ness Papa was wont to vent on anyone in the line of fire. On the
other hand, he was never unkind to me, except for his natural
roughness which I was sometimes oversensitive to.

I took advantage of several chances to take one of the cars
and drive with my old fly rod exploring some of the spring-fed
rivers near the height of land to the south and east of San Francisco de Paula. I had some small, cork-bodied bugs made for
catching crappie and bluegills. I tried these for the small-
mouth bass which had been introduced into these rivers, but
wasted my time fishing them natural-drift, like dry flies, and
did very poorly in general until I accidentally dragged one of
them across a likely-looking piece of water while preparing to
make a roll cast. A fine small-mouth bass of about a pound and
a half rolled on that bug with a vengeance and it finally
occurred to me that these fish might be more interested in
things that were trying to get away than in what was just floating along looking like nothing at all. The fishing was fun and
the surroundings pleasant, with green sugar cane fields bordering the steep riverbanks.

The only drawback was a common one in poor, heavily-
populated countries: privacy was nearly impossible to find.
Unless I managed to hide the car and sneak down to the river
without being detected, I was sure to draw a crowd of kids.
Even then, someone eventually came along and the word
would get out that there was a crazy American trying to fish
who obviously hadn't a clue about what he was doing.

There was one river flowing through a steep-sided valley on
the way to Matanzas where there were no cane fields and there
were spots where you could stay well-hidden from the road and
I could fish relatively unmolested. There weren't as many bass,
but I found, to my delight, that there were schools of mullet
that had come up the river from the saltwater and would take
a small wet trout fly in the fast currents between the deep, slow
pools. These mullet were as alike as peas in a pod within any
school of them I located. Silvery-sided, with steel grey back
and fine black lines running the length of their sides, they were
streamlined and active fighters on the light fly rod, often jumping and pulling off line in short lunges. In later years this
became a favorite family picnic spot, as it was just a short drive

from the old colonial city of Matanzas where we could buy fresh prawns or freshwater crayfish to amplify our picnic fare.

Before I left for Chicago, Papa gave me an advance copy of the collection of war stories he had selected and for which he had written an introduction. Published by Crown, it was called *Men at War*. In the introduction, the overriding thought he expressed was that the reading of these true stories and accounts of war would help any man to realize that no matter how bad the circumstances he might confront in battle, other men had confronted as bad, or worse, in times past. He also included a gratuitous comment that criminal military behavior, such as was carried on by the German SS, should be punished by castration. The remembrance of that comment would one day return to haunt me.

NINE

Now that I was out of college and the war was in the forefront of everyone's thinking, it was apparent that my next stop would be the Army Induction Center. I hadn't been back in Chicago long before I had to report for my physical, and on February 16, 1943, I became official government property. What a scroungy lot we were, totally bewildered by the battery of questions, tests, physicals, and other indignities we had to endure before being herded onto the train for Camp Sherman, Illinois where we had to go through the whole business again.

After being more or less fitted with uniforms, we were rousted out of our bunks at 5:00 a.m. and lined up in the company street by a tough-as-nails sergeant. "You men are in Company F for the rest of your time here," he growled. "Now you all know what F stands for, and that's exactly what's going to happen to you!" That was our welcome to the Army.

The myriad tests we took, including the IQ, were supposed to determine what branch we would be assigned to for Basic Training and eventually whether we would be qualified for Officer's Training. Although we were given three choices of branch, in order of preference, it apparently had no bearing since you were sent wherever the Army needed you at any given time. Most of us Company F men were sent to Fort Riley, Kansas for Basic Training at the Military Police Replacement Training Center on Republican Flats right next to the Cavalry RTC.

Like any basic training anywhere, it was dismal, and if it hadn't been for the war it would have been demeaning. As it was, I learned along with everyone else that there was only one way to do things, and it didn't have to be the right way, just the Army way. Mostly you knew you were doing something right if it hurt enough. If it didn't hurt, you could start worrying because a drill sergeant would come along and tell you it was wrong.

The part I liked best was weapons training where my familiarity with the Thompson submachine gun and my shooting experience stood me in good stead, though I still had to learn everything the Army way. We weren't allowed out of the battalion area for the first two weeks and then we were able to go to the PX where we saw our first "Junktown Debs" (young ladies from Junction City, Kansas) and drank our first alcohol, 3.2 beer. Some of us staggered back to our barracks, the result of our tough regimen and the shock of the weak beer on our systems.

A good deal of what we had to learn about involved the duties of a soldier, and guard duty was one of the most important of these. I'd learned quite a bit from my *Officer's Guide,* but being able to perform was a whole different matter. Some of us pulled guard duty off post on traffic control during an exercise involving the Armored Division which was training at Fort Riley. The Armored Division boys didn't much like MPs, so there were occasional fights in the PX but never in town, since we were never allowed off post the whole time of our training.

At first everyone lost weight but after a few weeks we started replacing it with muscle instead of flab. The training was hard for some of the older guys but was, generally, a song for us youngsters. The chow was substantial, but badly prepared; still, after the constant hyperactivity we wolfed it down with relish. One thing that put me off was some guy in the serving line pouring syrup all over my bacon and fried eggs, and as a result it was years before I could stomach pancakes or syrup in any form.

Another incident occurred during my first stint of real guard duty which might have affected my appetite had it not been somewhat stimulating for a young, sex-starved soldier. My guard post included a tour along one end of the mess hall. Guard duty was for twenty four hours with four on and eight off around the clock. We drew lots to see who started and I got in with the midnight-to-4:00 a.m. bunch. I was walking my post at slow cadence when I arrived at the mess hall kitchen and noticed some movement inside. My duty was to check out anything unusual, and this turned out to be unusual indeed. The main lights were out but there was a faint light from the open walk-in refrigerator door. I could see a WAC lying on her back on the meat-chopping block. Her face wasn't visible, but she had her skirt up around her waist and she was being plowed by the Mess Sergeant who was doing a stand-up job. He obviously didn't hear me: his ears were blocked by the WAC's heavy calves.

My orders failed to cover this particular circumstance so, after considering my alternatives, I continued walking my post. In a quandary about how to report the incident to the Officer of the Guard, I reported that I had seen movement in the mess hall and that, on investigation, it turned out to have been the Mess Sergeant cutting meat on the chopping block. The incompleteness of my report kept the sergeant out of trouble and me honest.

I also pulled guard duty one time when President Roosevelt visited Fort Riley. They put me on perimeter duty off in the hills beyond the rifle range. When the jeep dropped me off I was told not to move but not to allow anyone to move in my area. It was beautiful out there with some of the first signs of spring, and I saw quail for the first time since my visit in Piggott, Arkansas. I was armed with a riot shotgun, a useless weapon in the wide-open hills, but one I suppose I couldn't have turned into a sniper's weapon either had I been inclined to assassination. I never saw President Roosevelt, only the quail. Those who did see him were impressed with his big face, ever-present cigarette holder, his grin, and the sloppy homburg hat. They said he waved and smiled at everyone but never got out of the big, open car. It always amazed me that during all those years when he was in the limelight his personality was so strong that people simply forgot how immobile he was, despite the fact that they all knew he'd had polio. It wasn't until after his death that all the measures that had to be taken especially for him became public knowledge.

Finally they posted the announcements that applications were being accepted for Officer's Candidate School. Everyone knew that you had to have a minimum IQ of 120 to apply, but the Army wouldn't tell you what your score was, so you never knew if you were qualified until your application was either accepted or rejected. The main stumbling block, however, was not the application but how you did with the OCS Review Board which convened toward the end of every basic training period.

I had been a good soldier to the extent that I fiercely wanted the chance to become an officer. Perhaps it was the ghost of G.A. Henty or of my godfather, Chink Dorman-Smith, a great soldier in the British tradition I regretted never meeting. Probably, though, it was my hunger to do something well that Papa admired, as much as he admired good soldiering. I already knew he was disappointed with my assignment to Military Police, so when the chance came I stated my preference for Infantry, the branch I had been brought up to think of as "the queen of battles."

After reporting before the long table of what seemed to me to be very senior officers, I stood at ease and nearly shook from nervousness. I noticed that almost all of them were wearing the crossed pistols insignia of the Military Police; there was also one with the crossed sabers of the Cavalry. I managed to answer all their questions to their evident satisfaction, and the following week I was rewarded with my name posted on the bulletin board along with about twenty others selected for officer's training. I made it. Now all I had to do was get through OCS—Military Police OCS.

One Sunday near the end of Basic, we were lazing around waiting for chow time. The sky was not cloudy but not clear either. Suddenly a funnel cloud appeared from the southwest just like the ones I'd seen so many times in the Caribbean, which we called water spouts. Before any of us could react, it was roaring through the camp and we sprawled on the ground hoping to be spared. The noise was overwhelming, louder but much like the sound I had heard once when I had lain down by the train tracks on a dare when a train went by on the Skokie near Lake Bluff. I heard things flying through the air and saw one of the big horse barns from the Cavalry center land in the middle of our parade ground.

Miraculously, no one was killed, though a few were injured in the row of barracks next to ours which were flattened by the tornado. The clean-up livened things a bit while we awaited orders to our next assignments. Mine came in the middle of May and included a week's furlough in Lake Bluff before reporting to the Officer's Candidate School at Fort Custer, Michigan.

Camp Custer was situated between the towns of Battle Creek and Kalamazoo in the middle of Michigan's lower peninsula. There wasn't much to recommend it in the heat of the summer as a place to try to study and undergo the strenuous competition that went into the three months of OCS. There were just over 200 of us in the class. The two youngest were a boyish Southerner and I. A vast majority had come from the MP RTC at Fort Riley, though there were some from other branches and some who had been sent to OCS from the battlefield where they had earned the right to compete for a commission in active war service.

The schedule was more rigorous than Basic Training but with a lot more emphasis on classroom work and after-class study. My knowledge of the *Officer's Guide,* and the military reading Paul had given me, helped a lot. The toughest part was maintaining concentration during lecture classes in the stifling classrooms. What with the strenuous physical conditioning, the heat, and the often monotonous delivery of the lecturer, eyelids felt weighted. The competitive nature of the program, however, pushed all of us to our maximum abilities. One of the insidious extremes of the program was the student rating system, the rat sheet, in which we were all required to rate every member of the class in numerical order, from first to last, before the end of the course. This forced us to become acquainted with every classmate, to make a good impression and, at the same time, to evaluate each of them.

I found the courses stimulating, and my youth was a distinct advantage in keeping up with the coursework. A lot of the older candidates had been a long time away from school and they sometimes had difficulty with the demands of the course.

Unlike basic training, where we were never allowed off the military reservation at any time, OCS allowed us time off on most Saturday afternoons and Sundays. At first, almost no one took advantage of it, preferring instead to stay in the barracks and study or maintain their clothing and equipment which had to be spotless, pressed, and shined to perfection. After the first month, when we had the routines well organized and some confidence in our abilities, most of us younger candidates started taking Saturday afternoon and overnight off the post.

Through the USO we met some local girls and were wonderfully welcomed in their homes and invited to their social activities. Some of the families had summer homes and motor boats on nearby Gull Lake where some crazy parties were held. More than one candidate ended his course engaged to a local girl.

I remembered that the Muskegon River, where Paul had taken me for a day's float before I went out West a couple of years before, was not too far away and I wrote home for my tackle. I planned a Saturday afternoon and Sunday away by myself.

The problem, again, was transportation, the ever-present bugaboo during wartime. It turned out, however, that there was regular bus service from Kalamazoo to Grand Rapids, but I would have to hitchhike from there up to Newaygo and from there to Hardy Dam where I had seen fly fishermen plying big wets at the start of our float. I remembered being envious because we were fishing with lures and bait since we were planning to concentrate on bass and other warm water species that prevailed through the majority of the float section.

I had since read that the serious fishing was at night in the stretch below the dam during the giant mayfly hatch. Apparently there were very large browns as well as rainbows in this stretch of water and, although it was past the giant mayfly season, mid-July should be good for late evening and night fishing with big wets. I had one of Papa's old silk corona double-tapered lines that would sink well, helping to get a wet fly down. I didn't know then that a floating line would have been just as effective and that if I wanted to get a wet fly to sink deeper all I had to do was use a heavier fly dressed lightly on a long leader, which would allow the fly to sink deep as long as I drifted it at the same speed as the current. Anyway, I managed to get to my destination, having no problem hitching a ride in uniform and with my pack and cloth rod bag.

The water below the dam was broad with a strong current swinging first toward the north bank where I was standing and then in a broad fan toward the opposite bank. It was already past sundown when I arrived and I was glad of the warm, calm evening because the water was cold as I waded out in my sneakers and khakis. After a couple of hours, I was shaking, despite the still warm air. I had felt something a couple of times but wasn't even certain it had been a trout. I was working slowly downstream, one cast fished out then one step, casting across toward the far bank and slightly downstream and letting the fly swing around completely on its own without any twitching or pulling on my part, letting the current do all the work. I suddenly realized how wonderful it was to be alone wading a river. This was after all one of the true joys of fishing, the solitude which cleansed the mind of all its worldly burdens.

One of the things which almost never happens in the Army is being alone. Even going to the latrine is a communal event which must be performed not only with fellow sitters but in full view of shavers and toothbrushers. No giant trout was needed to make this a special treat and to reconfirm my values. Nor did any break the spell. The cold finally drove me to the bank and I built a small fire, ate the field rations I had cadged from the supply sergeant, rolled into my blanket and fell asleep staring into the embers, dreaming of Western streams with shadowy trout lying along the weed beds.

Time seemed to crawl by in OCS, but it finally came to an end. For me, it had been a success with an overall ranking in the top ten of the graduating class of about 200. None of my family could come for the graduation ceremony and the consequent initiation as a brand-new shavetail with second lieutenant's gold bars. Paul and Mother were away in Minnesota for a well-deserved fishing vacation in Itasca County. Since I had two weeks leave before having to report back to Custer for my assignment, I cabled Papa that I would be heading down to Key West where I would try to catch a plane ride to Havana.

My first night as a commissioned officer was spent at the Drake Hotel where a pretty girl desk clerk took pity on me and found me a closet-like room that turned out to be on the same floor as the visiting Brooklyn Dodgers baseball team. I couldn't believe it. These same guys spent part of their spring training in Cuba every year and Papa had told me about their coming out to the Finca where things ended up in a brawl with Papa and Hugh Casey squaring off in a doorway, each allowing the other to punch as hard as he could until one of them went down or quit.

I met Casey and he confirmed the story, saying both he and "Ernie" decided to call it quits simultaneously. Even Leo Durocher was nice. It helped to be in uniform then, and the girl camp followers who hung around the ballplayers like flies around honey were willing to put up with a new second lieutenant as a second choice. I enjoyed the leavings until the following afternoon when I was able to get a priority on a commercial flight to Miami. I caught the bus for Key West and spent a couple of days there waiting for the results of another cable to Havana. I saw some old friends and spent some time with Pauline and my brothers who were getting ready to go back to school.

While I was waiting at Pauline's, a call came from the Navy base where a Colonel Youmans wanted me to report right away, since he was flying that afternoon to Cuba. The name seemed familiar and it turned out he was the father of one of my friends at Dartmouth. As a Marine pilot, the colonel did liaison work between the Navy base in Key West and the Embassy in Havana. Papa had called the Embassy and the Naval attaché had laid on the flight. We flew in an obsolete Navy fighter/observation plane. I sat in the front cockpit while the colonel piloted from the rear seat. This time I saw no burning ships and we had an uneventful flight to Campo Columbia, the military airstrip in Havana. Before leaving the field, I lined up a return flight with the colonel for four days later.

When I got to the gate, Juan, Papa's chauffeur, was waiting for me. He drove me directly to the Floridita where Papa was waiting. Papa seemed very pleased with my progress in the military and we celebrated with a few drinks right there and dinner later at the Centro Vasco, followed by the fights where we saw Kid Tunero, who later became a good friend.

Papa was headed out the next day for a long anti-submarine cruise in the *Pilar*. He wouldn't be back until after it was time for me to leave. From his comments, I had the impression he resented Marty's absence, and was lonely and somewhat depressed about the lack of success in the Q-boat operation. Apparently they had made one sighting of a sub from fairly close but were unable to approach it. The German ship had been on the surface recharging its batteries but completed the job and submerged before the *Pilar* could work in close enough to convince them they were sports fishermen who might sell or give them some fresh fish. If they had gotten close enough, the plan was for the hidden combat crew to come up throwing grenades, sweeping the decks with automatic weapons-fire, and possibly to drop grenades down the conning tower. I am told they even had bazookas and anti-tank rockets. It seemed a far-fetched plan, but Papa was convinced it might work. The best they did was to spot one U-Boat on the surface and radio its position and heading to the Navy, who reported later that they had sunk a German sub, possibly the same one the *Pilar* reported. That gave Papa some satisfaction, but it was a far shot from his grand plan which, I must confess, seemed somehow surrealistic albeit well intentioned.

As usual, I promised to keep in touch, which I did poorly, and after seeing the *Pilar* off in Cojimar, I enjoyed the last couple of days reading and lazing around the Finca, swimming when I felt like it, and enjoying what was then a fairly pristine countryside. For once, I stayed out of the fleshpots and thought about the chances of a combat assignment. Had I known what was in store for me, I might even have shed tears.

On returning to Camp Custer, I found myself in an officer replacement pool. To keep us busy while awaiting a permanent duty assignment, we youngsters were assigned to teach whatever had been our strong points in OCS to some officer classes. I was amazed to find that the students were all real old-timers. Most of them had been in WWI and wore their victory ribbons. They had been recalled to active duty to be trained in military government and were to become administrators in liberated and occupied territories overseas.

These older students were referred to as "retreads," a new term at the time since the rubber shortage caused by the Japanese conquest of the rubber-producing East Indies led to the first mass tire-retreading in history. The silver-haired warriors were concentrating on civil administration courses but they had to be brought up to date on such things as weapons and tactics. I instructed weapons, for the most part, and it was excellent experience. The students invariably outranked me and I had to be on my toes. It wasn't like instructing troops who were a captive audience and who could be disciplined if they didn't pay attention. I was coming to understand what Paul Mowrer had once told me: that in the Army you're usually either going to school or teaching in one. Combat is the exception rather than the rule.

I began to have concerns about my future as a Military Police officer. From what we'd learned, the only real combat assignment a military policeman could aspire to was duty with a division MP platoon. At least you'd be close to the action and quite likely under artillery fire. Other than a transfer to Infantry, for which I had applied to the total bafflement of my friends who were convinced I was crazy, a division platoon would come closest to what I wanted in an assignment. I had marked it as my second choice. I should have known better. Maybe I'd have had a chance if I had asked for guard duty in Washington, D.C.

When my assignment finally came, I was disappointed. I was going to a Zone of Interior MP battalion at Fort Devens, Massachusetts. Two of us from my class were posted there without the vaguest idea what was in store for us. ZI battalions were normally assigned to stateside general guard duties involving security of both military and civilian installations with strategic or political importance. We picked up our orders in the adjutant's office and when we asked the clerk if he knew anything about the unit we were headed for he answered with a smile, "You'll find out."

To get to Fort Devens we took a bus from downtown Boston directly to the post. We reported to the post adjutant first and were directed to the headquarters of the 780th MP Battalion. Suddenly, we realized it was an all-black unit. Only the officers were white. The adjutant took us in to present us to the Lieutenant Colonel commanding the unit. The first thing that struck me was that he was a Southerner; it turned out the majority of the officers were. I was assigned to a company where I would take command of a platoon after a short training period in company headquarters where I first took over Supply with some stints of troop training.

The work was the sort of thing I had expected, but the surprise of being an officer with what were then called Negro, or Colored, troops was overwhelming. I didn't realize it at first, but this was a very unusual group of soldiers. The majority were well educated, and most came from the West Coast. They had been together for over a year at Fort Huachuca, Arizona, which they referred to as "the asshole of the universe."

When I took over my platoon, I found I had several college graduates, including one from Oxford. The Oxonian was an actor, a bit on the gay side, whose mother was a white English lady who had married a Black African commissioner in one of the British protectorates. He had come to the U.S. to act in films when he was caught up by the draft. Another of the college men was a squad leader who later became my platoon sergeant. His name was Chet Brown and he had been a running back at Kansas State University. We would eventually become great friends.

I was surprised that none of these men had tried for OCS but found that they had been discouraged from applying by the Battalion Commander. Eventually I recommended several of my men, only to have the recommendations sent back, and then I was given a "little talk between gentlemen" by the CO in which he made it eminently clear that so long as he was commanding the unit, "no goddam nigger is going to become an officer."

In such an environment, it took some time for me to gain the confidence of my men. Their morale was appalling. Conventional Army wisdom at the time was that Negro troops were inferior and not combat-worthy. There were a few exceptions to the rule that all black units should have all white officers, but they were rare, and only in certain branches, such as the Quartermaster Corps. Mixed units did not come into being, to my knowledge, until the Korean Conflict. Part of this was because many white soldiers, especially from the South, would have refused to serve in the same unit with blacks, or under the command of black officers. And since the peacetime Army had a preponderance of Southerners as a result of economic underdevelopment in the South, black and white relations in the military were a real problem. Frankly, I don't believe there was any real desire to make changes at that time, and only political pressure for equal employment opportunities in the civilian world could lead to the eventual changes that finally took place in the Army well after WWII.

The injustice was startlingly apparent to us in the 780th MP Battalion because of the self-evident quality of the troops involved. What efforts those few of us officers who cared were able to make were far outweighed by the prevailing attitudes of the cadre and the CO himself. What we didn't know was that the men were determined to do something about it themselves, and that they already had a plan up their sleeves. It caught everyone completely by surprise, including those of us on their side.

The battalion had received orders to prepare for overseas duty, and these orders were classified and not announced to the troops. Most of the junior officers were not briefed, except that certain changes in the training and in special equipment issues made the fact apparent well before we were let in on it. Finally, in December 1943, we were sent by convoy to Camp Shanks, New York, just above the New Jersey border on the edge of the Hudson. We were slated for overseas departure Christmas week. All the preparations were made. I had my last fling in New York, including a memorable evening at El Morocco where I met a literary fishing hero of mine, George LaBranche, who was enjoying an evening with a pretty young bimbo. He was well into his seventies, I believe, but more power to him so long as there was one left over for me.

All the playing was over. We were really going overseas. Everyone was confined to the post and even to the battalion area. Anyone going AWOL from that moment on would be designated a deserter. There remained only one final procedure before we would be cleared for departure: the Inspector General's inspection. Everyone was ready and each man had his full field equipment, weapon, and gear displayed for inspection. We had all our men turned out in perfect form when the senior officer representing the IG started his tour.

Before he got to my platoon, I could already hear the buzzing. Something was happening and I had no idea what it could be. I soon found out. The colonel came into our barracks and we snapped to attention. The first man questioned was an exemplary soldier. He was asked to recite his General Orders. He started bumbling almost incoherently in "Down South Nigger" talk and avoided answering the question. The next man was unable to fieldstrip his rifle and also lost his ability to express himself coherently. And so it went, all the way through the barracks. Men of intelligence and integrity, I had thought, were acting like cretins and demolishing their officers' reputations.

I was furious. All of us were. The battalion was refused by the IG and we were sent back to Fort Devens for further training. Our commanding officer was livid and our first officers' meeting was a dilly. We were all blamed for the incredibly poor performance, and our own credibility was suspect. We youngsters who had expressed sympathy for our troops were excoriated and held responsible for the debacle because we had been too soft on the black bastards.

There was a further visit from the IG and we were all interviewed individually. It soon became apparent that things were not what they appeared to be, which led to an understanding by the powers above us of what had, in fact, taken place. Our CO was replaced by an experienced but tough Lieutenant Colonel—not from the South. Several other officers were transferred out. We went back to work requalifying the troops all over again on a breakneck schedule. The trouble was that some of our men had been considered ringleaders in the plot to flunk the IG deliberately. These men were either transferred to other units or busted to lower rank. New men were transferred to the 780th from the Black Buffalo Division. They were a whole new breed of cat. Tough, ill-mannered, and insolent, they were the antithesis of the fine men who had been the core of the battalion.

During the next few weeks, I happened to run into a couple

of my men while on pass in Boston. One of them was Chet Brown. We went into a bar together and had a drink. It was then that I found out about some of the things that had bothered me about the foul-up at Camp Shanks. I knew it was deliberate, but I couldn't understand why the instigators felt it was necessary to make all the officers look like fools. Chet explained that they had hated like hell to shame us all, but that it would probably have been worse for us if they hadn't. The light began to dawn. We agreed on a program of accommodation and cooperation, and despite having a few "problem" men from the Buffalo Division in my platoon, Brown and Sgt. White promised to keep everybody in line.

I had a team, and from then on things went smoothly. The men had made their point and, despite a high price for some of them, they got rid of the commanding officer they hated so much and, more than anything else, they got the Army's attention.

*   *   *

One night in December 1943 while we were staying at Camp Shanks, I was staying overnight at the Algonquin Hotel. It was a favorite of Mother and Paul's and the manager could always find me a last-minute room. I had been out to dinner and a show and stopped in at the small bar, which was nearly empty though the light blue, mirrored walls gave the deceptive feeling that there were plenty of people in the place. A nightcap before bed seemed just the tonic. I shudder now to think that I had a dry martini straight up, the only way they served them then.

Besides the barman and me, there were only two others in the bar. The closer of the two men was seated two stools away on my left. They were having a heated discussion and, since they weren't exactly speaking quietly, I couldn't help overhearing the conversation, especially after I heard the name Hemingway used. It soon became apparent that they were arguing over the comparative literary merits of Faulkner and Hemingway, and also that they had had their full share of drink. The one closest, who had his back to me so I could only see him in profile in the mirror, was the vocal Hemingway proponent. He made the point that, "Sure, Faulkner writes beautifully, and I'll grant you he's a master of words, but he's too studied. He's too regional!"

His friend retorted, "Hell, he can write rings around Hemingway. And talk about regional, what do you call that Key West crap?"

I couldn't hold myself back. I interrupted with a "Gentlemen, please!"

They both turned to me with an obvious flash of anger which subsided immediately as they perceived my uniform. "May I have a word?" I pursued. They nodded assent. I continued, "I think you're both wrong. I know of a writer I think is better than either Hemingway or Faulkner. At least he's a hell of a lot better storyteller."

I had their attention all right. The near man snapped, "And who the devil might that be?"

"Maurice Walsh," I said, and then I started to detail his books I had read and that my father had told me he was a truly fine storyteller.

I stopped myself in mid-sentence as I noticed that the near man had blanched. I asked him what was the matter.

He answered, "I'm Maurice Walsh."

A shiver went down my spine and the back of my neck crawled. "I'm pleased to meet you, sir. My name is Jack Hemingway and my father is the writer you favored."

The drinks we had before us, needless to say, were not the last we had that night.

TEN

We sailed aboard a troop transport from Hampton Roads, Virginia without further problems. The transport was a converted passenger liner and was quite fast, so we went out of convoy without escort after the first twenty-four hours. The passage took seven days, much of which was spent in zigzag maneuvering.

Conditions for the enlisted men on troop transports were appalling. Troop quarters deep in the bowels of the ship were crowded, with triple- and quadruple-decker canvas bunks. There were so many troops aboard that the amount of time any group could spend above decks breathing fresh air was extremely limited. The rest of the time we spent in lines for chow, or going to the movies, but most of all in sleeping quarters where the air was fetid with the odor of vomit and stale sweat from the first day on. The capitalist system held sway and gambling, though forbidden, went on at all hours of the day and night. Small fortunes were won and lost, and there were occasional, but few, fights among the men. We all speculated on where we were headed and whether or not we would be seeing combat.

Officers were assigned duty below decks for four-hour periods at a time. It was a blessed relief to come back up for air to our more comfortable quarters on the promenade deck. We were four to a room, three of us from my battalion. The fourth was a first lieutenant named Bill Hall. He was a quite likable fellow who wore Engineer insignia. He wasn't attached to any unit but said he was going as a replacement officer. We talked quite a lot during the week at sea and he left a good impression. I heard about him again a year later. He had been captured while leading a mission to try to blow up railway tunnels at the Brenner Pass between Italy and Austria. He was tortured until one of his guards took pity on him and let him have a belt with which to hang himself. He had been a demolitions specialist. It was hard to think of him in such a role, remembering as I did the unassuming young man aboard ship.

When we finally sighted land it turned out to be Casablanca.

The port looked glorious from the distance in the bright African winter sky of mid-February. We disembarked and joined the advance party who had already set up quarters for us in a tent city on the southeastern outskirts of the city. Our battalion was completely self-contained, in that it had its own transportation, and getting it all unloaded and organized was a real task. There is little doubt that brilliant military thinking is one thing but without a fine logistical support effort, an army doesn't even get to battle.

During our short stay in Casablanca, the battalion supplied some men for guard duty in several locations around the city. Being the only French-speaking officer got me the job of coordinating guard postings with whichever local authorities were involved. It gave me a chance to have a look at the city which impressed me with its clean, well-ordered European quarter—and the sudden change to the Middle Ages when one stepped into the native quarter. Our men managed to stay out of the native area which was off limits to all U.S. personnel except the MPs who had to patrol there. Luckily, our battalion didn't draw that duty. The story that several U.S. soldiers had been beaten and castrated in the native quarter served as ample warning. But one of the officers stationed there offered me the courtesy of a visit with his patrol. The dark souks and alleys gave me the feeling of entering another world, a world I thought had disappeared since the fall of the Ottoman Empire.

The only other adventure worth recalling was a frolicksome night Lt. Moran and I spent with a couple of barmaids in the city. Mine was a red-headed Breton whose husband was in the Vichy Navy somewhere in the South Pacific. In any case, we provided each other with lascivious solace and, in my case, with a most pleasant memory.

Our final destination was Algiers where the battalion was to go on permanent guard duty at a variety of military installations. The whole battalion was loaded on a train, vehicles and all. There were no passenger cars, and this was my first time riding in the old forty-and-eights made famous in WWI. Contrary to what one might think, the journey across Morocco and Algeria was one of the most pleasant I have ever taken. The train dawdled along through lovely, pastoral countryside until we had gone inland from Rabat, the Moroccan capital. From then on the scenery seemed magnificent, reminding me of many parts of the West with touches of Islam thrown in haphazardly. Old Moorish castles, mostly in ruins, topped high, green hills, and almost every high place had its tiny, cylindrical, white mosque capped by a round dome.

The weather warmed for our trip and we were able to keep the sliding boxcar doors open and take turns sitting in the open door with our legs dangling in the breeze. We passed several mountain torrents which spoke to me of trout and, indeed, further investigation with the French authorities revealed that they were trout rivers, albeit heavily poached.

There were beautiful fields of oats just coming to head and still green. Peppering the fields were crimson poppies, and bands of European storks strutted majestically about in their pre-migratory nuptials. The names of the Moorish towns, Meknès, Fez, Taza, and Oujda, breathed the magic of the Thousand and One Nights. And, Sidi-bel-Abbés: who didn't know from reading *Beau Geste* that it was the headquarters of *La Légion Étrangere?*

When we first arrived in Algiers, we were stationed near Maison Blanche Airport until a permanent headquarters could be established in a more central location. Finally, a fine location was found near the suburb of Bouzaréa in the hills above the northwest end of the Bay of Algiers. We built our own tent city in a rolling field with vineyards behind us and the wooded edges of the grand villas and estates of the very wealthy between us and the city. Our only spell of bitter cold hit us when we first arrived. But once established in Bouzaréa, we had delightful spring weather. There was little sign that a military campaign had taken place here the year before. About the only indication of war was the blackout and an occasional air raid alarm, with the subsequent deafening noise of the anti-aircraft batteries. I never knew whether there had been, in fact, any enemy planes.

The war was dragging on in Italy where the weather, stiff German resistance, and the topography favored the Nazi defenders. I had again applied for transfer to Infantry but was turned down by my immediate superiors without so much as forwarding my application to higher headquarters. The reason was, of course, that I was the only French-speaking officer in our unit. Among the installations which the battalion was to guard were some scattered locations away from the city in places where the ability to communicate with the locals was absolutely essential. Partly for that reason, the CO decided to establish a small headquarters for a separate over-sized platoon under my command in Boufarik, a small town in the Mitijda Plain, some thirty miles southwest of Algiers.

One night before my move to Boufarik I pulled duty as Officer of the Day at Battalion Headquarters. During the course of the evening, Sgt. White, who had been deeply impressed by the horrors of venereal disease in our training films and lectures, overdid it a bit. There was a prophylactic station in the OD's tent and he used its services six times in the space of five hours. The procedure involved then wasn't particularly enjoyable, so I didn't believe he was doing it just for laughs. Not only impressed with his virility, but curious as well, I asked him where he was getting all this action. We were sufficiently good friends by this time that he confided in me that there was a marvelous group of "field whores" plying their trade in the vineyards.

The next day I made arrangements with Sgt. White to go into the vineyards after duty to see for myself what was going on. We had been having some problems with a high VD rate, and since our black troops felt uncomfortable patronizing the more or less sanctioned houses where many of the white troops went, they were often left with only one possibility: employing the services of streetwalkers, where there was no control over the sanitation, and the chances of disease were disproportionately higher. If there were a way to exercise some supervision over the "field whores," we might be able to get the VD rate down substantially.

We agreed that I would hang back behind the sergeant and that he would continue into the vineyards until one of the women approached him. He would then ask her to take him to her "patron." I would follow and, if I were noticed, he would explain that I was his officer and that I wanted to make an "arrangement" with the patron. Needless to say, this sort of enterprise would never have been condoned by higher authority.

Things went about as planned. The first man I met, however, was not the boss but an Arab ruffian who was suspicious of my motives but agreed to take me to his boss only if both Sgt. White and I were blindfolded. Walking on uneven ground with a blindfold is not easy, especially if you're not being led gently. It took about half an hour to get to the building where the patron was waiting. Even before my blindfold was removed, I could sense the dense, smoke-filled atmosphere. There were bongo drums playing and a reedy-sounding flute, and a crowd gathered around an open space where an Arab girl was doing a belly dance. The place looked like the interior of a large barn and I could see agricultural implements along the walls.

The patron was a tall, lean, quite distinguished-looking Arab who was the only neatly dressed person there. He wore Western garb with a white shirt buttoned all the way up, and no tie. He was very polite and invited me to join him first for some red wine which was in a giant green ten-to-twelve-gallon jug, then to share the pipe which was being passed around the circle. The smoke was hashish and I had some but felt no noticeable effect. The wine was strong and good, from the local vines.

I discussed our problem with him and suggested that he allow one of the battalion medics to set up a part-time dispensary at the barn. He thought it would do no good since the girls under his control accepted business from many sources and some would doubtless object to having a black medic on the premises when they were using them. I mentioned that I was going to have a detached unit of some fifty or sixty men with headquarters in Boufarik, at which point the patron suggested we might like to set up an exclusive arrangement for the duration of our stay there. He said he had been thinking of starting a house operation in a little agricultural village between Boufarik and the sea and that we could have exclusive use of it. If we gave his establishment all of our business, he would do his best to provide only new girls and we could keep a medic there during business hours who could take care of the girls as well as monitor the men. I told him I would have to talk it over with my non-commissioned officers, but if they agreed and we could reach agreeable financial terms, we had a deal.

Sgt. White and I went back to battalion with our new friend guiding us, unblindfolded. White left me to fetch Sgt. Brown to my tent for a planning conference. We agreed that what was not possible to do at Bouzaréa would be possible for our separate detachment operating out of Boufarik. It would require strict discipline and the agreement of everyone in the detachment to abstain absolutely from any sexual activity outside our own facility. I had been assured by the battalion commander that I could have all the men from my own platoon and would be free to pick the others to fill out the guard details from among others in our company. I instructed Brown, who was now a staff sergeant, to pick the necessary men, keeping in mind that they would have to be as reliable as possible. When all was said and done, we had much improved the situation and, that done, we returned to duty as usual.

I welcomed the move to Boufarik for a number of reasons. Probably the foremost was the opportunity to be on my own. I would only be reporting to headquarters once a week and would be living in requisitioned civilian quarters. While my relationship with my men was close enough, the atmosphere in the battalion as a whole was stultifying. No white man can ever truly be aware of what it is to be black. Just being a white officer in a black unit gave me an awareness of color and its concomitant problems I never could have conceived of otherwise. It must be considered to the everlasting credit of every black American who served in the Army that they were able to keep their sanity. I sincerely believe that none of us officers were not driven at least slightly nuts by the day-in, day-out contact with problems of race and race consciousness. While even with my own men this was true to a certain extent, in our new assignment we would all be on our own to a much greater degree. As it turned out, the most cohesive influence we would have was our mutual interest in our private bordello.

The British town major in Boufarik assigned me quarters in a French colonial house. The owners occupied the house but I had a comfortable, big, street-level room with the customary folding steel shutters looking out on a broad tree-lined street. The sanitation was primitive, but an improvement, nevertheless, over the slit trenches we had been using in the Bouzaréa tent city. There was a pleasant cafe just down the street where all the European residents gathered to discuss goings-on and where a light black-market meal could be had.

The largest single group of my detachment was quartered with a Signal Corps outfit just outside town which monitored all radio traffic for communications intelligence. I maintained a desk there where Sgt. Brown presided. For all intents and purposes, my men there and in other scattered installations around the Mitidja Plain to which we provided security were totally independent. My main function was rotating personnel, discipline, and troubleshooting. I conducted infrequent inspections since the units being provided security were the ones who dictated the arrangements. I saw to it that each party was satisfied. Chet Brown saw to it that everyone had their fair chance to visit our "facility." Along the way, I had an opportunity to see the country thereabouts, and even managed to get in some fishing of a sort.

I had my fly rod with me as always, and I took it with me whenever I drove around the countryside, just in case I should come across an opportune fishing situation. They were few and far between. The only stream that looked like a trout stream was the Ouadi Chifa which flowed through a picturesque gorge followed by the road from west of Blida to Médéa. If it had trout, I never found them, and I tried hard enough, even using worms and catching some eels. I did find some mullet in much the same sort of water as the ones in the Cuban stream; but in this case, at least ten miles from saltwater. There was a pleasant country inn where a tributary brook flowed into the Chifa, called the *Hotel du Ruisseau des Singes.* The Monkey Brook Hotel had good country bread and cheese and could fix you an egg dish to go along with the heavy red wine.

I had another good look at Algeria when I was put in charge of a convoy for a four-day assignment to fetch some supplies from Oran, about two hundred and seventy miles west of Algiers. The road lay inland through rolling highlands and along the valley of the Ouadi Chifa for a good bit of the way. I had high hopes for this river but it was a sea of mud in some parts and almost bone dry in others below the dams where water was extracted for irrigation. The country looked like parts of the West, except for the ubiquitous donkey, scruffy Arab farmhands, and the mosques. We had a bit of excitement on the way when we ran into a veritable locust swarm. We had just started down a steep slope into a valley when the windshield of my lead vehicle was completely obscured by giant grasshoppers about two inches long. We tried to continue but had to stop when we started to slip from the juice of the crushed insects under the tires. In about twenty minutes it was all over, though we had to proceed slowly until we were well out of the area. The swarm had come and gone less swiftly than the tornado at Fort Riley, but with almost as devastating an effect. The landscape was left devoid of any sign of green vegetation in a wide swath about half a mile across.

Two other unusual incidents punctuated the stay at Boufarik. The first started when an unhappy non-com from the radio monitoring station came to my quarters late one evening to inform me that they had heard a London news broadcast that my father had been killed in an accident during the blackout. Before finding out it was a false report, I had gone off by myself, completely stunned. There was nothing I could do so I did nothing but get stinking drunk by myself and awoke with a monumental hangover. But the hangover was cured miraculously when the same NCO knocked at my door the next morning, this time more cheerfully, to announce that the broadcast had been in error and that Papa was recuperating well in a London hospital.

A few weeks later, I had the pleasant surprise of a message that I was granted two days' leave to visit with Marty, who was now on her way to Italy as an accredited correspondent with the French forces under the command of General Alphonse Juin. She was staying at the Duff-Coopers', a beautiful villa in the hills above Algiers. Duff-Cooper was the British ambassador to the new French government, and his wife, Lady Diana, though already in her fifties, was still one of the great beauties of her time. As Lady Diana Manners, she had entranced the world with her beauty when she appeared on stage in a non-speaking role as the Madonna in "The Miracle." I was being invited to spend the weekend as their houseguest.

It was a weekend to remember. Marty was in good form, though she scarcely mentioned Papa. I only learned much later that they were already estranged and that he had taken up with Mary Welsh. In any event, Marty's visit was a welcome interlude with more than a touch of glamour. The dinner party given by the Duff Coopers Saturday night included Victor Rothschild, who had just been awarded the George Cross by the King for outstanding courage while dismantling dangerous unexploded bombs during the London blitz. Also there was Randolph Churchill, who had just returned from Yugoslavia where he had been parachuted with the British mission to Tito's partisans. He told us how he was saved by (Popovitch) Tito's chief-of-staff during a German surprise attack which nearly succeeded in capturing or killing Tito. Young Churchill was so impressed with Tito that he was instrumental in kindling his father's enthusiasm for the partisan leader and his cause, despite Tito's avowed Communism and loyalty to the Soviet Union.

Randolph Churchill was a Major in the British Army. He

seemed an earnest young man. While he resembled his famous father as a young man, he was slimmer-faced and perhaps lacking that special spark and redoubtable quality which kept Winston bobbing to the top no matter how badly put down. It is more probable, however, that it is only by comparison that he did not shine. It was a tough act to follow.

Ambassador Robert Murphy states in his memoir, *Diplomat Among Warriors,* that both the legendary Brigadier Fitzroy Maclean, who led the British mission to the partisans, and Major Richard Weil, Jr., the America OSS agent who spent a month studying the partisans, came up with the same opinion: that Tito was first and foremost a Yugoslav patriot and that his country's interests would come first in any conflict of loyalties. In the long run, their judgment was confirmed. In 1948, Tito stood firm against the threat of the whole Soviet Army poised on his borders and has since pointed the way to a possible accommodation between communism and capitalism.

I came away from that weekend wondering what the hell I was doing in the war sitting in North Africa supervising guard duty when young men were risking their lives in adventurous enterprises behind enemy lines. There seemed to be no way I could break the stranglehold the commanding officer had over me.

One of my most pleasant inspection tours turned out also to be the solution to my problem. The classified installation just outside the little mountaintop resort village of Chréa was my favorite to check out, and I soon learned to make my checks coincide with meal times. The food was undoubtedly the best I had ever tasted in a military mess. The reason for this was the French chef who took the trouble to round out his rations with locally-obtained products, including vegetables and fish. On one of my visits I asked jokingly how a fellow could get transferred to this outfit. I was told that all I had to do was to volunteer. I told the commanding officer about my repeated requests for transfer and he asked, quite seriously, if I could teach weapons in French. He knew that I spoke French fluently, so I replied that I believed I could if I had a French manual to work from or someone who could brief me on the technical terms. He said that if I were serious and willing to volunteer for hazardous duty, he would process my application outside of channels with a recommendation that I be accepted and that my unit commander would never know about it until the day my orders to transfer arrived on his desk. Furthermore, my current CO wouldn't even be able to protest these orders since they would come from the highest authority.

After I had completed the security clearance questionnaire, it only took about three weeks for both my transfer and my Top Secret clearance to come through. None of the officers in the battalion could believe it. Someone had actually managed to get a transfer out without a scandal of some sort putting a black mark on his record! My fellow lieutenants were pleased for me. They knew how much it meant. I couldn't tell them anything about my assignment except that I was transferring to the 2677th OSS Regiment, provisional. Since nobody at that time knew what the letters OSS stood for, it meant nothing. I only learned then, myself, that it stood for Office of Strategic Services. Most people thought it had something to do with entertaining GIs, Special Services, or sports. I confided in my men that I was going into paratroops since I couldn't tell them any more.

My official farewell to my platoon and to the other men in the special detachment came in the form of a party they gave me at our house of ill repute. Most of my original bunch managed to be there and it was a blast. The culminating point was their taking me to a closed door and telling me they had a surprise for me in the room beyond. The door was opened and there lay my surprise, a purportedly brand new (to the trade) young lady awaiting my pleasure with strawberry jam smeared all over her. They all roared with laughter and kept asking me if I knew what to do about the situation. After thanking them profusely, I insisted on closing the door and then asked the young lady to bathe.

I was very moved when they all announced that they were volunteering for paratroops as well. We all knew that even if they did, they wouldn't be accepted, but I appreciated their expression of fellowship. Such a fine bunch of men deserved better than most of them got from the Army.

Before reporting for duty at the training camp at Chréa, for such it turned out to be, I spent several days being given a general briefing and meeting people at OSS Headquarters in Bordj-el-Ahmin, a beautiful suburb of Algiers. The headquarters was in a lovely villa with dense planting all about which served to conceal the heavy security on the grounds. As it was, there was a heavy wire fence topped with concertina barbed wire and a control gate. I finally realized that, with a little luck, I might find myself really involved in the war after all.

While awaiting my orders, I received a message from Sgt. Brown. Our detachment had been recognized as the first VD-free unit in the North African Theater of Operations. He was delighted and wondered, in the note, whether battalion would be so pleased if they knew how we'd done it! I was delighted, too, but I felt as though I had been relieved of a great weight: much the same feeling my mother described to me many years later when speaking to me about her feelings when she and my father were finally divorced. She had loved my father but when the breakup was finally over the relief was palpable. In my case, I was fond of and totally committed to the black enlisted men in my Military Police unit. Nevertheless, my relief was real, though tinged with some guilt. They would never be able completely to leave behind them the ever-present consciousness of race as I had. That could only come with the passing of new generations brought up in a less-prejudiced world. The sad part was that many of them had come from California, where at least schools were desegregated, only to be thrust into the bitter race conflict by the war. Wherever they went from that day, my affection and good wishes went with them.

ELEVEN

The OSS training camp at Chréa, Algeria was as beautiful a setting as could be imagined. Located atop the highest point of the minor range of mountains immediately behind the provincial city of Blida, in a regal forest of blue cedars, the camp had a few small Quonset huts and a number of tents. On one side, the little resort village provided limited services for a small community of summer villas of the very wealthy who came to the 6,000-foot mountaintop to escape the summer heat of Algiers and the Mitidja Plain.

"Jumbo" Wilson, the British commander of allied forces in the Mediterranean since Eisenhower's departure to London, had a weekend retreat there guarded by the roughest contingent of soldiers imaginable. There were twelve of them, Scots Guards, all of whom had at least seven wound stripes acquired as desert rats in Egypt and Libya. Not only was their vocabulary limited to variations of the "F" word, used as noun, pronoun, adjective, verb, adverb, interjection or preposition, but they were always cheerfully spoiling for a fight at every opportunity. If you wanted to test your toughness, these fellows would oblige, and you'd better be good and willing to take as well as dish out.

The road up the mountain from the edge of Blida was narrow and winding and had the usual low stone walls on the outer edge, like French mountain roads. It wound first through small hillside vineyards, small farm patches, and sheep and goat pastures. Then the foliage became semi-tropical with lush vines and creepers until it entered spreads of live oak and scrub brush. At that point the view of the valley below was unhindered, and the whole of the Plain could be seen stretching to the sea in the north, rimmed on the west by the coastal range, and off to the right by the rising heights of Algiers and the Bay. Blida, below, was the site of a busy military airport where both British and U.S bombers were based—the latter as part of the U.S. XVth Air Force.

Driving down the mountain one morning at dawn for a field exercise, I was captivated by the sight of the whole plain below covered by dense fog. We were well above it looking down on the cloudlike surface when, as if by some sorcerer's incantation, B-24 bombers began emerging from the cottony blanket, rising in ever higher circles to form up together, then accelerating off toward a distant bombing mission somewhere in Europe. With the rays of the rising sun glinting off their cockpits and gun turrets, they were a stirring sight. The roar of all those engines filled the air space around and before us until the massive squadron reached altitude where, forming up, they lumbered on their way.

The camp itself was used for training both French and American personnel. There were courses being given in every conceivable type of weapon, including the enemy's. There was map work, demolitions and sabotage, use of radios such as "agent sets" in small valises, encoding and decoding, special devices, unarmed combat, and what has come to be known as "agent trade craft." I was assigned as part of the permanent staff, though I attended all the different classes when I was not teaching weapons to the French joes. I'm not quite sure where the name "joes" came from, but it was certainly not used in a pejorative sense.

The other instructors were a mixed lot. All were older than I and many had been in the field prior to being assigned to teaching duties. Security was excellent and, while many tales were told to illustrate points, the specifics of who, where, and when were left out. Everyone understood that the less any one person knew outside what he absolutely needed to know, the better off he would be in case of capture or torture.

Certainly I learned a lot more than I was teaching, and after a few weeks my commanding officer permitted me to assist in the instruction of some of the other subjects. The people who came to take the courses were given a first name when they arrived and they were never called anything else. It was forbidden to discuss one's own background or to question others about theirs. All soon understood that it was for their own safety, since these were all people preparing to go on missions in enemy-occupied territory.

In addition to the French joes, I was involved in training other special operatives. The school had a diversity of students, including Operational Groups (OGs), who were trained for disrupting rear areas in enemy territory by sabotage of railroads, roads, and communications, and by attacks on enemy units using hit-and-run tactics. There were also SI agents, though rarely, who needed some brushing up on weapons or map work or in communications. Their job was Secret Intelligence and all the ramifications of obtaining it and communicating it back by radio or other means. Occasionally Jedburghs used the camp, I was told. These teams were trained in Scotland and were comprised of three men from the three nationalities: U.S., French, and British. Usually two were officers and one an NCO radio operator, and their function was to provide staff leadership to existing resistance forces and to help coordinate their activities.

Among the teaching staff was a number of very tough, young men. They had all been to the OSS training schools in the States, and some of them had been through training in England as well. One of them impressed me especially. He was the only one of the younger men who had been in the field, and his toughness was not put on. In some ways he was crude. He was not particularly well educated, but you could sense his innate intelligence through the rough exterior. He did not talk about his prior missions, and they only came out to illustrate points he was trying to teach. I was to get to know him as well as anyone ever would, and I eventually learned that he had already made three jumps behind enemy lines prior to the assignment at Chréa: once in North Africa, once in Italy, and once in Sardinia. He had been commissioned in the field and, being several years older than I, he filled the spot one always has for a hero figure. His name was Jim Russell.

I was now totally involved with my new associates and, with only one exception, never saw any of the friends I had before my assignment to OSS. That exception was a young man I met at the Duff-Coopers, Piggy Warburg. He was an officer in the U.S. Army but I never saw him in uniform; he had some sort of special job which I never asked about. He was well acquainted with both the British and French hierarchy and I later found out he was a member of a prominent banking family. He knew I was with OSS now and got in touch with me to invite me to an afternoon and evening picnic with some of his friends. I mention it because that invitation afforded me a look at some of the incredible history of this part of the world. Our picnic site was not far from Blida, on the coast where the plain, the sea, and the coastal mountains meet. It was called Tipasa and was the ruins of a Roman settlement. Part of it was underwater either because of wave action over the ages or some earthquake. At any rate, we had marvelous swimming among the ruins and amphorae, where we collected sea urchins for our hors d'oeuvres. It was a complete respite from the military world and surely qualified me for the appellation so often applied to OSS staff personnel: "Oh, So Social!"

Jim Russell was the complete antithesis of the OSS staff person. In fact, he abhorred them. In his view they were nothing; only field men counted, and the tougher the better. I'm afraid I couldn't come up to the standards he set in that regard. However, the day he took me aside and told me the two of us would be going on a mission together I realized he had decided to accept me, if only for my ability to speak French. Jim's knowledge of French, or any other foreign language for that matter, was rudimentary at best. I remember, though, his getting results with the ladies using the phrase, *"Voulez vous promenade avec moi dans les buissons?"* I think it was the twinkle in his eyes that got results, not the words, which ought to have put any girl with sense off.

I knew that Jim must have approved of me or he would not have been told about the possible mission before I was. He was quite blunt about the circumstances surrounding our mission. He found out that one of his despised staff men, a full colonel, was supposed to have commanded the mission but had begged off for some obscure reason. It seemed that I outranked Jim by a month or two, having been promoted to first lieutenant just before we went overseas. As a result, I was to be in command, theoretically at least. I knew perfectly well that Jim would be the one calling the shots and that's the way it worked out, though we agreed in advance we'd be in joint command.

I damn near blew the whole thing. We had moved the whole school from Chréa to Koléa, on the beach, following an unfortunate incident when some young boys from the town had sneaked through the fence and gone exploring for empty shell casings on our firing range. They had gotten into the area where we did practice runs with explosives, grenades, and mortars. They picked up an unexploded mortar round and blew themselves to bits. Despite all we could do, it attracted too much undue attention to our operation. After a careful cleanup, we moved lock, stock, and barrel. We set up a new tent city right on the beach with an old, stucco bungalow serving as headquarters.

Shortly after hearing officially from Major Hendrickson that I would be preparing to go on a mission, a bunch of us went into Algiers for a Saturday night celebration. I hadn't as yet started being briefed and there were a few things I needed to buy at the PX. I think I was probably the only instructor without a pair of jump boots. I had the regular infantryman's combat boots which were ankle-high shoes with a two-buckle leather top. I had to get jump boots, especially since I would be going to jump school soon. So I got the guys to start in early enough to catch the PX before it closed.

We drove the three-quarter-ton truck in and left it parked near the Allied Forces Headquarters PX and I plunked down almost a third of a month's pay for the boots. There was no place to lock the boots safely in the vehicle so I kept them with me while we got started with our blowout. Despite visits to several approved bars, and the Aletti Hotel bar, which was supposed to be reserved for field grade officers but where we managed to imbibe for about an hour before being asked to leave, I managed not to lose the boots.

The crisis started when we decided to stop for one more drink at a civilian sidewalk cafe on the outskirts of town. Since we were seated within a few feet of the three-quarter with the seat in plain sight, I left the boots right on top where I could see them at all times. That was the first bad move. I forgot to reckon with the cleverness of Arab thieves. It must have been obvious that we had been drinking heavily by our loudness, if not by our actions. We were soon engulfed by a horde of threadbare urchins begging and asking to polish our boots. They were the diversion.

In view of my well-lubricated condition, I reacted very fast. I saw the boots disappear out of the corner of my eye and stood up, reaching for the arm and hand that had grabbed them. Too late, and the thief, an adult, ran down the street and into the nearest alley with me and the others, Jim included, hot on his tail. That was the second bad move.

The alley came to a T going only right and left, and before we could get to him the thief threw the boots over a wall into what was either a courtyard or a garden. He had been screaming the while and as he reached the T, three companions appeared, holding knives and advancing toward the four of us. The thief, behind them now, was also armed.

If I hadn't been full of liquor and wildly angry, I would have stopped. Instead, we all moved into them and had them disarmed or running within seconds. We were all qualified unarmed combat instructors, practicing every day. I think they were totally surprised that we didn't back off. We got in a few licks, but the boots were gone and it rankled. We got out of there, still angry, and with Jim driving we started back on the road toward camp.

If that had been the end of the story, the incident might have been forgotten. But it wasn't. A few miles down the road some Arab workmen who had probably been drinking, or smoking hash, saw the oncoming vehicle and started waving their fists and yelling angrily. One of them threw a stone, narrowly missing us, and we screeched to a halt. I think Jim just wanted to give them a piece of his mind, but the rest of us jumped out of the vehicle and started for the men. That was the third bad move. Jim grabbed me and held me back, telling me to stay out of it while the others jumped the angry men. I should have been keeping them out of it, too, but I didn't and they beat up the Arab workmen pretty badly, but very quickly, and then it was over and we piled in the truck and headed for camp.

We heard all about it the following day. It turned out one of the workmen had taken down the unit designation on the truck and reported the incident to an influential political relative who turned it in to the French authorities, screaming about American brutality.

Our being officers made it all the worse and the French authorities wanted us all to be made examples. They were already feeling political pressure from the fledgling national liberation movement, and Major Hendrickson leveled with us and said we might be thrown to the wolves. I must say I felt genuine contrition about my role in the business, though I also know that if the same scenario had taken place with enlisted men no one would have uttered a peep. Nonetheless, it was wrong and it looked like the three of us would be in hot water. We had unanimously cleared Jim.

The day of reckoning came on Tuesday when we all had to go in to headquarters to face the music. We each went in separately before a senior colonel in OSS Headquarters. I was last and it was apparent it wouldn't be pleasant when the other two had such long faces as they came out. I never saw either of them again.

When I went in and reported, the colonel went over the circumstances again and told me no charges would be pressed in my case because I could not be replaced on short notice for the mission to which I was assigned. However, I was not to return to the school but to report directly to the briefing officer in the compound who would explain the nature of my mission and send me directly to a security area from which I would not depart except under orders from him, and those would come just prior to our departure. The colonel then made it clear that he held me in utter contempt and that if it were entirely up to him I would have been court-martialed. I thanked him, saluted, about-faced, and left. It had been close, and to say that the whole affair had a sobering effect on me would be grossly to understate the case.

The mission, as first outlined to me by the briefing officer, was to parachute into occupied France in the northwest part of the Hérault department. The purpose of the mission was to establish and take over existing information networks in the area with a view to transmitting all available information regarding enemy force dispositions in the area, with particular emphasis on enemy defenses around the Port of Sète as well as the movements of the 11th Panzer Division. The 11th Panzer had the nickname, "The Ghost Division," and was scattered over a wide area of Southern France where it was resting and reorganizing after a severe mauling on the Russian Front, where it had distinguished itself valiantly and acquired a formidable reputation. The briefing officer confirmed the rumors we had heard that there would be a Southern France landing but said that the time and place had not yet been chosen and that the information we would gather and transmit would determine whether the landing would take place to the east or to the west of the Rhône River mouth.

Although Jim Russell was a competent radio operator and had "ham" experience, we were assigned two French radio operators, both non-coms, to free the two of us for action. Tall and lean, Julien had the rolling, heavily accented speech of the Toulouse area and the energetic cheerfulness of the Midi. Henri seemed more timid, though cheerful, and was short and pudgy. They were a sort of Mutt and Jeff team, but their role was invaluable.

A second aspect of our mission involved arming and training the local resistance and helping them in any action to impede German movements in the area. A concomitant of the latter aspect would be showing the presence of U.S. military personnel in the area which, it was presumed, would benefit the morale of local resistance groups.

With my agreement, it was decided to skip my jump training. With time so short, it seemed illogical to risk injury in practice. The sort of jump we would be doing was relatively simple and straightforward and didn't require the skills inherent in jumping out a door with a stick of troops. We would be going out the round hole in the floor of a B-17 whose belly gun turret had been removed for the purpose. There would be two planes, each with a load of containers full of arms, ammunition, explosives, and our radio equipment. Jim and I would jump with our personal armament, map case, compass, and the precious crystals for the agent set which would be our contact with base. Different crystals were to be plugged in for transmission at different scheduled times, making it possible to avoid operating on a single wave length for very long. These transmission schedules were memorized by both of us. Since I had no jump boots, I would tape my ankles inside the combat boots.

I spent hours at a time at the safe house where we were isolated, memorizing the maps of the area of the drop as well as our contacts and all available information about the area. There had never been an allied mission there before and the nearest ones were some distance to the north in the Correze and to the west-southwest near Mazamet, with the famous *Corps Franc de la Montagne Noire*. It was not a place of strategic importance in itself and had little industrial base of any kind except for a marginal iron mine and ore processing plant. The country was essentially poor, rough, and sparsely populated by French standards. The rail line running down from the *Massif Central* to the north followed canyon beds along stream banks except where it tunneled from one drainage to another or passed through short tunnels making shortcuts through rock outcroppings. It might become important to German troop movement out of the South after a successful landing in Southern France, though to rely on a line so easily cut would have been a foolhardy decision by any German commander and would likely be undertaken only under extreme circumstances.

Since I was forfeiting jump school, the briefing officer decided that I should participate in the last-minute preparations for several agent drops originating from Blida Airdrome in order to become familiar with the process. In each of these instances the agents were not among those we had trained at the school. The organization involved with the last-minute processing and on-field briefing seemed most efficient, though I had reason to wonder later on just how efficient it really was.

I was impressed with the fact that one agent was a girl and another a one-armed man. What was done at the briefing hut at the airfield was really a checklist operation to see that nothing had been forgotten. The briefing officer was British and supervised the equipment of the joes to see that nothing went with them that could give them away, and also that nothing vital was overlooked. His crew was expert at exuding confidence and helping the agents on with their striptease suit, a warm rubber outer garment which covered their clothing, and the foam-rubber-lined helmet to protect their head and, then, their single, British-made parachute.

Having seen this last-minute preparation, I began to fret about how I was going to get away with bringing along my fly rod, reel, and box of flies. I had managed to keep them with me ever since I had become an officer and I was damned if I was going to leave them behind. It might even be bad luck. Jim suggested I lie a little, and that's exactly what I decided to do.

TWELVE

Scarcely more than a week after the jump boots incident, Jim Russell and I were fully briefed and ready to go. We had been aborted once already, shortly after arriving at the airfield briefing hut. Something or other was wrong: the weather forecast or some other factor about which we could only speculate. The French joes, Julien and Henri, had been with us for three days and both remained cheerful, looking forward to the drop.

Jim told me of several missions which had been aborted when nearly over the target because of one thing or another. I could well imagine it wasn't easy on the nerves. For me the tension was mounting by the moment. It was almost a relief when we were finally at the briefing hut checking equipment and being dressed and harnessed. When the British officer saw the fly rod in the cloth case he exclaimed, "I say. You can't take THAT with you, you know." To which I replied, "Oh, it's only a special antenna. Just looks like a fly rod."

"I say. THAT's clever!"

I was relieved. I had twenty feet of line in my map case to fasten to the end of the rod just before the jump so I could drop it and have it hanging from me when I hit the ground, to avoid the possibility of injuring myself with the rod. Of course there was always the chance I might land on the rod and break it, but that was a risk I had to take. My reel, leader case, and fly box were in the map case as well.

Jim had rechecked the containers and the packages in which our radios and other gear were packed and we were ready to go. A late addition to our party, who we were told would be dropped in another area after us, went in the first plane with Julien and Henri. Once he'd boarded, Jim and I got aboard and settled in a small space near the belly hatch. The containers were loaded in the bomb bays but the smaller packages with our gear were in the hull of the plane, on the floor behind us. The section of flooring covering the hole through which we would exit the plane was in place to keep out the noise and the cold. Although it was August, the air at altitude was frigid.

As we crossed the Mediterranean, the dispatcher and his

assistant brought us sandwiches and coffee. I wasn't hungry but the coffee tasted good. Jim said to eat. It might be a while before we got to again. I chewed and swallowed without tasting. Then the pilot came back and chatted for a bit and I remember him pointing out the bright lights in the distance to our left. "Barcelona," he said. "No blackout." It struck me as strange that Spain, where it all started, was at peace.

We lapsed into silence, each with our own thoughts. As we came over land again we could feel the turbulence. Jim reminded me to be sure to keep my head up until the chute opened in order to avoid either knocking myself out against the edge of the hole on the way out or starting to tumble, which might cause my chute to malfunction.

It was considered very bad luck to wish anyone luck, so we followed the injunction all the French joes used, *"Mille fois merde!"* I managed a smile and the dispatcher removed the hatch cover and the two of them prepared the packages around the hole for the second pass, fastening each one's static line to D rings on the floor. I huddled out of the way and Jim stood above the hole watching for the signal fires and the code letter flashed by the head of the reception committee on the ground. Proper identification was imperative. There had been a number of incidents of jumps into false reception committees with tragic consequences.

Both the rush of air and the noise of the engines was deafening. The signal checked out to both the navigator's and Jim's satisfaction. We slowed and turned, dropping altitude. The second plane made its pass first to drop its containers and packages, then we followed as the dispatcher and his helper frantically shoved packages out. We could feel the plane jump as it lightened from the drop of containers from the bomb bays. We made a circle while the other plane made its second pass to drop Julien and Henri, then Jim and I sat on the edge of the hole with our legs hanging down, our feet just above the air-stream, and our static lines fastened to the D rings.

I grasped my fly rod by the center in my right hand, prepared to bring it parallel to my rigid body as I readied myself to stand at attention going out the hole. The red light was on and I couldn't help tensing. It switched to green and the dispatcher hit Jim's shoulder and, as soon as he was out, mine, and I was gone.

Never have I felt a greater sense of jubilation. After a short moment of total disorientation, the chute had opened with a snap and I was alive in what seemed total silence as the sound of the engines faded away.

"God damn, that was great!" I shouted without thinking, only to be admonished with a "Shush!" from Jim.

We'd been dropped from way too high, about fourteen hundred feet above the DZ, because the rough terrain had made the pilots nervous about going as low as they should have. For the moment it seemed wonderful to me but we would have to pay a price. Jim realized immediately that the wind was taking us away from the signal fires of the drop zone and he slipped away below me to try to land as close to them as possible. I followed as best I could but, suddenly, I was below the horizon and, an instant later, trying to fight the impulse to reach for the invisible ground with straight legs, the rod line went slack and I was tumbling through a thicket of bushes to the bottom of what proved to be a deep gulch. I had landed in France, whether safely or not remained to be seen.

I was unhurt, save for some bumping around on the rocks. Moreover, the rod was unbroken. After hiding the chute and striptease in some bushes and covering them with stones, I started climbing up the steep slope of the deep ravine. It was a hell of a climb, about three hundred feet through brush and thorn thickets to the crest of the ridge between me and the reception area. The night was moonless with a clear starlit sky, as planned. That was just as well because it was practically the only thing that did go according to plan.

When I finally made it to the reception area, after three bad spills coming down the hill from the ridge, Jim was there covering the lot of them with his Thompson submachine gun. I got everything sorted out quickly. It seemed the Frenchmen had not given any password, much less the right one, and since Jim's French was so limited he wasn't taking any chances. It turned out they hadn't received any information about a personnel drop and weren't expecting people, and certainly not Americans. Someone in Algiers had fouled up royally. They had been expecting a supply drop, nothing more.

They were, however, ecstatic that *les américains* had arrived; but first things first. We asked if they had seen Julien and Henri. They hadn't, so finding the joes and gathering up all the supply chutes before dawn became our first order of business. The maquisards had posted watchers on the ridges to mark the location of the falling chutes, but the country was so rough it was still a difficult and time-consuming operation. Although our personnel chutes were camouflage silk, the package and container chutes were bright and varicolored and would be spotted easily by the German observation planes that flew patrol over the area early each morning. Shortly after landing we had heard small arms and machinegun fire in the distance; it turned out a German armored patrol was trying to wipe out an ill-conceived resistance effort at the ore refinery in Le Bousquet d'Orb. While that action had nothing to do with the *"parachutage,"* as it was called, discovery of chutes in the area would certainly bring a German attack force into the area. We found out later that the German retaliation at Le Bousquet had brought plenty of force with it.

The next news we heard was catastrophic. Both Julien and Henri were badly hurt in the jump. Little Henri had landed hard in a live oak tree and the handle of his entrenching tool gouged out an eye. Julien had suffered a broken femur. Both required a doctor's help and would have to be treated by the local sawbones and hidden in the nearby town of Lunas. The nearest reliable doctor was in Le Bousquet and would have to be fetched.

The metal containers were scattered to hell and gone, and when each was recovered, men and oxen were needed to bring them back, though the first priority was still to get the bright parachutes out of sight. The latter task was completed, thankfully, before dawn, and about half the containers and all the packages were brought to the drop zone then loaded on an ox cart and trucked down a dirt track to an old, stone farmhouse where they were hidden under the hay. Jim and I, and our contact whom we called Robert, settled in a manger with a pile of hay in one corner and exchanged information. Robert had a bottle of rough country red and some *pays* cheese, the poor man's Roquefort, plus a half loaf of coarse country bread which he shared with us. It tasted wonderful.

The maquisards had arranged for an old gazogene (charcoal-burning) farm truck to transport the supplies out of the hills and down into the valley where they could be distributed to the local FFI (Free French) volunteers. Its first mission, however, was to take poor Henri and Julien to Lunas, three kilometers down the track from the farmhouse. Both of them were full of morphine. We injected them with the ampules from their first aid kits both to relieve their pain and to keep them from crying out and giving themselves away on the ride through town. The fewer people who knew about their plight, or their whereabouts, the better. The doctor would have to disguise his visits to them under another pretext when he made the trek from Le Bousquet to Lunas.

We dozed off in the hay while waiting to hear what had happened during the fighting at the refinery in Le Bousquet. The news, when it came, was not good. The Germans had evidently sent a company-sized reconnaissance in force to try to locate the resistance. The French, in turn, tried to oblige them by ambushing the Germans just as they were approaching from the south end of town where a foot bridge crossed the road at the entrance to the refinery. While the Germans, a company of Panzer grenadiers, had taken a few casualties, they had been able to dismount their vehicles and, maintaining good order and calculated efficiency, occupied the houses on both sides of the road and brought out hostages to the doors. The FFI kept up their fire and shot two townspeople held by the Germans, and it looked like the Panzers would mount a full-scale attack on the town. By this time there were about thirty FFI casualties and fifteen townspeople had been hit when the Germans stopped firing suddenly and pulled out back down the road toward Bédarieux.

The next news item we received explained why the Germans had broken off the attack. The BBC news reported that there had been a successful Allied landing in Southern France in the early hours of the morning somewhere on the Côte d'Azur. The Port of Sète, to the south of us, had been heavily bombarded by naval artillery for several days in an apparent attempt at deception. At that point, Jim and I began to wonder what the objectives of our mission would now become. The prime purpose, to supply intelligence for a possible landing west of the Rhône, seemed to have disappeared.

Still, information about enemy troop movements and dispositions would continue to be important to the forces on the new beachhead, and anything we could do to slow down enemy reaction to the landings would be worthwhile. The first part, it turned out, would be impossible because of the next bit of bad news. The chute on the package containing our agent radio, for which we had the special crystals, had failed to open and the contents, including the radio, were smashed beyond recognition. Our luck, she wasn't running very good.

The only thing that could save our chances of communicating information back to base in Algiers would be finding the radios of our two French operators. We believed they had been in one of the packages, but all those were accounted for. They might have been packed in one of the containers which hadn't yet been brought in. By noon all the containers were in and there was no sign of a radio. The leader of the local FFI came to see us and, after reporting the details of the firefight the night before, left us in Robert's care with instructions to move us and the containers via the old gazogene truck to a safer location up in the hills to the north. I don't think I ever saw a more bewildered look on anyone's face than when Robert told him I had parachuted with a fishing rod. That soon became legend.

Robert's crew consisted of young patriots, many of whom were too young to be drafted into the labor corps whose members were shipped to Germany to work on farms and in the factories. Some of the old men around the village had helped out the night before, but they had to make their appearance at their regular activities during the day. The youngsters had made a definitive move into the resistance and had, in effect, become outlaws. They had no uniforms and their sole means of identification as part of a paramilitary force were the blue, white, and red armbands with the letters FFI inked on them. If they were captured by the Germans, they could only expect to be treated as traitors and spies and would not be accorded the treatment required under the Geneva Convention.

The FFI commander was an army lieutenant who had recently defected from the Vichy forces and, according to Robert, was a better lot than Janvier, the head of the FTPF Communist resistance. Robert said you had to give the Communists credit, though, because they had been at it a lot longer than the FFI in the area and had strong support from the union members working at the mill and in the mines. The attempted ambush of the German reconnaissance force the night before had been a joint effort and the only one to date. It hadn't won any supporters, unfortunately, for either side. I explained all this to Jim and he said he'd already run into the problem in Italy where many of the local resistance groups were Communist-run. He thought we should distribute the arms to either or both groups, provided they were ready to go ahead and use them. I agreed, and since we had had no specific instructions in this regard except to keep from getting embroiled in anything political, that became our plan.

As soon as it was dark we heard the gazogene huffing and puffing its way up the track from Lunas. We loaded as many of the supplies as we could on the truck and started the long, slow drive to the area where we would be holed up: what we came to think of as "The Hideout." It took us about three or four hours to get there, just creeping along the dark roads with Robert lighting the way ahead with a hand-held flashlight. The truck had no windshield. We were ready at any time to abandon it or, at best, to get it off the road into the bushes on the side of the track. Traveling at night was strictly against the law, and any official forces that discovered us would have us dead to rights. The patrol would have to be a substantial force, however, since we were armed to the teeth and lacked only mobility.

The hideout was a deserted village of old, half-ruined, stone houses huddled together under the brow of a cliff which formed a long rampart along the north and west side of the Plateau du Guillaumard, one of the many *causses* in the region. The settlement had been abandoned late in the last century when the water ran out. Earlier there had been a full-blown spring a little below the base of the cliff which had served as the genesis of the village centuries before. It had been a place of few crops and much grazing, but the depletion of the spring caused its evacuation and now there was only a trickle of water in a hollowed-out rock pool. It was enough for our purposes for a limited time.

Among the items that had been parachuted were some field rations. We shared these with the boys who had been assigned to us and many of the things included were a treat to them. The French had been on short rations for a long time. During the next weeks we were provided with some delicious farm food by the locals. It was very basic and reflected the innate poverty of the region. There was fresh ewe's cheese, made by the farm women. Whatever they could sell, beyond the local need, was picked up by a small truck which made the rounds to deliver them to the caves in Roquefort-sur-Soulzon, less than thirty miles away by sharp, winding backroads. Meat was rare and what there was, was made into strong, tough sausages which were smoke-cured by hanging from the ceilings in front of the wood fires used for most cooking. Both as an aid to security and for more practical reasons, we set snares along the trails approaching the settlement. They were for rabbits but they would trip a man trying to approach in the dark. We ate rabbit stew and rabbit roasted over a fire on a predictably regular basis.

Quite aside from anything else, it was almost impossible for us to find out what the hell was going on outside our region. Jim finally got one of the boys to bring up a battery operated radio receiver. He did so for two reasons: with it we could at least get war news firsthand from the BBC, and Jim was sure that he could get a transmitter of some sort going, given enough time and the parts from the broken set.

In the meantime, men from the different units in the area would appear at our door every day. After undergoing a thorough security check from Robert, they were supplied with arms, ammunition, and rudimentary instruction. The FFI commander had some sort of demolitions project he wanted to do, so he sent up some youngsters and we taught them how to work with primer cord, time fuses, detonating devices, and plastique explosive. They were bright boys and quick studies, and their enthusiasm was boundless. When we felt they were qualified, we sent them back to the FFI headquarters to prepare for their mission.

I'd give anything to have been able to plan it properly for them or not to have sent them to do it alone. It ended up in the worst sort of tragedy. Their commanding officer sent them off to try to blow one of the many tunnels along the rail line down in the valley between Le Bousquet and our hideout. Neither Jim nor I was ever consulted. I believe the FFI may have felt it important that they pull off something important to offset the stature the FTPF had gained locally. At any rate, the tunnel and that particular segment of line were of no measurable importance that late in the game. Nevertheless, the boys were sent out to try to blow it up. They were sent out without a sound plan or anyone responsible to oversee it. They were just boys, and all of them wanted to be the boss. It became apparent afterward that they had not posted guards outside the tunnel while they planted charges, and they all wanted to be in on setting the explosives.

They had the bad luck not to get away with it because the first patrol the Germans sent along the track since the landings on the coast caught them red-handed. When the soldiers were through with them they piled the young bodies onto one of the ubiquitous old gazogenes and ordered an old man from the nearest village to drive them into the hills and deliver them to the "bandits," as they referred to the resistance. The old man drove the truck up from the valley to Le Clapier, two kilometers from the hideout. Jim, Robert, and I went over to see them, piled neatly like cord wood in the back of the truck. There were sixteen or seventeen of them, and that figure was probably pretty close to their average age. They had all been mutilated, organ stuffed in mouth, and eviscerated. The old man couldn't say anything, but tears ran down his dried-up cheeks. We all cried, trying unsuccessfully to hide our tears.

Every day Jim worked on trying to jerry rig a transmitter. He had everyone on the lookout for radio parts, and he felt he was getting close. The tunnel tragedy had knocked the fun-and-games aspect of resistance out of the local gentry and there was a discernible lull for a few days. In the meantime, Robert had his contacts trying to find out which German unit was responsible for the brutal massacre.

I decided to explore the stream down in the valley below the settlement. I hadn't had a chance to put the rod to work yet and this was my chance to fish in occupied France. Everyone was working at something, and I had nothing to do. It was about twelve hundred vertical feet down to the valley floor where the Verene, a small tributary of the Orb, flowed north to south in a deep canyon along a stretch of the rail line between tunnels. This area had never supported agriculture and, consequently, there were no ancient terraces along the valley walls as there were at Lunas. It was just rough country with steep pitches, broken by small, meadowed flats.

The surrounding country was solid limestone and I had high hopes for the stream. Limestone means rich aquatic life and healthy, well-fed trout. I was in khaki, a civilian garb not uncommon at the time, but wore no cap and there was a U.S. flag sewn to my right shoulder, but no insignia on the left. I wore the shoulder holster and a .38 inside my OD shirt. I fastened the reel onto the rod butt, left the rod case behind, and stuck the fly box and leader damping case inside my shirt beneath the pistol. I allowed myself the whole day and started down toward the stream while it was still cool. I had barely broken a sweat by the time I got there. Nervous at first, I had finally been overcome by the joy of going fishing. Despite the incongruity of the circumstances, I broke into a wild, leaping run down the mountainside, totally oblivious of the risk to life and limb.

I didn't even bother to study the stream carefully as I should have but stepped right into the water which, at low summer level, reached only to my knees at the deepest part of the run. The cold was at once shocking and delightful. I set up the rod and jam-knotted the leader on, fastening a wet leadwing coachman on the 3X tip. I had jumped into what was the best-looking water around and, of course, had completely ruined any chance at a trout, if such there were. The railway tracks were some forty yards away, above and to my left as I faced downstream. I started casting across, letting the fly swim down and across the current in classic wet-fly style. Nothing hit, but I saw fish below me dart away at my approach and knew they were trout by their speed and the manner of their movement. I had to be more cautious, get lower, and move more slowly, since the water was crystalline and the fish spooky.

I hunkered down and kept my casts horizontal, to fish out the tail of the pool where the water roughened a bit before leaving the pool for a short series of chutes down to the next deep water. I had become totally concentrated on thoroughly covering the last few yards of possible holding water when I heard a most unwelcome and frightening sound, that of marching boots close by. With the sound of the stream through the nearby riffles, I had been caught completely unaware. I looked up and, marching at route step with rifles and machine pistols at sling arms, was a patrol in German uniform. They were all looking toward me and making what sounded like derisive, joking comments as they went along.

For the first time in my life I made a silent wish that came as close to a real prayer as I had ever come. Above all, I wished not to hook a fish at that moment. If I had, the whole patrol would have halted to watch. Then there would have been conversation and, if I had turned to any degree, the U.S. flag would have been visible. The powers above were with me; I hooked nothing, and the Germans kept on marching down the track. I started to shake, but with far better reason than I had when I lost the big steelhead on the Pahsimeroi. I got the hell out of there and started the long climb back up the *causse*.

A few hundred feet up, at the first flat ground above the level of the tracks, I stopped and scanned the valley bottom. The foot patrol was out of sight around the bend, but I spotted a figure wading in the stream a quarter mile downstream. I watched curiously as he waded slowly upstream, stopping periodically to lean down and reach under stones, then put whatever he'd got into the willow creel hung over his shoulder. He was too far away for me to see exactly what he was doing, and it wasn't until I asked Robert about it that I found out what the fellow was doing. He was a professional trout fisherman who fished for the local inn at Avènes which still served the occasional meal for a price. He walked slowly up the current of the long, shallow pools and spotted the surprised trout shooting off their feeding locations to hide under a rock. He then calmly approached the rock and put his hand in the water for a moment to let the water cool his skin then reached under the rock skillfully and grabbed the trout around the middle and lifted it, immobilized, into his creel. The manner of grabbing around the middle was obviously a much-practiced skill, but it seemed so deliberate it gave the impression of utter simplicity. This fisherman was well-known for his skills, and few others could come even close to filling a creel with lively trout for the trade as he could. I had heard about tickling trout before but had never thought it could be done in so seemingly easy a fashion.

The war news kept getting better. Apparently the landings on the South Coast had been a huge success and the consequent rapid advance toward Toulon and Marseilles, and up the Rhône Valley, was pulling all, or most, of the German forces out of Southern and Southwest France toward the Northeast, to avoid entrapment. Paris had been liberated by the Allies, and German armies were in full retreat on every front.

We were still unable to get a message out and, by this time, must have been considered lost by our headquarters in Algiers. It seemed the best we could do now was to arm as many men as possible and try to prevent, or at least slow down, any attempt by German forces to evacuate through the area under our control. We decided to move down into Le Bousquet d'Orb where we could hear in advance of anything coming up the valley from Bédarieux or Lamalou toward us.

Jim, Robert, and I settled into an empty apartment above a corner pharmacy which gave us a good vantage point overlooking the southern approach into town, where the firefight had taken place on the night of our jump. We were invited to eat at the inn at Avènes, where there was a low weir across the Orb and some inviting weedy water where I caught several trout on dry flies. We ate crayfish *à l'américaine,* a great but messy delicacy, followed by trout doubtless caught by the hand fisherman. The old grandfather of the family was in the bedroom listening to the personal notices on the BBC and suddenly burst into the dining room with tears in his eyes, crying out, *"J'ai pleuré de joie! J'ai pleuré de joie!"* It was the personal message which meant that the following night there would be a parachute supply drop in our sector.

After a brief discussion, we decided to change the location of the drop zone by a few kilometers to an open field close to the valley bottom near a cluster of farm houses called Jonçel. Since we had a good handle on the valley, it would give us a much easier time gathering and disposing of the containers since it was much closer to the road than the DZ above Lunas at Les Pascals where we had landed.

The *"parachutage"* turned into a great social occasion. Gone was any semblance of security and the whole population of the valley seemed to know about it and had apparently turned out to help with the work. These people quite evidently felt that the war was over for them, what with the presence of Americans in uniform and the Germans not in evidence for some time. We had sentries posted all the way down the valley to warn of any danger. Even Jim let down his guard and there was quite a lot of wine consumed by all present, and the ladies were flirtatious. We kept our heads in that regard, however, because the worst possible thing we could do would be to fool around with some local girl and create internal problems with the resistance people. We would await a better chance somewhere else for any catting around.

Everything went off perfectly except that there was no message for us from base and no replacement radio. We came to the conclusion that they must have written us off completely.

Janvier, the FTPF chief, paid a call shortly after the drop requesting a large share of the weapons which he said the local commander wouldn't give him. I got both groups together and stated our policy that we must arm any group that would fight, and settled the matter temporarily. It was becoming obvious that a serious rift was developing between the two factions, the FTPF and the FFI, and now that the Germans were becoming a minor problem, politics were upstaging patriotism. I could see that it was heading for an ugly showdown at some point.

The following night I was awakened by Robert shaking me. The guard had reported that an enemy column was headed up the valley and would reach the edge of town shortly. Our dispositions, in such an eventuality were already planned and we gave the necessary instructions. No one was to open fire until Jim and I did. Jim stayed upstairs and I went down behind the glass door of the pharmacy, opening it just a crack. In order to avoid the mistake which had been made in an earlier firefight, it was agreed to let the point of the column enter the town so we could ambush the main body from the flanks, not giving them the opportunity to reform and establish position in the buildings. By the time the point men reached the pharmacy, the main body would be well into the ambush. All the civilians were told to get down in their cellars and stay out of the way. We had men scattered from below the mill all the way through town.

The point man in the German column carried a Schmeisser machine pistol at the ready and marched up the middle of the street until he was opposite Jim and me. We opened fire with our Thompson guns. He went down without firing a shot and the second man, fifty yards behind, threw down his weapon and put his hands in the air. Unexpectedly, there was no firing from below where the main body of the column should have been. It turned out there were only three men and they had been trying to bluff their way through by pretending to be the point scouts of a larger formation. Word sped to us that that was all there was, and our sentry had been carried away in his first report. We brought the wounded German into the pharmacy where he was made comfortable, though his wounds were in the gut and he had little chance of survival. Amazingly, no one had fired at the second and third men, who threw down their weapons and surrendered; they became our first prisoners and were put into the jail where they were the sole occupants. All were very young and I had fired my first shots in anger, and I didn't feel all that good about it. The wounded youngster died the next day.

By now we were known to all and sundry as the lieutenants Jimi and Jacques *le fou*. I had my first fly-caught trout in France, and on a dry at that. Robert was wild to engage the enemy and Jim was coming close to having a functioning trans-

Papa with Mr. Bumby (my childhood
nickname) in Paris, 1926.
(Photo by Man Ray)

The photo of my mother, Hadley Richardson, in her wedding gown, was taken in 1921 before her marriage to Papa. The portrait of Hadley, taken in Paris, 1929, is one of my favorites.

(Below) The young family on vacation
in Schruns, Vorarlberg, Austria.
(Right) Papa took the photo of me on
the beach at Juan-les-Pins with my
nurse, Marie-Cocotte Rohrbach, who
was also Hadley's housekeeper.

(Top) Papa at Pamplona, circa 1927,
with oxen, used in the running of the
bulls. *(Bottom)* Posing with Papa's
sailfish, caught off Key West in 1929,
when I was six. *(Right)* Papa and
second wife, Pauline, on the beach at
Hendaye in 1932.

(Top) The recent success of *A
Farewell To Arms* cheered the
young writer, here shown relaxing
in Key West. *(Below)* At Bimini, in
1934, aboard the *Pilar* with Papa
and Winston Guest, I learned all
about the Thompson submachine
gun.

With one of Averell Harriman's black Labradors,
Papa, Jack, Gregory and Patrick as we appeared in
a magazine feature. (Sun Valley Photo)

(Left) Papa and John Dos Passos landed equally impressive catches during their convocation in Key West in 1929.
(Above) The young Max Perkins, Papa's editor at Scribner's, proved he could fish with the best of them. During his distinguished career, Perkins helped develop many of the brightest talents of our time.

Part of our OSS team at Le Bousquet, with a downed U.S. flier, seated left. I am in the center, Jim Russell, right, and two French "Joes."

Captain J.H.N. Hemingway, far right, training officer with the 10th Special Forces at Ft. Bragg, N.C.

**Skiing at Sun Valley after the war
with, from left, Rocky Cooper, J.H.,
Ingrid Bergman, Gary Cooper and
Clark Gable.**

(Above) After a hectic courtship, I finally
got Puck to the altar in Paris, 1949. *(Top
Right)* Matron-of-honor Julia Child and
best-man Lt. Jack Kelly attended Puck
and me at the American Church in Paris.
(Photo by Paul Child) *(Bottom Right)*
Bride and groom on our honeymoon at
Crécy-en-Brie.

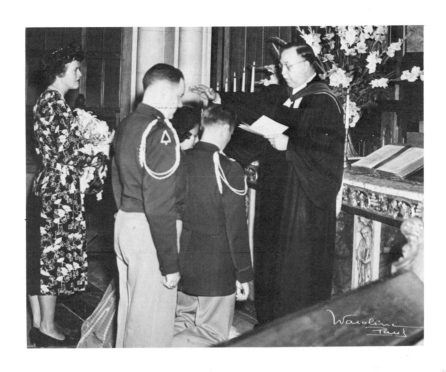

(Right) I claimed at the time to have caught this six-pound rainbow on Silver Creek with dry fly, but actually used minnows, as proved by the tell-tale minnow bucket at left. *(Below)* Papa in Havana with Little Miss Muffet, in 1952. He was just getting accustomed to the idea of being a grandfather.

mitter. Robert had managed to requisition some gas at gun-point somewhere and was in control of an *onze cheveaux traction avant,* the first Citroën with front-wheel drive. The FFI had commandeered one of these admirable vehicles before our arrival but it had been shot up the night we landed and barely made it to Les Pascals farm before collapsing per-manently. We had pushed it down into the ravine where it lies rusting to this day.

While we had no knowledge of other Allied missions in the area, it was common knowledge among the FFI that there were Americans with the *Corps Franc de la Montagne Noire* near Mazamet. Robert thought we might be able to contact them and perhaps solve our communications problem. Jim decided to stay at work on his set while Robert and I set off in the *trac-tion avant* for a thriller-chiller of a ride down the valley through Bédarieux, Lamalou, and along the base of the Espinousse Mountains through St. Pons to Mazamet. The windshield was open and I sat on the passenger side with the Thompson sub-machine gun sticking out the front. Robert drove like a mad-man and, luckily, we encountered nothing on the road until just outside St. Pons where a German jeep with four men in it sat parked by the side of the road just as we came around a turn. Robert floored it and I let go a couple of bursts at the jeep and we went flying through the winding streets of the town and out the other side with no pursuit behind us.

We made it all the way into the town square at Mazamet without further incident. Robert may have been wild but he was good, and the *traction avant* really held the road well on the curves, though it had a distressing tendency for the rear end to drift, which I wasn't used to, and that action scared the hell out of me.

Mazamet was celebrating its official liberation and the square was crowded with people yelling, laughing, and drink-ing. We stopped the car and put it under guard at the city hall and went in. The mayor and the local resistance chiefs greeted us but told us the Americans had left. We'd missed them. With little hesitation, we circled around the square and headed back the way we'd come and, this time, encountered nothing at all. At Mazamet we had heard that the Germans were still around Montpellier and we decided to head down there with two cars armed and see if we could help. This time Jim didn't want to miss out on the action so he came along.

Robert drove the lead car filled with armed men and Jim drove the second car with me at the gun beside him. Three of our guys were crowded in the rear. Jim couldn't believe what Robert was doing in the front vehicle: we barely managed to keep within sight. We headed toward Béziers and cut across the back roads to Pézenas where the people told us the Germans had all pulled out toward Montpellier. So we drove along the road to the coast where we saw the hillock of Sete across the lagoon, then drove along back roads inland parallel to the national highway number 115 until we were approaching a crossroads just outside Montpellier.

There was a new burned-out panther tank in the crossroads and small arms fire coming from close by. We conferred and decided to bypass to another entrance to the city which Robert said he knew. We ended up following a maze of small streets all the way to the central square where we were told the German forces were evacuating to the northeast and only fighting rear guard actions to protect their convoy. At that point we realized we were out of our league and called a halt. People were just starting to come out of their houses, aware that the hated occupiers were indeed gone. Spirits soared with every hour that there was no sign of a return by the Germans.

Since it was late, we decided to spend the night at Montpellier. Everyone was on his own and we agreed to meet in the square the following morning. Robert stashed the cars with a cousin then joined the celebration. There was no danger of any problem with the local populace. We joined the throng and were soon accompanied happily by some very attractive local ladies and, since the mood was one of such complete abandon, we just allowed matters to take their own appointed course.

The next morning, badly hungover, our little group joined forces in the square where we satisfied our need for a hair of the dog that bit us. We sat at an outdoor cafe watching the crowds when, suddenly, a great cheer went up. We heard the roar of tank engines, then watched as the lead elements of the French Armored Division clattered heavily into the city with General De Lattre de Tassigny in the lead tank waving to the multitudes and being cheered in return. It was a historic occasion I would recall with some amusement several years later when attending a diplomatic reception in Washington, D.C. A young Frenchman told me about being an aide to De Lattre and when I questioned him about what battles or campaigns he'd participated in he told me about the battle of Montpellier. I was unable to refrain from laughing as I told him of having been sitting in the Place when he arrived. It did not amuse him, I'm afraid.

Without further ado, we headed home to Le Bousquet where Jim finally got his jerry-rigged radio to function with our crystals. Transmitting at one of the scheduled times, he actually made contact with Algiers. We were told to stand by, and after a long wait, we received a message of congratulations on our survival and were ordered to proceed forthwith to Headquarters SSS (Strategic Services Section) 7th Army, at the beachhead at St. Maxime.

THIRTEEN

After farewells to our friends at Le Bousquet d'Orb, Jim and I drove off in one of the requisitioned Citroëns. All we had with us were our personal weapons, OD blanket-sleeping bags, clothing, and maps. One other thing we had, which we had not even thought about until then, was our operational money. We each carried a considerable sum of cash in thousand-franc bills rolled up and inserted into condoms with the end tied off to protect them from moisture. In addition, we each carried emergency funds sewn into our clothing and, attached to our buttons, *Louis d'or* coins, which were highly prized at the time. Until then we had had no need of either kind of currency. Had we jumped in early enough to set up an information network, we would probably have had to use funds to finance various aspects of our operation. The gold coins were for bribery in case we got into a jam. The only other item we had jumped in with were "L" pills. We had each been issued one of these rubber-coated cyanide tablets which were to be kept in our mouths in times of emergency and the likelihood of capture. They were guaranteed to take you into the next world within thirteen seconds, and painfully. Jim and I had discussed them prior to the jump and once we appraised the situation, and the evident stage of the war, we destroyed them.

Almost anything could be had by military personnel during that period by issuing *bons de réquisition.* These were hand-written promissory notes issued by officers in the name of the military authorities. We acquired some gasoline this way. Later we got it from the military once we'd arrived in an area where U.S. forces were active. We drove to Avignon where there was a functioning Bailey bridge across the Rhône and spent our first night there. It wasn't smart to try to travel by night, since there were a lot of trigger-happy citizens around, and we knew no passwords and didn't even have documentation, except for the famed Eisenhower passes which stated that we represented Supreme Headquarters Allied Forces Europe and should be accorded any assistance possible, signed by Eisenhower himself. That was fine, if you could get to the point of showing a pass. In the dark, if you didn't know the password, you were in for serious trouble.

Both armies had recently rolled through Avignon, the pursued and the pursuers. As all normal services were in a state of disruption, we had difficulty getting a meal. However, we finally met some local girls who took us to the home of one of their families where we were treated to a fine black-market meal with all the things that were supposed not to exist. Finally, we were allowed to use the bedroom of a lost son and happily spread our sleeping bags on the big double bed.

Next morning we headed for Marseilles where we hoped to get some more gas and find out where our unit might be located. We wasted most of the day running down the gas and could find no practical information and had to drive on to the beachheads at St. Maxime and St. Raphael. Jim and I spent the night in Marseilles with a couple of the toughest bimbos I had ever come across. They were beauties, though, and just what was needed for the occasion. Mine had the foulest mouth I have ever heard, and I could only decipher half the filthy colloquialisms she was using. She had the face of an angel and a body that wouldn't stop and, somehow, these considerations seemed more important than propriety at the moment. The ladies of the night and the fabulous dinner we had at a black-market restaurant just outside the *Vieux Port,* which had been totally flattened by air bombardments, were the only expenditures we made from our "operational" funds. As I remember it, when Peter Sichel, the unit financial officer, asked for an accounting, he received a somewhat different report on the funds expended.

The next day we made it all the way to the beachhead, detouring around Toulon where the French were still mopping up after a heavy siege. There we saw the devastation to the resort villas along the coastline wreaked by the Navy's bombardment preceding the Allied landing. Inquiries at 7th Army Headquarters about the location of our unit finally hit pay dirt. They were somewhere near Sixth Corps Headquarters, which was supposed to be somewhere north of Lyons by now.

The Allied landings had been a fabulous success and objectives which were expected to fall in a month had fallen inside a week. It had been a complete rout, and significant elements of the German Army had been destroyed along the highways

by Allied Air Forces as the Wehrmacht beat a wild retreat up
the Rhône Valley to try to reassemble. They were hoping to
establish a more defensible main line of resistance between the
Swiss border and the northern end of the Vosges Mountains
and then along the Siegfried Line.

Jim and I were shown the course of the campaign on a map
so we would know what lay ahead of us. We decided to head
north directly over the mountains following the Napoleon
route via Digne and Gap to Grenoble. Butler's Task Force,
under the command of Brigadier General John Butler, had followed the route part way after the landings, then cut over to the
Rhône Valley at Montelimar where they intercepted the main
body of the retreating German Army and impeded the retreat
until, using up all their heavy ammunition, they were firing at
the Panzer tanks with their .45s. At that point, the Air Force
came in and finished the job.

The country along the route was wild and mountainous and
much more like the American West than the mountains of the
Cévènnes where we had been holed up. Considering the condition of the roads, we made good time. There was no traffic, so
we arrived in Grenoble in time to grab a meal at a cafe on the
main *place*. Unlike the South where the food was fair, the
bread here was brown and sticky—you could mold the dough
into any shape you wanted, like modeling clay. Portions were
tiny, and it was obvious the war had been a heavy burden on
the local population. Passing through, I also saw several likely-
looking streams amid the alpine landscape. I marked them
down for a future visit.

From Grenoble we drove toward Lyons where we skirted
east of the city heading north through Bourg to Lons-le-
Saunier where we found Sixth Corps Headquarters and spent
the night in a classroom, part of a school requisitioned for officers' quarters. The next morning we were directed to Voiteur,
only seven kilometers north on the road to Poligny and Besan
çon where the front, if you could call anything so fluid a front,
was indicated on the Corps' war room map.

Military traffic crowded the roads, with priority given to
convoys carrying gasoline and supplies. With our civilian
Citroën, we didn't stand much chance of getting through the
various checkpoints, so we ditched the car at city hall and the
Corps Headquarters Motor Pool assigned a driver to take us to
Voiteur.

Imagine the French village of your dreams, right down to a trout stream running through it and past the beautiful chateau on the edge of town, and you have Voiteur. The town is a few kilometers off the main highway but has a small rail station. The Jura Mountains are off to the east of it with their foothills starting just outside town. The Strategic Services Section had pretty much taken over the town and we were dropped at the motor pool inside a walled courtyard with an iron grill atop the wall. The Jura is slate country and the roofs are steep-pitched so the snow will slide off. All in all, the picturesque buildings and lanes gave the headquarters a most unmilitary look.

A Major Crosby first greeted us and, after seeing that we were assigned rooms in the manor house at the bottom of the hill, ushered us into an office where we went through our debriefing, accounting of funds, and were then given an overview of what roles OSS personnel were playing with the advancing 7th Army. Both Jim and I were to be assigned to teams working in direct conjunction with the American divisions of Sixth Corps. Jim was to go to the 45th Division and I to the 3rd. We would have a day or two at headquarters to rest up and to be given an overall briefing. Lastly, they asked, wouldn't we like to come up to the chateau for drinks and dinner that evening?

I took a walk down to the bridge across the Seille where the stream left the town and ran north through some fields to disappear in woods about a kilometer away. It really looked trouty, with good weed growth but a clean gravel bottom and a harmonious mix of riffle and rill with the obvious possibility of some undercut banks on the outside of the bends where the gradient wasn't very steep. The map showed that the stream started from a spring only a short distance above the town, so it ran as close to perfectly clear as it is possible for a stream to be which has passed through a small town and is obviously used to flush its effluent. At any rate, the stream looked great; and if I were given the time, I was determined to give it a try.

Returning to the manor house, I encountered one of the ubiquitous types that populated OSS, wearing military clothing with no branch insignia or rank, but who behaved more like civilians. This chap asked if I could spare a few minutes to give him a hand with something. He explained that the unit had just moved in and there was a shortage of fine wines for the nabobs at the chateau. For expedience, he intended to use his talents to liberate a few choice bottles from the wine cellars without going through the difficulty of a formal requisition. He informed me that he had discovered that the best wines had been moved out of the chateau to keep them out of German hands and were hidden in a sub-cellar under the manor house.

I followed this furtive character down into the cellars and through a trap door into the sub-cellar where I held the flashlight while he performed a most unusual feat. Withdrawing a set of lockpicker's tools from his pocket, he went through two sets of locks in a few seconds commenting the while on their primitive design. Inside the vault, he made a careful inspection of the bottles ranged along the walls. Everything was covered with dust and he made a rapid selection of a dozen bottles of the best, secreting one small bottle in one of his trouser pockets.

He motioned for me to carry out the bottles and put them in a gunny sack we had brought for the purpose, then he proceeded to replace the bottles we'd taken with inferior wines which had been standing upright on the floor. He even blew dust on the newly inserted bottles with a rubber bulb and carefully replaced a few cobwebs along the front of the bins. Only a careful inventory would reveal what had been taken.

This man was obviously a pro, as he went on to explain after we had taken the bottles up to the mess at the chateau. Before being recruited into OSS, he'd been a professional thief, and a most successful one at that. He'd never done time, and when a friend of his who had been recruited from prison told him that men with his talents were needed in the service of their country, he volunteered immediately. He assured me that his talents had been put to good use on a mission of some importance prior to his current assignment.

That evening at the chateau was an impressive occasion. Drinks were served in the salon by the regular servants who, while not quite in livery, were most appropriately dressed. The wife and daughter of the owner acted as hostesses and seemed very distinguished. When introduced to them, I learned that they were marquises. The daughter was quite beautiful with unusually well-toned skin for a natural golden redhead. Neither wore makeup—it was practically non-existent, though, oddly, the tarts in Marseilles wore plenty of it—and their appearance was radiant.

There was a most diverse group of people at the chateau and

I sensed some of them were true VIPs. The talk during drinks was fairly general, though about the war. Jim was not comfortable in this environment. These were, for the most part, the people he despised. Notwithstanding, he made his normal move toward the daughter whose haughty demeanor fazed him not at all, and soon his natural charm had her smiling and laughing.

We went in to dinner, which was formal and very good, especially with the excellent wine being served. The best was the farm bread which had been baked with white GI flour the mess sergeant had supplied to the local baker. When the ladies, including several American civilian secretaries, had excused themselves and the men remained to smoke and sip brandy, shop talk came to the fore.

A late arrival at the dinner, Henry Hyde, had just come from a border crossing out of Switzerland where he had conferred with Allen Dulles. I was asked about our mission, since Jim had excused himself before dinner, and garnered some amused laughter about my deceiving the briefing officer about my fly rod. There was also considerable interest around the table in the political bickering which had started in our area between the FFI and the FTPF forces over the distribution of weapons. Before I left, I was told that I was needed as soon as possible with the 3rd Division team, and that they would send a driver to take me up by jeep the next morning to report to Captain Robert Thompson, the team leader.

When I got back to my room, my new friend the lock picker was waiting for me with Jim. They had hoisted a few and eaten in the mess hall at the manor house. Sitting on top of the dresser was the small bottle he had slipped into his pocket that afternoon. Since this looked like the parting of the ways for all of us, that small bottle was to be our farewell toast. It was rum, from the Canary Islands, and the label was handwritten: the date, 1812. We opened the bottle and poured the entire contents into three tumblers, clinked glasses, and each took a sip. There was no odor and no taste. Just as we started to comment that it had gone bad, the spirits hit with a punch. First a warm glow turning to fire and then an aftertaste unlike anything I had ever had. It was magnificent. We toasted again with *"mille fois merde!"* and finished it off: the wages of sin. I slept soundly.

Third Divison Headquarters was located in the town of Luxeuil-les-Bains, about 155 kilometers to the north. I noted that it was in the foothills of the southern end of the Vosges Mountains. The commandant had chosen a school, as they did so often. There were plenty of bathrooms, and the classrooms made fine offices. Furthermore, school is always out when a military campaign moves through an area. I reported to Captain Thompson and was pleased to find him friendly and informal. After the usual brief discussion, he told me he had to go out to reconnoiter a possible crossing point and asked if I'd like to come along. It would give us a chance to get acquainted, and it would be on-the-job training as well.

Before we left, the captain took me into the war room, introduced me to the staff, then showed me the dispositions of the two regiments in our sector on the map. This was the first time the advance had slowed down significantly, he told me, due to strengthening German resistance and the natural defensive advantages afforded by the rugged, mountainous terrain. He showed me where we would be going and explained that in all cases we were to check through the command posts of the units we were passing through, all the way down the line, regiment, battalion, company, and platoon. This was the surest way to avoid serious trouble. If the unit commanders knew where we were and where we planned to be, the chances of accidents were much less. Such lessons had been hard-won in earlier campaigns, especially in Italy.

Our job, the captain told me, was to recruit, train, and infiltrate agents through enemy lines to report enemy dispositions, movements, and numbers, for the tactical use of the division. We generally knew in advance what the division objectives were going to be and acted accordingly. Occasionally, a division in the line would be pulled out and switched to another sector like an end-around play, in which event strategic information was passed on to the division taking its place, and it took a bit of good liaison work to handle the recovery of overrun agents in such cases.

Information was transmitted by agents in a number of ways, including short range 300 voice radios. Sometimes messengers were sent back with information, or it was left at a point between the lines where one of us could infiltrate to pick it up at a prearranged time. The people we were using were all local civilians who knew the country well. They were the ones who selected these drops or rendezvous points.

In addition to the office we maintained at division headquarters, there were "safe houses," generally close to division headquarters, where the agents were housed, trained, and prepared for their missions. These people were all volunteers who were checked as thoroughly as possible, given the circumstances and the urgency of the situation. Most of them were known to the resistance or had been a part of it. They ran the gamut from priests and young girls to mailmen and woodcutters, mostly ordinary people who happened to be considerably braver and more resolute than most.

As we drove from division to a regimental command post at La Bruyère, the captain asked me about my mission in the Cévènnes; he, too, was more than casually interested in the large supply of small arms still in the hands of the resistance groups at Le Bousquet. It seemed that there was a real need for such weapons in Sixth Corps' area of operations. Thompson introduced me to each of the unit commanders as we passed toward the lines until, finally, we reached a point several hundred yards before the hamlet of Faucogney where we stashed the jeep. The village had taken a beating. The American forward units were, for the most part, situated along the crest which passed through the village. The German MLR (main line of resistance) was across a shallow valley on the opposite crest, which was the high point of this part of the Vosges range. The valley between Faucogney and Le Tholy was irregular pasturage with scattered copses and a few stone fences. There were a few low-grade farm roads in the valley and a small stream of no military significance.

When Thompson and I reached the company command post, we found that one of the forward platoons was entrenched in foxholes on an exposed point near a line of sheltering timber. He decided we should sneak in low, following the timber line, to a point where we could determine if this would be a suitable place to try to infiltrate our agents. The company commander had not sent any patrols into that section yet and it was generally felt this area might remain the leading edge of the front line for a while.

We kept low, moving along the bushes until we reached the ridge line, then crawled to a point where we could get a good view ahead. Thompson kept the lead, but when he reached a certain point he waved for me to come up. Peering through the bushes, we saw that a German patrol was approaching in our direction less than forty yards away, and about two hundred yards farther out, other German soldiers were digging in, setting up defensive positions. We crawled back to where we could stand up, then, keeping low, ran back to the crest of the ridge PDQ.

At the company command post we pinpointed the spot on the map where the German patrol was coming through. The CO immediately called in mortar fire followed by a mortar barrage from battalion on the area where the men had been digging in. The point they had chosen would have been a perfect staging area for a counterattack, if we hadn't spotted it; even though our foray hadn't turned up a good passage point, it did serve some purpose. On the way back through the lines, I was struck by the look one of the dogfaces gave us: he expressed unfeigned admiration for our bravery. Thompson said it was a good thing he didn't know that while he was shivering tonight in his foxhole under the constant threat of an enemy attack we would be sleeping in a warm room, drinking whisky in the drawing room, or enjoying the company of attractive young women. In any event, there would be retaliatory German artillery fire and, likely, mortar and machinegun fire on those American front-line positions. Such were the ironies of war.

The following day, Thompson decided to send me back to Le Bousquet d'Orb to gather up as much as possible of the small arms, special equipment such as prismatic compasses, and demolitions equipment. When he called headquarters for the OK, they said they were all for it and had already considered the same idea. I hated the idea of leaving the team so soon—I had barely gotten to know Voiteur and a few of the other team members—and I had serious concerns about the willingness of the two politically embroiled forces to relinquish the weapons. Major Crosby told me to get rough with them if I had to, and it turned out that's just what I had to do.

I was assigned a supply sergeant and a 2½ ton truck. Our orders were good anywhere, which allowed us to cut out a lot of red tape. We took turns driving and made it back down the Rhône Valley in record time. Jim and I had missed seeing the devastation of the fleeing German Army along the Rhône because of the mountain roads we had taken north from the beachhead. Now, seeing the skeletons of all the German tanks, half-tracks, and other vehicles made us appreciate what a luxury we had with our air supremacy, and what it must have been like without it. Around Montélimar and Orange there were literally miles of burned-out vehicles, including the scattered gazogenes, hand carts, and bicycles. We saw where Butler's Task Force had hit them from the flank.

We crossed the Rhône on the Bailey bridge set up by the French Army with a plentiful supply of jerry cans, and after a few stops, our orders and 7th Army passes cleared the way to Le Bousquet. When we arrived in the little town, we were greeted joyfully—until I told the lieutenant, now a captain, why I had returned. I explained that I intended to be completely fair and assemble as many weapons from the FTPF as from the FFI, but that didn't make all that much difference to him. He gave me hours of argument about the dangers of giving up those weapons, especially the automatic weapons which we needed most. Janvier, leader of the FTPF, couldn't meet until the following morning, but the young FFI captain assured me the FTPF would hold back and that they would use their weapons to turn over France to the Communists. I was sure I would hear much the same from Janvier, and when he showed up I was right.

Janvier arrived early the next morning and asked to speak to me in private. Since I'd spoken at length with the FFI leader, I felt I had to accord him the same opportunity. He already knew why I had come and he urged me to leave the weapons as they were. Without further argument, I told him I would meet with both of them together. When the captain was brought in, the three of us sat down. I announced that I was leaving with the two-and-a-half filled with all of the automatic weapons from both camps plus all the plastique explosive, related equipment, and the pistols. They were to be used, I explained, in parts of France where the war was still going on, by Frenchmen who were still fighting to liberate their country from the Germans. I said they could keep the rifles and any other supplies, but they both started yelling at the same time, and wouldn't listen to reason.

Stoically, I picked up a fragmentation grenade and pulled the pin. "Gentlemen," I said, "I am under direct orders of the Commanding General of the U.S. 7th Army and I will not return to the 7th Army without fulfilling those orders. If you do not agree to comply with my order to you, none of us will leave this room alive." They sweated visibly. "I will accept your word given here and now, and I expect that each of you will see that the other complies, but I want your agreement now."

Then the miraculous happened. Both officers broke into smiles at the same time and couldn't assure me quickly or profusely enough of their complete willingness to cooperate with the 7th Army. I thanked them, reinserted the pin into the grenade, and went on to express the gratitude of 7th Army which was, after all, still busy liberating French soil.

The weapons were brought in, cleaned and checked under the sergeant's direction, and piled carefully into the back of the truck. I'll never know if I could have carried out my threat, but I know I was determined to at the time. I did, however, remember my father telling me of an incident involving a challenge to a duel and, since the choice of weapons was his, he had elected .45 caliber pistols with each party holding onto one corner of a knotted scarf in his teeth. The challenge had been dropped. The psychology involved in each instance was essentially the same.

The sergeant and I were out of there that same night, since I wanted to be clear of the area as soon as possible. The more they thought about what had taken place, the less the two factions would like it and I didn't need any more hassle. We got across the Rhône, slept and stood guard alternately until early light, then gulped some K rations and headed back to the war.

FOURTEEN

The next few weeks were some of the most memorable of my life. The OSS team members, who were almost never all together at the same time, were a fascinating collection of characters and as diversified in every possible way as could be imagined. Jean Poniatowski, called Ponia, had climbed the executive ladder in the corporate world and typified the *beau garçon, boulevardier* image, telling stories endlessly of great romantic conquests and adventures. Nevertheless, he was a first-class field man who could handle and motivate agents as well as take the necessary risks to put them into place. Jack Niles couldn't have looked less like a man who would drive a jeep through an enemy roadblock under fire as part of his routine job. He was a man of the theatrical world but he understood people and he was brave. Both Ponia and Jack were close to middle age and taking young men's risks.

Cesar Moretti was a young man of indeterminate age who had been a professional bicycle racer in Argentina before the war. He was tough but seemed to have an innate gentleness. A jack-of-all-trades, he was Bob Thompson's personal assistant. The team was rounded out by Don McAfee, a Navy lieutenant, who had served with Admiral Leahy's embassy in Vichy until interned and repatriated to the States where he was recruited into OSS. Don didn't seem much older than I and had made the assault landings with the team in Southern France.

Right from the beginning, the team had had tremendous intelligence successes, first making contact with organized resistance groups and enabling the landing forces to have complete and accurate estimates of enemy troop-strengths and dispositions as well as subsequent movements. The single most devastating action used by the Germans against the assault forces had been their use of radio-controlled bombs, one of which made a direct hit on a troop-filled LST, inflicting heavy casualties.

German forces were caught by surprise and spread out too thinly to be able to mount an effective counterattack. Furthermore, the manner of the assault with the paratroop drop, much more successful than the one in Normandy, resulted in a well-coordinated operation which moved with amazing speed to seal off Toulon and to liberate all territory east of the Rhône. The success was made possible by highly developed new methods of resupply through a beachhead, plus the early capture of Marseilles which provided a huge port facility for the landing of supplies and reinforcements.

The highly mobile nature of the campaign created challenges for the OSS teams assigned to the combat divisions. There were wide open flanks on both sides of the advance much of the time, which the OSS teams exploited to the fullest advantage. They commandeered civilian cars and ran agents recruited from the local resistance around the ends of the combat zones and deep behind the Nazi positions. Using radios, they kept contact with dozens of infiltrated agents whose up-to-the-minute information kept the assault divisions as well informed as any army in history.

An amazing coincidence occurred the day of the landings. Don McAfee ran into the girl with whom he had been keeping company in Vichy months before. Apparently, she had been evacuated to the South and was living in the first building Don entered after hitting the beach with one of the assault waves. Until that incredible moment, they had not seen each other since November 1942, almost two years earlier. Both were overcome with emotion and she volunteered immediately to stay with him and help in any way she could. By the time I joined the team, she was as much a part of it as any of us. She did everything from clerical work to cooking, and helping with the training of new recruits in the safe houses. Along with everything else, she was very attractive and had a special quality of seeming helplessness which disguised her underlying courage and determination. We all thought of those two as a team: a most unusual circumstance in the middle of a military campaign.

When I returned from my supply mission in the South, the division had moved farther north and was now headquartered in Remiremont, again in a school. While we had the usual office in Division Headquarters, we were all billeted together in a large requisitioned house that must have belonged to an important man of the town. It was a three-story house which would be our domicile for some weeks to come. A niece of the owner kept her room there and assisted with the housekeeping, though it became obvious that she was really there to protect her uncle's worldly goods from the barbarian Americans. Unlike other requisitioned houses we had occupied where we had been made to feel welcome, as liberators, here we were treated not as occupiers, perhaps, but certainly as unwanted nuisances. Remiremont is not quite in Alsace but the niece seemed more Germanic than French both in appearance and in manner and was, in sum, the only rotten apple in an otherwise well-ordered household.

I became the second assistant to Bob Thompson and so it worked out that one of us, or occasionally Cesar Moretti or Don McAfee, was on duty at all times at division headquarters. It was important to be in constant contact with the ever-changing disposition of U.S. troops, and especially to know what division plans were at any given time in order to coordinate our activities and order the emplacement and priorities of our agents. As a result, the four of us took part in line-crossing less often than the others. Because the division was constantly changing its position with respect to the other divisions at the front, some of our team members ended up in another division's sector helping retrieve joes who had been infiltrated into the area when it had been a 3rd Division objective.

Because we maintained such a close relationship with the Division Headquarters, and especially with the G2 (Intelligence) section and its two officers, we became close friends and spent much of our non-duty time together. I was impressed with their tales of the Anzio landings and the fantastic fighting that went on before the breakout. The 3rd Division already had the highest number of casualties of any infantry division in the U.S. Army: something over three hundred percent of its effective strength of nearly 15,000 men. The Commanding General, Iron Mike O'Daniel, was one tough cookie. On any given morning, he could be heard checking with his regimental commanders by field telephone. "How's it going? Did they take the objective? Kill lots of Krauts? Good! Good!"

The Assistant Operations Officer (G3) became one of our closest pals and kept us abreast of division tactics and plans. The most significant thing about the whole operation was that the work done by the team, and its agents, was valuable and was appreciated and used. Often this is not the case and, indeed, many Regular Army types are deeply suspicious of anyone serving in Intelligence; as a consequence, an Intelligence section assignment tended to be the graveyard for military careers, which reinforced, in turn, the basic suspicions.

It had been a long time coming but it was becoming more apparent all the time. Don's girl was dissatisfied with the role she was playing. She was only too aware of the risks being taken by the volunteers she helped, cooked for, even trained on the SCR 300 radio, and tested on vehicle and armaments identification. While it was equally clear that she was in love with Don, her sense of patriotism and duty was causing her to chafe at the bit. Her conscience would not permit her to continue in her relatively safe role as a girlfriend and general helper. She felt strongly she should go on a mission. She knew she was qualified to do it, and she understood the risks involved as well as anyone can who hasn't taken them, but when she approached Don with her idea he ridiculed the notion and then became dead set against it. He had not, however, eliminated the idea and it grew within her.

It came to a head one day when Don had gone off for several days with one of the other divisions to participate in a recovery operation. She approached Bob Thompson, not for the first time, and made it clear that she was determined to go. She knew we had had great difficulty getting anyone successfully into the Gerardmer/Col de la Schlucht area which was the 3rd Division's present objective and more or less directly above us to the east on the highest ridge of the Vosges Mountain range. The part of Remiremont where we were set up was at the foot of a west-facing slope of steep, wooded terrain and was relatively safe from enemy artillery fire. Although the south end of town was exposed, one of the regimental command posts was located about eight kilometers east of town with forward elements dug into positions three to five kilometers farther east in the valley, and one in the steep, pine-clad hills on each side.

It was a difficult and terrible decision for Bob to have to make, but realizing that she was determined to do it, and in view of our great need for information, he decided to go ahead and put her through. We briefed her as thoroughly as we could on where she would have to go, her cover story, and what she would have to do in any of the various circumstances which might arise.

After a light meal, the three of us drove in the jeep to St. Amé where we were to check in with regimental headquarters. To get there we followed a white tape which had been laid through the trees at waist level and could just be seen in the dim glow from the slits of the jeep's blackout lights. At the end of the trail we had to leave the jeep and proceed on foot. From there I carried the heavy 300 radio set, but she would have to carry it through the lines herself, like a backpack, and cache it somewhere in the woods where she could find it again when she was ready to contact us with information.

We continued to follow the white tape on foot, past the forward batteries of division artillery. The outgoing 105 rounds passed with such force we felt as if they would take our heads off. There were also occasional incoming rounds from the German 88 batteries high on the mountains to the east. It took us an hour to reach the point just to our side of Julienrupt where the most forward company command past (CP) was located. I stayed with the girl while Bob checked in with the CP. When he returned, he brought a runner to lead us to the forward foxholes of a platoon dug in along a forest track several hundred feet up the slope to our left.

The path we followed appeared to be little more than a cart track and was very steep. We crossed several of these in the dark and could have become lost quite easily except that the runner knew the way so well. We came to where the platoon leader sat huddled by his field telephone in a hut on the edge of a small cluster of woodcutters' houses, called Cleurie, only a few hundred meters from a second cluster of huts called Flaconnières. The platoon leader said a German patrol had come through Flaconnières in the afternoon but, from all appearances, had pulled out. He had sent a patrol to the very edge of the village and drew no fire.

Bob decided it was a good point to take the girl to, since there was a network of trails we could follow through the woods and then along below the crest of the ridge to Le Tholy where she could cache the radio and slip into town and figure out how to get to the Gerardmer area about ten kilometers further on. The platoon leader was right. Flaconnières was empty and we sent her on her way with the 300 on her back, making her look small and helpless. We waited a half hour before heading cautiously back to Cleurie to listen for any sounds, or shots. Aside from the sound of artillery overhead, the night was silent.

The next few days were tense. We monitored the girl's channel and heard nothing. Don came back. He was upset but not angry; though I had the feeling it troubled him more than he showed.

I met a very nice nurse who was staying over at the field hospital in Remiremont before going on to the main hospital at Épinal. We spent a lot of time together, and what we did we did from loneliness. We did not make love but, instead, we held each other in the dark, under a blanket, with our clothes on. Our relationship never progressed beyond that point even when I drove over to Épinal to see her on several occasions. I couldn't get the picture of the girl climbing up into the night with the SCR 300 on her back out of my mind. There were probably plenty of things my nurse wanted to blot from her memory as well.

The days turned into weeks when, suddenly, news came that our girl agent had crossed the lines farther south in the French sector. Bob was contacted and went down to debrief her. She had never been able to get back to her radio but she had located the positions of all the principal German headquarters, plus the unit designations and the map coordinates of a number of artillery batteries, fuel dumps, and more. Her memory was amazing and the information she gave Bob later proved invaluable.

She was badly in need of medical attention so Bob arranged to pick her up about a week later and bring her back to the headquarters at Remiremont. Bob didn't go into detail, but he said she had done a hell of a job and been through a very rough time.

The week went by and Bob went down and got her and brought her back. They arrived in the evening and came into the big room where we were all sitting around on the blanket-covered furniture. We gave a small cheer as she entered the room, then fell silent. She looked at Don and he looked up at her for only a second, then looked away. She turned away and asked Bob to arrange for transportation to take her home right away, then she left the room. That's the last any of us ever saw of her.

*   *   *

The next series of events caused a violent warp in the weave of my memory through the war. Bob Thompson told me I would soon be going on leave to Paris where his friend, Mike Burke, had told him my father was holding court at the Ritz after a long session with the 4th Infantry Division in the "rat race" across France. But something came up and it turned out that Bob had to go to Paris instead on official business, and would then take his leave. Cesar Moretti and I were left in charge of the office for the last week of October.

What happened next has been recounted in an article by a Lt. Cdr. Richard M. Kelly in *Blue Book Magazine* of August 1947, an article entitled "Spy Work Ahead." It was based on an interview with a man who was to become a good friend, and a much closer companion than either of us ever anticipated. His name was Justin Greene. There are several discrepancies between Greene's account of events and mine, which I'm sure he would be the first to admit is not an uncommon phenomenon. He is, after all, a psychiatrist. The discrepancies are not, in fact, very significant except to illustrate how differently two people can view the same event. I was tempted to recount the events just as he described them, but I have opted instead for my own memory's version since it is what has served me thus far. I learned many new things about both the function and malfunction of memory in the next six months.

On the 28th of October 1944, Captain Justin Greene, who commanded the OSS team with the 36th Infantry Division on our northern flank, hd a problem. He needed to put an agent in the field in an area which was on the very edge of the 3rd Division sector. The location was important because there was a house that he had used in the past for a letter drop. It was a place where he could pick up important information and, at the same time, be assured of help for the agent he needed to infiltrate. Because of some slight readjustment in the division sectors, it appeared that the exact location, or the best approach to the house, was through the northern edge of 3rd Division's sector.

Greene came to ask Bob Thompson's help, but Bob was still in Paris and not due back for another day or two. I was pleased to give any assistance I could and went over the operations map very carefully with Greene to try to find the best possible route. I was not aware of it at the time, but apparently the "lost battalion" incident of the 36th Division was already in progress and there were enemy forces between the battalion and the main body of the division. I had no idea of the situation and had not been briefed on it.

We drove north along the west bank of the Moselle River to Poueux Fort d'Arches where we crossed and headed northeast on Departmental Highway D44 to Bruyères. On the way we saw considerable air support activity from P-47s dropping bombs along the horizon ahead of us in support of a U.S. attack through the *Forêt de Champs* toward St. Dié. We could hear the bombs over the noise of the jeep and see the dark smoke rising from the explosions. Everything to the right of the road was 3rd Division territory; to the left was 36th Division's.

Bruyères is a fair-sized old town in rolling foothill country not nearly as precipitous as the mountains east of Remiremont. Units of the 36th Division were in the town but just east of it and to the north were 3rd Division troops. I believe we made our first mistake at that juncture. We did not check in with either battalion or regiment but just asked any troop commander on the spot what his assessment of the situation was. Granted, it would have been awkward to make a long detour to observe the rules, but it might have been well worthwhile.

At any rate, we tried several approaches before ending up in a small valley where a 3rd Division aid station was receiving a large number of fresh casualties from a firefight a few hundred meters up a gully behind Belmont-sur-Buffant, a tiny hamlet on the edge of the forest. The officer there told us that the troops on his left flank had advanced much farther and that we could go that way without encountering resistance. We climbed over a high hump of open wooded hillside until we were suddenly right in the middle of a forward platoon of Nisei from the 442nd regimental combat team which was attached to the 36th Division.

As I remember it, we tried to question them about the situation ahead and the ones we questioned, who were regular GIs, couldn't tell us anything. Again, we didn't take the time to check with their commander or higher headquarters, but now that we were definitely in 36th Division territory, I was just along for the ride. Any purpose I could have served from that point on was clearly ended. The French joe who was with us never spoke a word and was clearly spooked.

We were now on the forward slope of the hill and could see that there was a long, narrow clearing in the hollow ahead and to the left of us. The place we were trying to reach was called Gr ébéfosse, another cluster of three or four houses a few hundred meters up the hollow from the *Commune de Bois de Champs* which was not much bigger. The people who lived here were woodcutters whose families kept a small kitchen garden and a few chickens. Justin said he was fairly certain this was the spot and that the letter-drop farmhouse would be just a little farther down the hollow to the left.

We stayed in the woods going to the left around a turn until we suddenly saw an American light tank hunkered down on the opposite side of the clearing. The big gun was facing left, positioned on a track running along the bottom of the opposite wooded hillside. Justin wanted the joe to cross over and, using the tank for cover, to proceed along the track to the left for another hundred meters until he came to Grébéfosse. The letter-drop house, he said, lay back in a little cul-de-sac at the bottom of the opposite hillside. We held a whispered conference with him and the joe refused to go on alone. Justin then asked me what I thought we could do, since his man wouldn't go on alone. Like a damn fool, I went along with the suggestion that we take him ourselves. With the tank there covering our approach, the path looked clear.

Justin hid something under some tree roots—which he later told me was incriminating stuff—and then we edged to a point just opposite the tank and all three ran across the thirty-five or so yards of open ground into the shadow of the rear of the tank. The joe and I stayed hidden there for a minute while Justin climbed straight up into the woods above us where he thought he heard some voices. Meanwhile, a closer look at the rear of the tank revealed a clean two-inch hole made by a Panzerfaus anti-tank shape-charge grenade. The tank was dead. We should have been suspicious that it had remained in position so long without even moving its turret, but by that time Justin had stepped right into a hornet's nest and awakened the hornets.

It was hard to believe, but there was a whole unit of *Alpinjaeger* mountain troops digging positions along a sunken road about six or seven yards up the slope in the thick forest and, experienced though they were, they had not posted sentries and had not even noticed us crossing the open ground. Justin reacted as quickly as if he'd stepped on a snake and came crashing back down the slope with small arms fire popping all around him. The joe panicked and broke for the other side of the tank only to have a grenade explode right in front of him, tearing out his guts. I hit the ditch at the foot of the slope and scrunched down as small as I could get while Justin went down, followed by more grenade explosions and small arms fire.

Two soldiers came down and I tried to open fire with my M3 submachine gun but was hit immediately by a single round from above. I let out a cry and tried to hide in the ditch again. Within seconds someone above me fired several more times, hitting me in the right arm and shoulder each time. I felt no pain but was conscious of being sprayed with grenade fragments along the right side. My right arm and shoulder were the only parts exposed to the firing from above. At that point I figured there wasn't a whole hell of a lot that could be done to save this situation and joined Justin in crying out, *"Kamerad!"* German for, "I surrender, dear!"

We were both disarmed and helped up to the road where, dazed, we were given rudimentary first aid. I remember the aid man cutting off the right sleeve of my tanker jacket and emptying it of at least a pint of jello-textured blood, then applying several large patches of bandage which he wrapped with a long, wide strip of gauze. They injected us with the morphine ampules from our own first aid pouches to relieve the pain which still hadn't cut through the shock. One of the men laughed and pointed at a new type of carbine they had been using, and kept repeating, *"Schiessen, Schiessen,"* over and over again, pointing first to the carbine and then to my wounds. Justin had been hit in the foot and they had his boot off with some difficulty and, though it bled almost not at all, you could see bone. He had also had a bullet hit his helmet and follow the helmet liner before exiting without so much as scratching him. Then they blindfolded us and half led, half dragged us to their company CP which, Justin told me later when we could talk, was the very house we had been trying to get to.

The fatally wounded joe was brought in, too, and I could hear him groaning outside in the hall where he died within the hour. Justin and I were taken right into the room where the company commander, an *Oberleutnant,* was seated at a table. I was having a hard time staying alert because of blood loss, but I heard him questioning Justin through an interpreter and Justin's explanation seemed to be something about our being with a French guide who was taking us to catch a Frenchman who was collaborating with the Germans. I was wearing my MP insignia, so the story made some sense and appeared to pass muster with the officer. Then Justin was taken into a bedroom and I was seated before the *Oberleutnant.*

Through the interpreter, he asked my name, rank, and serial number, which I gave him. He looked at me quizzically and asked to see my dogtags. I pulled them out with my good left hand and he read them carefully and asked in German if I spoke German. I answered, *"Nein."*

He then asked in French if I spoke French, to which I replied in the affirmative. Then, in French, he asked if I had ever been in Schruns.

I answered that I had, long ago as a child. He asked me the name of my nurse. I told him she was called Tiddy. He broke into a broad grin and said in French, "We drink a toast to Tiddy. She is my girlfriend!"

All this took place about mid-day, and by the end of the "interrogation," which ended with a toast of Schnapps, it must have been two or three in the afternoon. Justin and I were kept apart until late that night when we were told we were being evacuated. I never saw the *Oberleutnant* again, but I heard about him many months later. After Justin and I were carried up the forest trail in the midst of a mortar barrage from our own troops, and finally arrived at what I assumed was a battalion CP, a hefty-looking *Hauptmann* quickly ordered us evacuated to an aid station in the custody of four orderlies. The *Oberleutnant,* I heard later, was captured in a counterattack by the 442nd RCT and, when questioned later, turned out to speak perfect English and even suggested to the interrogators that it would be futile to attempt to mount a rescue operation for Greene and me. He explained that the severity of our wounds precluded our being able to participate in any way. He was then interned for the rest of the war as a prisoner of the French.

We lay in the aid station for what seemed hours before being loaded into an ambulance which seemed to hit every pothole in the Vosges Mountains before finally delivering us to a small town where we were transferred to another ambulance for the rest of the trip to the German field hospital at Colmar.

We were treated well enough at the field hospital, though I went through a bad time when I was told by the *Stabsarzt,* a surgeon major whose name I remember was Peters, that my arm would have to come off because of gangrene. Since it was my casting arm, I respectfully told him I'd prefer to chance dying rather than lose it. The Germans seemed to amputate at the drop of a hat, and the place was full of new amputees. The surgeon said there was a chance with sulfamide, their version of sulfanilmide, but that it wasn't a good one and that I would have to drink enormous amounts of water or I would surely suffer severe kidney and liver damage. I told him I'd drink until I burst if I had to. It worked out, and the wounds, which were kept open with drains rather than closed as our medics would have done, lost their sweet smell of putridity after a couple of weeks and I began to feel itchy from the healing. Still, I had to wear an airplane splint to hold my elbow away from my body.

The nurses in the hospital were very friendly and generous to us. They were religious sisters and I thought they were Alsatian since they spoke German, and French with a German accent. Justin Greene managed to talk them into getting a letter out for him, which he says got through to his home. My mother said she heard from a Catholic organization that I was wounded and safe before she was ever notified that I was missing in action by the War Department. When I went back to Colmar years later to try to repay in some way the kindness of the sisters, I had the whole religious establishment, as well as the medical establishment of Colmar, trying to locate the order which had served in the hospital and they could locate no records of it and, sadly, came to the conclusion that it must have been a German religious order which was working in the field hospital. The building itself had since become a police prefecture.

Although our wounds were by no means healed, we were considered well enough to evacuate to a prisoner of war hospital eighteen days after our arrival in Colmar. God knows they needed the beds. There were five of us, all officers, in various states of disrepair. We were put under the guard of three very ancient NCOs from the *Luftwaffe* and marched from the hospital to the railroad station one fine morning in the latter part of November. I had been issued a light wool, green Italian Army shirt which stretched quite well to cover my bandages. We were a sorry lot as we hobbled along. Justin was on crutches with a cast still on his foot. Ray Saigh, a lieutenant from the 45th Division, had been a forward observer for the artillery, and before that a running back at Florida State, but I don't recall the nature of his wounds. Dewey Stuart, a second lieutenant from the 36th Infantry Division who had received a battlefield commission after fighting the entire Italian campaign, had a leg wound that was healing fine, but had had the trigger finger of his right hand and the finger next to it amputated by a surgeon who told him he would have a better chance of repatriation with no trigger finger. He threw the second finger in for free.

Our travel group was rounded out by a French officer, a lieutenant of *Spahis,* who had served with those tough Moroccan troops in North Africa and taken part in the siege of Toulon where he was wounded and taken POW near the Belfort gap.

We didn't know it at the time, but we were headed for Ludwigsburg where the POW hospital was located, some ten to fifteen kilometers north of Stuttgart. We traveled in a coach compartment for the first part of the trip and then switched to an open coach for the rest of the way. We had privacy in the compartment but had to suffer a certain amount of indignity in the open coach, mostly from civilians who resented POWs being given space in the crowded train.

The entire trip, which, taking the most direct route, was no more than 275 kilometers, lasted well over twenty-four hours. There were constant delays for re-routing, switching, being put on side tracks to allow priority trains to pass, and to shelter several times in tunnels during Allied bombing attacks. Most of the actual movement was at night, at dawn, or at dusk. The rest of the time we would be hidden on some stretch of track in a deep forest or a deep cut or tunnel, hiding from what the German civilians referred to as the "Luft Bandit," the U.S. Air Force which had almost total control of the German skies at this late stage of the war.

At one station in the middle of that endless night, there was an air raid alarm. We were standing with our guards on the platform, stretching our legs and getting some fresh air. During the *Voralarm,* everyone was supposed to take shelter. Our guards moved swiftly for old geezers and disappeared down some steps into a shelter and, quite suddenly, we were all alone. Whenever we had been left alone in the train car, we had discussed the possibility of escape. It was obvious Justin and Dewey couldn't move well enough, but Ray, the French officer, and I might chance it. We started for the end of the platform and had almost reached it when we heard the all clear and our guards were back on the platform and yelling at us in German which clearly meant, "Get the hell back here and make it snappy!" It was a very cold night and I was already shaking in my light wool shirt; my wound had opened up and was bleeding through the bandage. I, for one, would not have gone very far.

Our French officer friend was a cheerful soul and, besides being full of stories, loved to sing. He taught us the words to several French marching songs, all of which would qualify for a new version of "Songs My Mother Never Taught Me." Much to the consternation of our guards, who were sour-faced throughout, we were all soon coming in for at least the chorus of *"Joli Battalion," "Chevalier de la Table Ronde,"* and *"Aupr ès de Ma Blonde."* I think the guards were only too relieved to turn us over to the permanent guards at the *Kriegsgefangener Lazaret* at Ludwigsburg.

The POW hospital more closely resembled the Tower of Babel than anything else. Every nationality who had fought against the Third Reich was represented there. It was part jail, part hospital, and, to top it off, seemed to be run completely by committee. The German presence was there, of course, but much of the administration was left to the prisoners themselves. For example, we were checked in first by German security and searched for weapons or other illegal items, then registered formally by a French NCO and assigned to our wards. Our next contact was the "man of confidence," a sort of prisoner representative selected from a list approved by the Germans. He was a British NCO.

The senior Allied officer was a marvelous man from Perth, West Australia, Lt. Col. LeSouef; he was a surgeon captured at the first battle of Tobruk. The principal surgeon was a Polish major we all called "The Miracle Man." The hospital operated on a shoestring and very little was available for serious surgery because it was assumed, erroneously, that anyone there had been properly treated before arrival. Of course, many were in bad shape and needed further treatment. LeSouef told us the miracle man literally earned his reputation by doing the impossible in a completely jerry-rigged operating room with inadequate instruments, poor lighting, and often without proper drugs or anesthetics. The place was really meant to be a convalescent center but, because of heavy pressures on the German military medical establishment, it had been forced to assume the role of a real hospital, a role for which it was ill prepared.

Part of our regular routine, I shall never forget, involved Col.

LeSouef. We younger officers managed to stay together in one ward and LeSouef would come in every night to bid us good night. Almost invariably, he would prolong the event with the following:

"I say, chaps. You do realize, don't you, that the lack of phosphorus in our diet affects our memory? Phosphorus is most important for one's memory and the lack of it may cause you to be forgetful. Not to worry though, as soon as the phosphorus is restored the memory is quite as good as new."

He would give us his big, beaming smile and remind us to study our copy of the Geneva Convention to keep "the Hun at bay, so to speak." Then, just as he was about to leave the room, he'd do an about-face and start out, "I say, chaps, you do realize how important phosphorus . . ." Then, finally, "Well, good night then."

LeSouef was adamant about the Geneva Convention. Once, when we had just been through the charade of being paid in prisoner scrip, which would be confiscated that night during security inspection anyway, Col. LeSouef asked me if I had received the proper amount. I should have kept my mouth shut, but I replied that, indeed, I had been shorted, though I couldn't see that it made any difference. There was nothing to buy and, in any event, we wouldn't have the money long enough to spend it.

LeSouef became apoplectic shouting, "You're not going to let them get away with it, by God! We'll get a special pass to go to the *Commandantura* and you'll stand up for your rights!"

"Yes, Sir," I replied with more enthusiasm than I felt. The man I would have to face was Chief of Security for the whole installation, an *Abwehr* captain named Haas. He was number one on our s--- list and had recently deliberately caused the death of one prisoner who was in serious condition and confined to his bed. During a surprise night inspection, Haas, obviously drunk, became furious when the weakened prisoner did not leap from bed to come to attention in the presence of a German officer. The senior man in the ward explained the situation but Haas insisted the prisoner come to attention. Since the prisoner could not stand on his own, one of Haas's goons grabbed him and stood him to attention by force. The prisoner died later that night.

Col. LeSouef made the arrangements for our visit to Haas' office, signing a form stating that on our word as officers and gentlemen we would make no attempt to escape during the visit. LeSouef had been there before, but for me it was an eerie experience to be allowed out of the prison courtyard without guards. We walked, side by side, down the street and down the hill into Ludwigsburg to the *Commandantura.* Our clothing was marked, of course, so that anyone seeing us knew that we were prisoners, but we arrived without causing a stir. After reporting the purpose of our visit to the adjutant, we waited outside the captain's office until ordered to come in. I had, of course, expected the colonel to come in with me, but he demurred, saying he would wait outside and listen to be sure I stood up for my rights properly. I heard Haas's loud command to enter, then stepped into the office, coming to attention in front of the captain's desk, and reported, saluting and announcing my name and rank.

There was another captain with infantry insignia and a *Ritter Kreuz* hanging from his neck sitting in the chair next to the captain's desk. Haas asked me calmly what I wanted and I explained that I was an *Oberleutnant* and that at the recent payday I had only been paid the pay of a *Leutnant* and that I had come to insist that I be paid the difference.

His face turned beet red and he exploded in a stream of invective which I did not understand but the meaning of which was quite clear and it ended with the familiar word, *"Raus!"* which means get out! I remained at attention and as the enraged officer ran out of breath, I ventured in English to the other captain, "After all, you too, Herr Hauptman, will surely insist on your rights when you become a prisoner," to which he chortled while Haas roared on. Finally, the security chief seemed to calm down, the pressure lessened by the stream of invective, and he sighed . . . yes, sighed . . . then sputtered, "Ach, you Americans. Such fools." He then opened his file drawer, took out the five Marks difference, and counted it out to me while the other officer smiled. I saluted smartly and left the office and was greeted by hearty congratulations from LeSouef who then admitted that he never really thought Haas would give in on the issue.

"The secret, my boy," he said, "is to keep Jerry off balance at all times." "The secret of what?" I wondered to myself.

The steady trickle of new wounded increased as casualties from the British Airborne Brigade's Arnhem airborne assault started coming in. There was a marvelous SAS captain who taught me a lot about the Bible, and the nephew of some friends of Mother's and Paul's, Charley Magnusen, whose right elbow had been shattered by machine gun fire. Charley could think of nothing but his farm in Pennsylvania and swore he would never leave it again if he ever got out of this damned mess. He was very pale and deeply depressed about his chances of making it, though I believe he did.

And so we made it to Christmas, which we celebrated rather dourly though there was one bright moment when "The Miracle Man" invited all the officers into the surgery supply room for a thimble each of surgical alcohol. I damn near passed out; it hit us all like a ton of bricks.

Our main holiday present came from the skies, in the form of an air raid. The siren went off and everyone who could headed for the cellars. Some of us stayed above to watch an F-47 dive to strafe a flak tower a few hundred meters away from the hospital in the edge of the woods. As he pulled up from his dive, one of the 20mm cannons in the German battery opened up on him and got him with a lucky round. The plane erupted smoke and fire but the pilot managed to stay with it until he had gained enough altitude for his chute to open when he bailed out; we watched him disappear below the rim of trees. An hour later he was amongst us with minor wounds from 20mm shell fragments and forced to answer the thousand questions we all had about the latest news from the outside world.

The pilot's name was Al Ligon, from Michigan, and his nickname was Sleepy Lagoon. He did a lot to cheer us with his tales: "There I was at 30,000 feet; the flak was so thick you could walk on it; so I got out and walked!" or "The safest place in the world is behind that 2,000-horsepower engine. There's no way they can get to you there!" to which we would all chime, "But what about when they're behind you?" Ligon got a lot of kidding because the Air Force was supposed to have their own separate camps and hospitals, and here he was with the common folks.

The hospital was bursting at the seams by this time and Justin Greene got in some sort of hassle with the authorities about distribution of Red Cross parcels, so we were transferred out as troublemakers and, though his foot was far from well, my wounds were fully closed now and there was no more separation or bleeding. We were put out in the *Flieschling Lager,* a large single-room building only a few hundred feet from the hospital, where the only heat was the crowded bodies of the inmates. The conditions were appalling; this was where escapees, Russians and Ukrainians, or any others not considered as having rights under the Geneva Convention were kept, wounded or not. The ration, which had been about 1,300 calories per day in the hospital, by Justin's estimate, was barely 900 here. But fortunately, we did not have to stay there long and, after several days, we were shipped northeast in the same fashion as before to a permanent *Offizier Lager* (officer's camp) at Hammelberg-am-Main: Offlag XVIII B.

FIFTEEN

Hammelburg was different from anything I had yet seen. The POW complex, made up of several different camps, sat on a plateau above the Saale River Valley where the old town lay. Since it was not visible from the camp, I only saw the town itself during our arrival on the train when we were marched from the railway station up the long hill to the reception area which was part of a permanent military farm complex. There we had our clothing taken away while we went through delousing showers. At that time we didn't know about the fake showers in the concentration camps which sprayed gas instead of water; perhaps it's just as well we didn't. As it was, these were the most luxurious moments we had enjoyed to date in Germany. Unlike Ludwigsburg, this camp was under the complete control of the Germans when we arrived and the prisoners seemed totally disorganized.

We were put in a compound where there were only Americans and it was filled with a substantial portion of the officer cadre of the 106th Infantry Division. Most of these men had been captured with hardly a shot fired during their first week of combat in a quiet sector of the line as a result of the highly successful surprise of the Von Runstedt offensive. It was their introduction to combat and they didn't see much of it, or at least, not for very long. As a consequence, their morale was about as low as it could get. They just went through the motions of standing up for their rights under the Geneva Convention and, as a result, the conditions of their imprisonment were abysmal.

There were no organized prisoner activities in the camp. There was insufficient food. Red Cross parcels were seen arriving but were never distributed. There was no fuel for the single stove in each of the leaky wooden barracks. The straw-filled ticks on the wooden slats of the triple-decker bunks were filthy and lousy and were never changed. Officers were filthy and unshaved, and no shaving gear of any kind was made available. Between the two roll calls each day, prisoners spent the whole day in their bunks trying to keep warm with thin blankets and suffering through their private thoughts. I believe I saw one book the whole time at Hammelburg, but much later. The only reading material when we arrived consisted of OKW *(Oberkommando die Wehrmacht),* bulletins recounting the glorious German victories as the Nazis continued to consolidate their fronts, and an occasional copy of a German publication much like *Life* magazine.

A "man of confidence" represented each barracks. Ours was a chaplain from the 106th. It did little for our religious zeal when we caught him stealing food for himself from the common supply which it was his duty to pick up and distribute to the men in the barracks. At that point, he lost his job and was ostracized. For a time at Ludwigsburg, when Justin was very ill, I had been senior American officer and, as such, had been requested by a French Army priest to perform certain functions in his stead in the likely event of one young American Catholic boy dying before the priest's next visit. He instructed me and, understanding that my faith was not deep, he confided that if I made a sincere effort the effect would be the same. The young soldier, having been assured by the priest that I was okay, didn't mind.

If one spends a lot of time alone with one's thoughts during a prolonged period of cold and hunger, thought patterns can be very revealing. At one point I dreamed of a small paradise on earth that I had seen once with Papa. It was down in the Snake River canyon close to Twin Falls, Idaho, and had bountiful clear-flowing springs alive with trout and cress beds and was surrounded by the high black lava walls and the dry desert. He and Gary Cooper were planning to buy this place and I visualized myself as the permanent guardian of this paradise. I think everyone dreamed of a somewhere that would never be short of food. Strangely, the lack of food took such high precedence that sexual thoughts, even if deliberately entertained, simply had no substance. The planning of menus was a much more popular pastime.

I also wonder if the LeSouef Phosphorus Effect wasn't leaving its mark. Many things about this period are not at all clear in my memory, though I do remember one incident which I found frightening. One day after morning roll call formation, my name was blared out on the loudspeaker with the order to report to the *Oberleutnant* who called roll each day. As I crossed the parade ground I remembered, with some trepidation, the commments my father had written in *Men at War* suggesting that SS officers should be castrated.

I felt some relief in noting that this was not an SS man, but I was nervous nonetheless and would have preferred total anonymity. The *Oberleautant* was a well-fed, clerkish-looking fellow who wore Himmler-style *pince nez* glasses. I reported properly and was told, in perfect English, to stand at ease. He hesitated, then asked if I were by any chance related to the writer, Ernest Hemingway. I acknowledged that I was, upon which he went on to tell me that he was a great admirer of my father's work and had taught about his writing as a university lecturer in American Literature. He smiled broadly, shook my hand, and that was that.

None of my friends were housed in the same barracks with me. There was minimal intermingling between barracks; no one had the energy. Justin estimated the caloric value of our one slice of sawdust bread, ersatz coffee, and bowl of rutabaga soup as barely 900 calories a day: not even a maintenance diet. The one cheerful event was running into two of the guys from the OSS camp at Chréa. We were exceedingly careful about betraying our recognition and only got together to speak when it would appear coincidental that we were together on the parade ground, searching ostensibly for wild onions and garlic cloves among the clumps of dead grass. They told a grisly tale of treachery and deceit by the Russians in Czechoslovakia where they had been parachuted into an area controlled by the Czech Brigade. They said they had been under attack from the Germans and that the Soviets deliberately held back though they were within easy reach for a rescue operation. The Czech Brigade was predominantly a nationalist group who would eventually have opposed the Sovietization of their country. Knowing that, the Soviets chose to let them be destroyed. Don't ever try to persuade me that cynical U.S. leadership started the Cold War. Those who believe so obviously never saw the early Soviet machinations, provocations, and power plays. These friends had been through a series of brutal interrogations but, fortunately, in being handed over to the *Luftwaffe* their records had been scrambled and they were transferred to a regular prison camp.

An incident occurred later which profoundly affected everyone in the camp. The German commandant, a colonel *(Oberst)*, made the announcement at roll-call that, henceforth, a new set of rules was going into effect. Previously, no one had been permitted to leave the barracks to go to the latrine during the air raid alarms, which could often last a long time. It had been decided, the *Oberst* told us, that in the interest of sanitation one man at a time could go from the barracks to the latrine during the *Voralarm,* but if the full alarm should sound while in the latrine he would have to remain there until the all-clear was sounded. That was good news. The only problem was that the *Oberst* hadn't bothered to inform the guards.

That night there was a *Voralarm* about eleven o'clock. Several guys leaped from their beds and headed for the latrine, each trying to be first since only one could go at a time. In fact, they all had to stop since an officer from another barracks had beat them to it. But, suddenly, a long burst of machinegun fire shattered the night. We crowded around the door to see what had happened; a body lay crumpled twenty feet from the latrine building. There was shouting and anger throughout the camp but we had to wait for the all-clear before recovering the body. The young man we discovered there was a lieutenant, a lawyer in civilian life, who had been well liked by all who knew him.

We were permitted to hold a funeral procession through the compound. During the procession, a platoon of German Officer Candidates marched by on the outside of the fence singing the Horst Wessel song in their full, proud Germanic voices. I believe every man in that compound felt hatred stirring in his guts. There was never any apology for the "incident," only the cursory explanation that there had been a "misunderstanding."

It was early March before there was a real change for the better. It came about as the result of the arrival of a large contingent of prisoners from the East: American officers of mixed branches who had been captured earlier on and been sent to the Offlag at Schuben, Poland. They arrived after a long march of hundreds of kilometers across Central Germany brought about by the evacuation of their camp before the Russian advance. In this latter stage of the war, the value of American prisoners as bargaining chips was increasing daily.

Pop Goode, Colonel, U.S. Army, had commanded an infantry regiment of the 1st Infantry Division in Normandy. He had been assigned to the division before the Normandy landings straight from Camp Hale, Colorado, where he was a regimental commander in the 10th Mountain Division before the unit was shipped out to Italy. At the time, he claimed to be the senior colonel in the U.S. Army, and I'll tell you he was some kind of fine soldier. His capture in Normandy may have hurt his career chances, but we all soon became grateful he was among us. Within twenty-four hours of his arrival, the American officers' compound underwent a total change. The way I heard it from one of his staff, Pop Goode reported to the Camp Commandant and faced him down, refusing to accept any order from him since the Commandant was junior in date-of-rank. He demanded and got all the items necessary to clean house: razor blades, distribution of Red Cross parcels, coal for the stoves in the barracks, a new commandant, this time a Brigadier General, all within a week.

Suddenly we all ceased being slovenly, despairing, and dejected. Leadership made all the difference. Classes were organized, some of them serving as cover for committees on subjects from weapons procurement to escape. Hope made its appearance and soon even the weather started showing signs of improvement.

Col. Goode's executive officer in the camp was Lt. Col. John Waters, who happened to be General George Patton's son-in-law. He had been taken prisoner during the North African campaign in Tunisia, foreshortening what would doubtless have been a brilliant military career. A fine-looking, soldierly officer, his flair helped bring a quick resolution to a tricky situation during the event of our first, but false, liberation.

The incident took place in the early afternoon of a spring day in late March. It was the first in a rapidly unfolding series of events which are still nightmarish in retrospect, over forty years later. We had been hearing the distant thunder of artillery fire for several days, but on this day it seemed to be getting closer. Beyond the wire on our side of the camp we could see a partially cleared hillside on the edge of the woods. Farther to the right, where the Serbian general staff was quartered with most of its entire officer corps, were the administrative buildings of the POW complex. A dramatic increase in the noise, and the clank of armored vehicles approaching, drew many of us to the wire facing the clearing on the hillside. We could see a haystack on the hill, which burst suddenly into flames, and the sound of 50-caliber machine guns and 20mm cannon fire rent the air as the horizon was filled with the dark shapes of American light tanks, half-tracks and tank destroyers.

The U.S. Army had arrived, or so we thought. The guards all disappeared from the towers and their walking posts. Word reached us to get inside and down under the bunks, which we did immediately. The camp commandant apparently was prepared to turn over the camp to Col. Goode but, as I heard it afterward, another German unit housed at the camp refused to go along. Lt. Col. Waters was wounded trying to assure the turnover of the camp without unnecessary casualties or bloodshed. The U.S. forces held back while the Germans withdrew and then came roaring to the edge of the camp, several tanks penetrating the wire by the simple expedient of driving their tanks through it.

Next we were ordered to assemble and Col. Goode explained to us the risks involved in trying to make it out with the armored task force. It seems the armored unit had blasted its way fifty miles behind enemy lines in a planned breakthrough with the express purpose of liberating the U.S. officers in the camp. The problem was, their intelligence reports had been mistaken and there were ten times the number of prisoners they had expected. There was a total of only twenty-three vehicles in the task force, over half of which were lightly armored half-tracks intended to carry out POWs. They had taken casualties in several firefights during the day and had managed to reach Hammelburg only because of the close fighter support which would not be available if the evacuation continued into the hours of darkness. Furthermore, their last functioning radio to call for tactical air support had been knocked out.

The time lost by the confusion and the unexpected numbers at the camp delayed the departure sufficiently to make a return to Allied territory the same day impossible, especially now that the element of surprise was no longer in their favor. By now, German forces were fully alerted to the armored incursion and would be mounting an organized counterattack.

Even though all of this wasn't spelled out at the time, we knew that the odds were poor for those who chose to go with the armored column, and Col. Goode gave us the choice. The result was that everyone who felt up to it boarded the half-tracks, and others, including me, crawled up on the tanks, hanging on wherever we could. Even Justin Greene, with his bad foot, got aboard one of the tanks.

It was already almost dusk when the task force leader gave

the signal to start back. He had selected a different route than they had followed to Hammelburg; unfortunately, that route turned out to be through an area used by the German Army for maneuvers and artillery practice. They knew it, literally, as well as their own backyards.

As we started out, the atmosphere was one of great exuberance. Everyone thought the war was finally over for them. Some of the tankers had liberated some hooch, giving some to the prisoners. You can imagine the effect: noise, cheering, pandemonium where there should have been discipline, silence, and attention. Ray Saigh and Dewey Stuart had come to Hammelburg and I was with them behind the turret of the lead tank.

The first attack hit us just as darkness settled over the area. We were moving along a narrow defile beside a hedgerow. The hedgerow concealed a platoon of attackers who fired several *Panzerfaus* projectiles at the tanks. This German version of the bazooka was a one-shot, hand-held shape-charge which had to be loosed at its target from close range to be effective. The hedgerow was hardly three yards from our vehicles, plenty close enough, and the first hits threw us rudely off the tanks. The tracks on the lead tank were blown away and we clambered aboard another tank, just barely hanging on as it worked its way around the first tank and the armored infantrymen cleared the hedgerow with automatic weapons. By midnight there had been several more attacks of the same nature and the column had made precious little progress when the commander decided to halt for the night and set up a defensive position and await the return of close air support at dawn.

The area where we set up was in rolling country with scrub woods where the road wound in a horseshoe deep into the fold of a hill. I had become separated from my friends during the shuffling; everyone was either asleep in the vehicles or camped on the ground nearby. Sentries had been posted on all sides.

Another fellow and I decided it wasn't a healthy spot and, about an hour before dawn, we decided to part company with the column and try to make it across country on our own. We reported our intentions to the commander who did not try to discourage us. We then started up through the woods toward the top of the hill where we felt we could see what went on and case the country ahead to the west where eventual safety lay.

It turned out we weren't the only ones with the same idea and we ran into some other prisoners on the way. We must have been a half mile away from the column when it became light enough to see the column in the fold of the hill stretched out like a snake that had been cut into pieces. Within minutes we heard the ominous roar of heavy tanks and the clangor heightened sharply as, one after another, six Tiger tanks appeared around the bend in the road from a distant hill. It was too late for the column to take defensive action and they were fired upon by the overwhelmingly superior guns of the Tigers.

The sound was deafening and most of the vehicles of the column, tanks as well as half-tracks, were totally demolished within minutes. We heard later that casualties were not so heavy as it appeared from our vantage point. The survivors dispersed, and we headed out as quickly as we could to avoid the inevitable roundup by German infantry.

Our main priority was to stay as far away from other prisoners as possible, so long as we were headed in the right general direction. I don't remember clearly just how long we were out there, but I believe it was two days, possibly more. We had eaten the K rations our would-be liberators had given us and I remember, at one point, coming to a small house in the woods with a kitchen garden. The proprietors had heard something and panicked, leaving unfinished food on the table.

Another time, we sneaked by a farm and liberated a white Angora rabbit from a hutch, wrung its neck and, totally famished, tore off the skin and ate it raw. Several times we dug out rutabagas from the earth-covered piles where they were stored.

When we were finally caught, it was one of the most frightening moments of my life. Famished, thirsty, cold, and stiff, we were starting out one morning when we were taken completely by surprise by a patrol made up of young boys in uniform, armed with side daggers and an assortment of weapons, including one Schmeisser machine pistol. The problem was that they were as frightened as we were. We were obviously unarmed, but we must have looked pretty desperate to them. The boy with the Schmeisser was visibly trembling and his finger was on the trigger with the weapon pointed at my belly.

The Schmeisser has a rate-of-fire of about twelve hundred rounds per minute and, while it is hard to hold on target for a long burst, it can do stitches on you mighty fast. There was total silence and I could sense the wheels turning in their little heads. I spoke as softly as I have ever spoken, and as slowly, hands in the air, *"Bitte, kanne wir sprechen mit ein unter Offizier?"* Lousy German, but slow and clear. The kid with the Schmeisser stopped trembling and yelled in a squeaky voice to one of his buddies to go get the *Feldwebel*. Within a very short time the bad moment was over and we were once again guests of the Third Reich.

With the sergeant now in charge, we were marched to the railroad station at a nearby town where they reported our capture and were apparently told to hold us there until a prisoner train would come by some hours later. The timing was good. It turned out to be the train taking the recovered prisoners from Hammelburg to evacuate them south to Nürnberg.

The column from the 4th Armored Division which had caused the great ruckus was a forerunner of the whole 3rd Army which liberated the prisoners left at Hammelburg on April 6. Justin Greene had been retaken and put into the infirmary and was home within a week. Someone tried to make a scandal out of the prisoner relief column, saying that it had been sent by General Patton for the sole purpose of rescuing his son-in-law. Later, a whole book was written about it.

We were transported in ice-cold freight cars to a massive Luftwaffe *Offizier Lager* just outside Nürnberg where there were literally over ten thousand Allied Air Force officers incarcerated. On the way, we were shunted to a siding while a German armored train moved by going north with tanks and troops. The tanks looked new and the troops fresh. It was demoralizing. The good news was hearing how light the casualties had been when the Tigers had attacked our tanks. From our viewpoint on the hilltop, it had looked like a charnel house.

At the new camp we were spread out among several compounds which were well organized and relatively cheerful compared to where we had been. We heard tales of the great escape through tunnels dug under the wire, and we saw the first combat jets which were being flown from a nearby airport by the Luftwaffe. Also, not far away was a V2 rocket launching ramp and we saw several of the hideous buzz bombs sent up into the sky on their way to England.

We had only been at Nürnberg about a week when the word came down that the whole camp was being evacuated; which meant everyone who wasn't seriously ill or incapacitated. We started out the following day immediately after the morning slice of bread and bowl of ersatz coffee. Like all military move-ments, there was a lot of waiting around which wasn't surpris-ing considering that the column of marching prisoners was, lit-erally, miles long. I never knew just how many men there were, but I heard an estimate from Col. Goode that there were over ten thousand. I never saw the head of the column so I have no idea what was in the lead, but I suspect there were supply trucks, or wagons, both front and rear, which carried mess facilities for all of us.

Once we were out of Nürnberg, we traveled mostly on the secondary roads, probably to ensure that we didn't interfere with military traffic in the area. We climbed a long hill onto a plateau and, just as my part of the column reached the top of the grade, we were treated to a sight which was as ghastly as it was cheering.

The sky was clear and it was a bright, spring day. It must have been around noon or shortly after when we saw the first silver cigars high in the sky. They just seemed to keep on com-ing like migrating geese: vee after vee after vee, with their con-trails streaming behind them in the high, cold air. The sight was hypnotic as the cylinders covered the sky in their thou-sands. They were B-17s and we almost forgot what they were there for until the moment the first booms and thuds reached us, as the thousand tiny flashes of light, like silver crystals rain-ing from the sky, struck the city below. Nürnberg which we had seen stretched out behind us was suddenly hidden from view by the rising clouds from the massive incineration. At its peak the raid gave us a sight I have never seen since: we could actual-ly see the shock waves rising out from the epicenter of the attack, rolling waves of super-heated air reverberating out-ward over the land.

There was a spontaneous cheer from ten thousand throats as the realization spread through the column that Nürnberg was buying it. The guards scowled or looked away but made no move to stop us. But our euphoria was drenched quickly enough when, a few moments before the last of the silver bombers disappeared, two explosions in a row shook the ground around us and a barrage of 50-caliber machine-gun rounds bit the earth along the length of the column. We all dived for the nearest cover and I found myself in the ridiculous position of being scrunched in a ditch with my head snuggled in the crotch of a guard who had beaten me to the spot. It reminded me of my father's comment when he heard that the newest saying from the Pacific War was that there are no atheists in foxholes. "Of course not," Papa replied, "the Christians beat them to it."

For the next half hour the guards took their turn laughing at us and joking about our *"gute Freunde,"* meaning our own pilots who had fired on us. From that point on for the rest of the ten-day march, prisoners were assigned to put out panels of paper or cloth spelling out "US POW" on the ground along our route during daylight hours. After that first day, we actually had a P-51 Mustang escort within sight most of the time.

We were headed generally south, shuffling along at a snail's pace, which seemed to the Air Force people like a forced march. Most of them had last marched in cadet training and they suffered badly from sore feet and blisters, keeping the medics busy. There were guards strung all along the column and others farther out on both flanks accompanied by their war dogs. The total distance we covered in the ten days was something like 200 kilometers, an average of about twelve miles a day. In fact, that's a lot for men on near-starvation rations and in poor physical condition. What helped most was that we had Red Cross parcels distributed before leaving Nürnberg. Those were the basis of our travel rations so we ate better than normal and were able to barter with locals along the road for eggs, onions, potatoes, and some grain which we toasted, ground, and then boiled to make a wheatena-like mush.

The long-time prisoners all had small, cleverly-designed stoves built of old cans with crank-driven blowers which made it possible to make a very hot flame with little fuel. With the exception of the sick and, strangely enough, the tall, lean basketball-player types, almost everyone benefited from the march. Those exceptions never recovered from poor circulation in the extremities and suffered the worst from cold and poor diet. Now they were having the most difficult time.

Depending on where we were in the column, we sometimes spent the nights under trees along the roadside clustered together so the guards could keep track of us. On other nights we might end up in the haylofts of big barns, or in a vacant school building.

One evening we were halted on the edge of a small village awaiting arrangements for night quarters. There was a small brook running through a culvert and it looked fishy. While no one was watching I ducked into the water and hid below the bank while I scouted the bottom for a holding rock where I might try for a trout. I spotted a likely place a few yards before the entrance to the culvert and moved cautiously toward it. This was the technique I had seen the hand fisherman use back in Le Bousquet. I put my hand in the icy water and let it cool off, then reached under the rock and felt way back underneath. There was a fish and I sneaked my hand and fingers around it, pinned it to the rock, then with my left hand lifted the whole rock out of the water with the wriggling trout pinned against it. Seven inches long, and three of us shared it, broiled over one of the blower stoves with no salt or seasoning of any kind. It may have been the best tasting trout I ever ate.

There was one emotion-charged day on the long march when a rumor flew down the column that President Roosevelt was dead. The guards were the first to say so, but none of us would believe it. We thought it was just another cruel rumor meant to demoralize us further, but finally word came down from Col. Goode that it was, indeed, true, and there was open weeping amongst us, even some of the violent Roosevelt haters.

We got to be on fairly easy terms with some of the older guards, and for a small commission, we could get them to help us with our bartering. In truth, their rations were not much better than our own. As they often said, *"Alles kaput in Deutschland. Ya. Ya."* A couple of us worked on one of the old guys with the hope of talking him into helping us get away. Whenever we were alone with him, we would talk about his village just south of Ingolstadt, where we were apparently headed as our crossing point on the Danube. We tried to get him to say that he would go home when we got close to his village, and that we could help him. We suggested that he could pretend to be taking us on a work detail and escort us, under guard, past the dog patrols. At that point, he could take off and we would go our own way.

We finally crossed the swollen Danube on a pontoon bridge—the regular bridge had already been blown—and renewed our persuasions on the old man. He was at least sixty, the bottom of the barrel! He finally agreed and we decided that only three of us could go because it would have been unlikely, and suspicious, to take more than three on a work detail. When we got within fifty yards of the perimeter guards with their watchdogs, the old man lost his nerve. He stopped, turned to us, and shook his head. We couldn't blame him. We were pretty scared ourselves.

A few days later we arrived at Moosburg on the Isar river in Bavaria. This was the largest prison camp we had yet seen. On one of the last days I got to carry Pop Goode's bagpipes for a short way. He had managed to retain the eccentricity of keeping his pipes with him throughout his captivity. While I admired his spunk, I wished to hell I'd been able to hold on to my own fly rod all the way through. I wondered what had become of it and if it were still all right, and if maybe someone had caught a handsome trout with it back at Voiteur—where it had doubtless been sent to SS headquarters along with my other personal effects when I'd been reported missing. As it turned out, Don MacAfee held on to it and saw to it that it was sent on to my father.

The day after our arrival at Moosburg, a rumor of some concern reached me. The gist of it was that selected officers were going to be evacuated to Hitler's redoubt to be held as hostages against the safety of the leading Nazis. Those being selected were the prominent and the relatives of prominent people as well as the higher-ranking officers. I had an idea that I stood a good chance of being chosen and determined to do something about it. The compound next to ours was filled with enlisted men who moved around quite a bit since they were sent out on work details: something which officers were not permitted to do under the rules of the Geneva Convention. One of them had slipped through the wire into our compound to do some bartering and I approached him with a deal I hoped he couldn't refuse. I suggested to him that we trade dogtags and insignia and that he take my place in the officers' compound, where he might be interned longer but where he wouldn't have to pull any work details and would, supposedly, get better food. The latter was untrue, of course, but he would avoid the danger to which many of the enlisted men were exposed when on work crews. While clearing away rubble around railroad yards they had often been subjected to strafing by Allied air strikes.

He decided it was a good deal and I became an EM and he a first lieutenant. I don't know if he was one of the ones sent off to the redoubt or not. I have since talked to some of the officers who were, and they told me they had waited about three days longer for liberation than the rest of us at Moosburg and that was about it.

At any rate, the great day came in very much the same fashion as the false liberation at Hammelburg. We heard cannon fire and then small arms, but the compound was so gigantic I never saw anything until we knew everything was all right. There were U.S. tanks in the streets and, wonder of wonders, within an hour there was a Red Cross doughnut truck complete with Red Cross girls serving them. Unfortunately, several men became violently ill from the doughnuts, and we were told that a couple of men had died from eating them. Their stomachs simply couldn't take the heavy, rich food so suddenly after near starvation.

The first thing the U.S. Army did after the liberation of the camp was to put all the American POWs under guard and forbid them to leave the premises. Foreign prisoners were allowed to roam freely wherever they wished, and the Russians and others were apparently having a field day raping and pillaging.

My own first priority was to make contact with my unit in some way. I had had no success escaping from the Germans; now I would try my luck with the 14th Armored division of Patton's 3rd Army. It was a pushover.

I made contact with my friends from Chréa and we talked our way out and hitched a ride on a truck to Army Headquarters, which was in Regensburg at the time. There we checked in with the OSS section and, after a cleanup and issue of fresh clothing and insignia, we were taken to the staff officers' mess. Seated at one of the tables was Marlene Dietrich in field gear, looking glamorous, and I wanted to go pay my respects because I knew she was a friend of Papa's. But shyness overcame me and, to my everlasting regret, I didn't.

We spent the night at Regensburg and heard the news that Admiral Doenitz was negotiating the surrender of all the German armies. The news was already out that Hitler was presumed dead, though the fact had not yet been confirmed. We were given highest priority for a flight to Paris the next morning on a staff liaison plane. Things happened so fast and so efficiently it all seemed like a mad dream sequence.

I remember looking at the odd geometric patterns of the fields as we crossed the Jura and the Vosges, thinking about all the fighting those fields had seen over the span of time, and about the ways of men, and how those fields got to be so small through subdivision by inheritance, and of how people have always managed to survive, one way or another.

We landed at Le Bourget Airport, where Charles Lindbergh had first set foot after his historic crossing when I was still in kneepants. I had an address to get to once we had checked in with our headquarters in a building on the Rond Point des Champs Élysées. The Rond Point is about half way up the Champs Élysées and we were taken there in a military vehicle, by the back way. They didn't want us for long. There was only a skeleton duty staff and we were given permission to report back in a couple of days.

I headed on foot for the *Étoile* and the *Arc de Triomphe,* from whence I planned to head down toward the *Place des Ternes* where Dave Niles had told me he lived with his wife, a noted choreographer. Except for the difficulty I had getting there because of the packed VE-Day mob, it proved the best choice of destination a man ever made.

The walk, if it can be called that, took over two hours. I took one hour to get from one side of the *Champs Élysées* to the other. The city was a madhouse of joyous delirium, though perhaps a different sort of delirium from that which reigned after the first liberation the previous August. There was, of course, a party in full swing when I arrived at David Niles' flat. His wife, it turned out, did the choreography and managed the two theaters, I believe, where the USO gave its shows for GIs on leave or stationed in Paris, and the apartment was alive with the most beautiful women I had seen for a long time. I won't bore you with details except to say that it was almost a relief to report back to headquarters thirty-six hours later to be sent off to London for a short stay before heading home.

The forty-eight hours in London are completely forgotten except for a two-hour visit to X2, the OSS counterintelligence section where I filed a report regarding the actions of certain Germans I had encountered during my six months imprisonment: namely, *Hauptmann* Haas at Hammehburg, negatively, and the *Alpinjaeger Oberleutnant,* very positively. I later received indirect news about both. In Washington I received an officer's belt with a note saying that the prisoners at the POW hospital in Ludwigsburg had choked Haas to death with it and wanted me to have it. It had the *Gott Mit Uns* buckle and was of beautiful leather, and of large size, so I later gave it to Papa.

Years later on a short visit to Schruns where Tiddy had been my nurse, I inquired about the Austrian officer who had been my benefactor. Tiddy, they told me, had died the year before my visit, never having married, and no one knew anything about the *Alpinjaeger* officer.

Another visit to the area where Justin Greene and I had stepped into the hornet's nest yielded more information. My pal, Dan Callaghan, and I had tried to retrace the events of that day just as they had taken place, but I was having some trouble finding the exact places where I had been. Finally, I found a middle-aged man in a small house near where I thought it had happened. After I'd recounted the events of that day, so many years ago, he burst out with the story of how he had watched the events of my capture from his home, when he was eleven years old, and then he explained why we had not been able to find the clearing and the sunken road. A whole new forest of robust pine trees had been planted after the war and were now over forty feet high. He led us to the place and we found the emplacements the *Alpinjaeger* had been digging and the house where we had been taken after our capture. It now belongs to a German who uses it for a summer vacation home.

The people of Grébéfosse and the *Commune de Bois de Champs* were welcoming and made wonderful *framboise eau de vie,* raspberry brandy, which they served in thimbles from old Johnny Walker Red Label bottles. They still remembered *le Capitaine Grin,* as they pronounced Justin's name.

From London we flew to Washington, D.C. in a C-54, stopping at Prestwick, Keflavik, and Gander on the way. After reporting to OSS Headquarters in the Q Building, I was given two months' leave and almost nine months of accumulated back pay. At the time of my capture I had weighed about 210 pounds and I now weighed just over 140. I neglected to mention that the business about sex going out the window during periods of cold and semi-starvation more than reversed itself after a few good meals. The effect had become most apparent during the VE-Day celebrations in Paris.

At that point I got a priority commercial flight to Chicago to see my mother and Paul Mowrer. I tried to telephone, but there was no answer, so I decided to go ahead and surprise them. I also hoped to see Mary McNulty who had been much in my thoughts the whole time, despite my obviously having been true only in my fashion.

But Chicago was a disaster. Not only was there no one home

in Lake Bluff, but our house had just been sold. With some difficulty, I finally found out from a friend of my mother's that Paul was in France and Mother was in New York about ready to go join him, frantically trying to find any news of me. She was staying at the Algonquin Hotel, so I phoned and arranged to meet her as quickly as I could. I performed my prisoner-of-war act for the ticket agent and managed to wangle a seat on a flight back to New York, after learning from the McNulty family that Mary was away at Vassar.

My mother, whom I called Mamie just as in old times, was radiant and we had a wonderful reunion. The event was marred only for a few moments during the course of the dinner when I suddenly realized that she had been staring at me in a most unusual, somewhat bemused fashion. I tried to think what might be wrong then I realized what I had just said. Without thinking, I had lapsed into the sort of talk that had become habitual in the six months in the company of men only. Totally unaware, I was speaking more nearly in the manner of the Scots Guards at Chréa than as an officer and a gentleman (by act of Congress) should be. I apologized, and we had a good laugh about it.

Mamie had to leave the next day for Paris where Paul had accepted the task of starting a new Paris edition of the *New York Post*. The challenge, which he had taken on at the behest of Ted Thackrey and Dolly Schiff Thackrey, the owner-publishers, turned out to be complicated by post-war conditions in Europe and, finally, became impossible because of the long-lasting newsprint strike. The competing *Paris Herald* had been fully prepared for the strike with a stockpile of paper, which made the *Post's* challenge untenable. Paul and Mother managed to keep things going, including the Villa des Tilleuls in Crécy, until the summer of 1949, an accomplishment for which I was ever thankful.

SIXTEEN

The summer of 1945 was spent doing all the things I'd daydreamed about during prison camp: eating too much, playing too much, and not thinking a whole hell of a lot about the future. In New York, after Mamie left, I made contact with Marty and we had a big evening out which ended up at the Stork Club. I got the news from her about the breakup with Papa and about the new woman of the house, Mary Welsh. I had telephoned Papa in Havana and been invited to come down as soon as possible to spend my leave there. It sounded good.

Papa was enthusiastic, if slightly sheepish at first, about Mary. At the time I remember thinking that at least he had good taste in girl's names—I was still thinking in terms of seeing Mary McNulty as soon as I could. I finally did make phone contact with Mary in Poughkeepsie. She was a freshman at Vassar and, though it was late in her freshman year, she said it was still difficult for her to get off campus for very long. I told her I would be right up, and I told Papa I would be right down after a short visit to upstate New York.

Mary McNulty and I had one of those dates which ought to be forgotten but never is because it comes at such a pivotal point. It started out being great fun in some local place but ended after she let me down as gently as she could with the clear message that someone else was her main interest, and a very serious one at that. We parted permanently that night and I will never cease to admire her complete kindness and the effort she made to be as gentle as she could with my feelings. Still, it hurt a lot for a long time.

I had no trouble getting to Cuba where Papa met me with open arms at the airport. On the way to the Finca he told me more about Miss Mary and he was, clearly, completely under her spell.

My introduction to Mary Welsh was not propitious, or perhaps actually it was. It depends on the point of view. Papa said to go on down to the pool; Mary would be there and was anxious to meet me. I went down in shirt sleeves, planning to change to trunks after the introduction. As I walked around the bend in the path and down to the pool I could clearly see that she was swimming. As I approached the edge of the pool, she reached the far end, climbed out, and turned to face me. She was completely nude. Startled, I began to turn away, but she called for me to come ahead, then introduced herself as she wrapped a giant beach towel around herself.

That was the beginning of a long and sometimes tumultuous relationship characterized by one overriding fact: she was the only one of my three stepmothers I never loved. I did not immediately dislike her. Quite the contrary, I liked her at first and saw no reason to believe that I would not become truly fond of her in time.

During that visit, a major crisis occurred involving Papa and Mary. I had remained at the Finca to laze about and read while they went off in the big, apple-green Lincoln Continental convertible along the back road behind Luyano on the periphery of Havana. I think they were headed for a visit to some friends in the fashionable west end of Havana—something which would have been unheard-of in the "old days" when Papa could scarcely be dragged to any sort of social function and insisted on either entertaining at home or meeting people in bars or restaurants. He was driving and it started to drizzle just as they were entering a stretch of undulating, winding road. Something or someone darted onto the roadway ahead just as they were topping the hill and Papa hit the brakes. The big, soft-suspensioned car went into a slide, swerving from side to side. When Papa tried to pull back onto the road they ran into a line of trees along the road, and both of them were hurt. Papa suffered broken ribs and hit his head again but, as usual, made little of it at the time.

When I got a call at the Finca, I drove out to the aid station with Juan, the chauffeur. The medic had taped Papa's chest and put a bandage on his forehead where he had struck the rearview mirror. But he was more concerned about Mary who was agonizing about the gash on her face, which had already spewed a lot of blood, and the small glass-cut on her forehead.

Papa went home with Juan once I had assured him I would see that Mary was all right. I was to accompany her to Rodrigo Diaz's clinic where the well-known plastic surgeon, who was also a good friend from the *Club de Cazadores,* would make sure her good looks were unimpaired. Mary was clearly demoralized at the possibility, and who could blame her? She behaved well, though, and I admired her "grace under pressure." I think it was the closest we ever came to being good friends, and the key moment was when I remembered how much she liked to smoke, and, since she couldn't light her own cigarette at the time, I lit one and held it to her mouth. Her reaction at that moment was the closest thing to gratitude I ever had from her.

There were several old friends around at this time, including Tommy Shevlin who was on leave from the Coast Guard where he had been serving in the Miami area. Also there was another Coast Guardsman, Carl Bottume, who was a great favorite of Papa and Mary's. He had served in the Pacific for a long time aboard an attack transport as well as on an ocean-going tug. An aspiring writer, Carl was now assigned to Havana and on his time off was seeing a lot of a very attractive German girl, Lydia Ludke. Lydia was very tall, graceful, and pale-skinned with black hair and icy blue North Sea eyes. She worked in the Bohemia Bookstore where we bought all our magazines and newspapers, and she was the daughter of the principal German agent operating in Cuba before and during the war. He was now in a Cuban prison and near death. Lydia did not appear to share her father's loyalty to the Fatherland and was much sought after by the young men about town, but she would not have anything to do with the locals, only the Americans, whom she seemed to consider better company. She and Carl were good pals and I soon began going places with them in the evenings, or taking long walks with them out in the country near San Francisco de Paula.

One day Carl was asking me about my imprisonment and I told him about the time the chaplain from the 106th Division was caught stealing bread from the general barracks supply. Carl said he could top that. On the attack transport there had been a chaplain who was well known for his successful forays among the nurses, WACs, and other assorted American ladies serving their country overseas. He had a knack for getting them back to his cabin aboard ship where he presumably committed his foul deeds.

Needless to say, the chaplain's unpopularity among the men and officers of the ship knew no bounds and they were intent on finding a means of retribution. One reason they felt certain the chaplain was doing more than help cleanse the souls of the misguided ladies was that he made a fair dent in the supply of condoms with which all branches of the Armed Forces were well supplied, in the interest of hygiene.

Carl was the one to come up with the solution. One evening when the chaplain was ashore on one of his dates, Carl and the other officers took the remaining supply of condoms and proceeded to blow them up into long, sausage-like balloons and tie them tightly, then filled the chaplain's room to the ceiling with them. When the unsuspecting man of God opened the door to his cabin with his date on his arm, its packed contents caused considerable embarrassment and spoiled an evening of frolic for the chaplain, who soon thereafter requested, and received, a transfer to another ship. That operation was carried out to the immense satisfaction of the whole crew, whose religious zeal had dimmed measurably during the whole period of his duty among them.

The three of us often went to the Centro Vasco together. Located on the Malecón close to where it meets the Prado, the club was a wonderful landmark of Cuban culture, so to speak. It was a typical old-fashioned Spanish club with its regulars there every day playing dominoes and the drinkers holding down the bar in Basque fashion, usually given to song. Sometimes Papa and Mary joined us for an evening, but more often they stayed home or went out to the Floridita or to the El Pacífico for Chinese food on the roof garden. Papa loved the shark fin soup at the El Pacífico which he was convinced was a great contributor to "lead in the pencil."

One time at the Centro Vasco, Carl, Lydia, and I met Eddie Chivas, a liberal Cuban politician, a senator at the time. We all had *caracoles en salsa verde* (snails in green sauce), a specialty of the Basque kitchen. We had had quite a lot to drink and were feeling jolly, with the cool evening breeze blowing in through the tall, thin, louvered shutters. Chivas, a balding, thick-spectacled idealist, was talking volubly about the dangers inherent in the resumption of power by Fulgencio Batista. He was convinced Batista was no longer the idealistic young sergeant who had saved his country from the dictatorship of Machado in 1934. When order had been restored, Batista was to step down so that general elections and the Democratic process could take its course, but Chivas doubted Batista's resolve and his honesty.

One of the points we heard him proclaiming was that perhaps democracy as practiced in the U.S. was inappropriate to the Latin temperament, just as the British parliamentary system was inappropriate to the Yankees. American democracy simply broke down too easily, allowing grand theft on a monumental scale at every level of bureaucracy. The answer, he suggested, certainly wasn't military supervision but a better system: one more suited to the Latin way of doing business. Chivas was so carried away with his fear of impending injustice, and with his suspicions of Batista, he said he refused to exist in an atmosphere where any more of Cubans' personal rights were taken away. None of us took him as seriously as we should have.

Much later, after it had been announced that some further constitutional rights had been "temporarily" suspended, Eddie Chivas stood up in the Senate, in full view of the television cameras which were focused on him, denounced the actions of the Batista government, then pulled a Colt .45 automatic from his shoulder holster and shot himself through the head. So much for not taking Latin American politics seriously.

The next few weeks in Havana passed quickly with much pigeon shooting, some fishing, forays to the boxing matches to see Kid Gavilán and Kid Tunero's last fights, *jai alai,* tennis, fencing, and my gradual return to some semblance of my former blooming good health.

One day, I thought I was alone at the Finca. I was ensconced in one of the big oversized easy chairs in the living room where the large Roberto Domingo bullfight paintings occasionally drew my glance away from the page. Had anyone asked me, I would have said that I was fully recovered from my POW experience and those thoughts were far from my mind. The doors and windows onto the patio were open allowing the afternoon breeze to flow through the house. I was in that semi-somnolent stage of concentrated reading when four or five loud blasts exploded around me, one of which seemed to be in the room with me. In an instant reflex, I hit the floor like a wounded groundhog and started foxholing my way under a table to find better cover. I was shaking all over when laughter exploded in the room almost as loud as the bangs. I had been frightened by cherry bombs and firecrackers thrown by my two brothers, Pat and Greg, who had just arrived for the Fourth of July from Key West. At first I was furious, not just at them but at myself for thinking I was back to normal. The fear I felt in those few moments was worse than any I had known before and I can only explain it by assuming that I was not as fit as I had been when I was in action in France, and I was not mentally prepared.

I have since reflected on the tenet that Jim Russell spent so much time pounding into me during our OSS training. He said one should always have in mind a place to dive into the instant you hear gunfire. If you can dive soon enough, there is a good chance they won't be on you with the first burst, but they will immediately correct their aim. Dive before the second burst. Always having a place in mind to dive into keeps one alert, and it never hurts to be alert, I discovered, even in peacetime.

At the end of my two months, I said farewell to Papa and his new wife and headed back for my next duty assignment in the nation's capital. After France, Germany, and my repatriation gauntlet, I wasn't sure what to expect, but I was prepared for anything.

OSS duty in Washington, D.C., was just about the softest thing that ever happened to me: what the British call a "swan." After the formalities at the Q Building, I was assigned to a general personnel replacement pool out at the Congressional Country Club where I ran into some old friends and met a few new ones. There were aspects of OSS which were definitely advantageous, and this was one of them. Along with many others who had served in the field in Europe, I had volunteered for duty in the Far East. In order to do that, I was required to give up my points for release from active duty; the release point program had been set up in the final stages of the war in order to create a fair way of determining who could get out and back into civilian life first. While I didn't have enough points for my time in service and overseas duty, the POW time gave me enough bonus points to get out right away had I wanted to. But the lure of another mission in the Far East overrode my desire to become a civilian. Now I was spending my days at the Country Club sitting around, exercising, and taking overnight passes into the city where I immediately discovered a marvelous phenomenon of the war: the girl desk clerk.

An OSS veteran I had known at Chréa, Pat Patterson, introduced me to the concept. If one is a young, healthy officer, and reasonably acceptable in appearance, the girl desk clerk suddenly finds it within her powers to find one a room, provided, of course, that one goes along with the idea of entertaining her when she gets off work. I found the idea challenging and, since we only had to check in at the Club once a day, my Washington duty at the Shoreham Hotel was a continual delight for several weeks.

When my orders finally came through, I was assigned to a series of courses being given at various training facilities in the area where, for the first time, I was exposed to the kinds of instruction my comrades at Chréa had been through before going overseas. Specifically, I was being trained for service in China, where there was a large OSS contingent in Kunming, the center of Far East operations.

After completing my first course I was sent on temporary duty to New York where I was to report to one of the major hospitals noted for its psychiatric facility. I was not told what it was about but that I was to cooperate in whatever they wanted me to do. When I reported to the doctors, they put me through a battery of tests which lasted almost two days. I had a small room in the examination ward where I was locked in at night. After the more formal tests, I was given a script with several different cover stories which I was supposed to memorize. Among them was one story which was my own operational history. The various stories had been supplied by the Q building people in Washington, and the purpose of the exercise was to determine, by the use of polygraphs, which of the stories was the true one. I was told I could use any means I could devise to stop them from determining which was the true story. I was given a day to study the cover stories and then the polygraph exams would begin the next morning.

It was quite an ordeal but the results were amazing. They failed to detect which story was the real one, and even failed on their second choice. When it was over they told me that I was the first one of the thirty field veterans they had tested to that point to beat their interrogation system; then they asked me to what I attributed my success. I explained that, since they had told me anything was okay, I had simply picked the lock to my door and gone out on the town with my old journalist friend Leonard Lyons. Lenny never drank himself, but I had spent the night with him cadging drinks from all the celebrities and near-celebrities he was interviewing. We had had a great time and, in the process, I had gotten thoroughly sloshed and sneaked back to my room very shortly before getting-up time.

I had a super hangover and was able to respond to the questions untruthfully without any emotion or guilt, or whatever is measured by the polygraph.

Fortunately, my examiners had a sense of humor and laughed as well as thanked me for my help. Before I left to return to Washington, they gave me a personal evaluation based on the tests and the upshot was that they recommended that I pursue a career in diplomacy.

I was about to go off to another tactics course when the news of the atom bomb broke, and within a few days VJ Day came and, with it, the end of the war. There was great joy everywhere and I looked forward to immediate return to civilian life. Within the week I had my first serious lesson in the treacherous way of military bureaucracy.

I had applied immediately for relief from active duty and was eagerly awaiting an early favorable decision, but it was not to be. When I had waived my points for early discharge to volunteer for duty in the Far East, I had committed a grievous error and now I could not undo it. There was nothing for me with OSS now, so I was returned to the regular Army where someone took delight in inflicting retribution for the time I had shirked my duties by serving with OSS. I was assigned as one of the officers commanding a German POW installation at Camp Pickett, Virginia. For the next two months I spent my time trading insults with a crew of Afrika Corps soldiers and NCOs, and engaging in knife-throwing contests with their administrative staff at camp headquarters; the object was to win away their cigarette ration, which was larger in a week than I had enjoyed during six months as their guest. I was appalled at the luxuries and freedoms they were given. Some of the shrewd ones were even managing assignations with girls from the nearby town. Such is the American Way. After they had been repatriated, I received letters from a few of those men; all of them wanted us to send cigarettes. A few years later I found out why.

I finally got out of the Army altogether in November 1945 and headed for Havana on terminal leave. Carl Bottume was gone and I heard later he had died of a rare malady. I missed his cheerfulness, but Wolfie Guest was back from China where he had been on an OSS mission on the Shantung Penninsula, and the lovely Lydia was available so we spent quite a lot of time together discovering some delightful walks along the deserted trolley tracks of an abandoned line which cut through the countryside west of San Francisco de Paula.

Major Richard Cooper, Papa's old friend from East Africa days in the thirties, was in Havana with his new bride and the level of drinking at the Finca, and elsewhere, increased markedly. Dick Cooper was a friend of Baron von Blixen (Isak Dinesen's white hunter husband), and, after a brilliant WWI record, subsided into remittancy only to find great wealth on his own in Wyoming oil. We had visited him at Casper before the war. He was the first white man to try to kill a lion with a bow and arrow, at least in modern times, and had done so under Blickie's tutelage. The result was catastrophic for one gunbearer who was mauled to death on the lion's hundred-yard charge. Blickie actually finished him off with the express rifle at point-blank range. Dick Cooper was knocked down and unhurt, but he didn't try for lion with the bow again.

Now, with his young American bride, Cooper seemed to be embarked on an endless party which eventually led to his untimely end when he drowned in East Africa in shallow water, incapable, because of his condition, of extricating himself. Those with him were unable, for the same reason, to help. I remember him as a man as charming as one could ever meet.

Our neighbor, Frankie Steinhart, who lived in the hollow below the Finca, pulled one of the great social coups of the season when he had the heiress, Marjorie Merriweather Post, owner of the *Seacloud,* the magnificent square-rigger which had once belonged to the Kaiser, and her guests, the Duke and Duchess of Windsor, for a party at their home. Papa hated formal parties and declined the invitation, but Mary and I, who were pals of the Steinhart daughters, Peggy and Ann, went down and met them all. We pulled our own small coup by talking the Duke and Duchess into walking up the path to the Finca to see Papa, whom they had met some years before.

As had the whole world, I had heard much about David Windsor and his American bride, for whom he had given up the England's throne. To me he looked very worn and his fine manners did not permit much insight into his true personality. All in all, he was most cheerful but I could begin to understand the attraction of the fascinating Wally. She was much more attractive in person than in photos. Her features were far from strikingly beautiful but her eyes were truly special as was her voice. The eyes were a shocking blue in a pallid face and were piercing as well as beautiful. Her voice was best described as warm and persuasive. After a quiet talk with Papa, I escorted them back down the hill with a flashlight on the path before the Steinharts had a heart attack. All this led to a later visit to the *Seacloud,* and that was one beautiful ship. The quarters were unbelievably lavish, and we were stunned by the ship's gold service for formal dining.

During my stay at the Finca I had heard a great deal about Freddy DeMarigny and his young wife, Nancy. Freddy had occupied the front pages of the papers for some time when he was accused of, and stood trial for, the murder of his father-in-law, Sir Harry Oakes, in Nassau. Freddy had been unfortunate in earning the enmity of the then governor general of the Bahamas, the Duke of Windsor and former King of England. Freddy was always an operator and, while living in Nassau during the early part of the war, he managed to get around some of the strict currency export regulations to the obvious consternation of the powers that be. After a particularly obvious incident in which he brought back a new automobile and a new Star boat from the States, both items of far greater value than he could possibly have acquired legally, the governors called him in for a direct confrontation, sure they had him dead to rights.

When asked to explain, Freddy told them that, as much as he disliked saying so, he had been unusually well endowed by fate and that whenever he traveled in the States he came across wealthy women who, having heard about his endowments and his prowess, were more than willing to give him large sums of money or other objects he might desire in return for his favors.

The Duke and his deputy stood open-mouthed. Freddy had totally avoided their trap; however, he had not made friends of them either, and when the murder took place it was a decidedly unfriendly government making the key decisions about whether or not to prosecute on very flimsy evidence. It became a *cause célebre* and finally, after a lengthy and tawdry trial, and just when things were looking very bad indeed, two local ladies stepped forward to testify that Freddy and his friend, George, had been on the opposite side of the island *in flagrante delicto* with them; and could not possibly have committed the crime. Freddy and George were such gentlemen they would never have testified to such effect themselves; it would have contravened their code as titled gentlemen. Despite the complete exoneration from guilt, the Duke found it in the best interests of the colony to declare Freddy DeMarigny *persona non grata*. It cast a stigma on Freddy that made life most difficult for many years, but he was a great sailor and a first-rate wingshot and spent some time with Papa in Cuba in his wanderings.

Freddy was in Montreal when Nancy came down for a visit. They were separated and she wanted to spend a few days relaxing in the country. Papa and Mary had made plans to go to Cayo Paraiso in the boat for a week of camping, so Nancy arrived just as they were leaving.

I played host to her and I don't think either one of us could tell you who seduced whom. I guess it was sort of even. The conditions were ideal with the bucolic surroundings of the Finca and we decided that when Papa and Mary returned we'd continue our idyll in the Bahamas where she had a home, a hotel, assorted properties, planes, automobiles, and boats at her disposal.

Papa was furious when he got wind of our escapade and an unsent letter published in Norberto Fuentes' book without permission, (along with every other letter published in it) quotes Papa as saying that "Bumby is sleeping with anything that moves, is hollow and warm." I avoided Papa until he cooled off, but Nancy and I spent several days at an isolated house on Grand Bahama where she flew us with champagne, caviar, and ourselves for company and sustenance. Neither of us found it boring at all.

We flew back from Nassau to Miami with Bill and Ann Woodward in their plane and arranged to meet later in New York. I returned to Havana where, after Papa vented his spleen, we got down to serious talk about my future. It was agreed that I was to go back to school. The GI Bill made that an easy possibility and it was the feeling then that a man without a college education could get nowhere in the world. I mentioned that Papa, himself, had done well enough without one, and in a field usually populated with educated people. He insisted that things were different now and that I must be properly prepared to face the challenges of a new, peaceful world.

I had led such a dissolute life in my last days at Dartmouth that I immediately ruled it out as a possibility. Princeton sounded good, but inquiry revealed that they were accepting no new students since they had given priority to their own returning veterans. I suggested a Western school and the University of Montana became an obvious choice based on its location within easy reach of Sun Valley and the best fishing in that part of the West.

I wasn't yet sure what I wanted to do for a living and, strangely, I still don't know, though I've done a hell of a lot of things, a few of them well. Papa agreed to Montana and promised me fifty dollars a month to supplement my GI Bill money. School was to start in January so I left a bit before the holidays to join Nancy in New York.

Tommy Shevlin had offered me his apartment for my stay there and it was the fanciest setup I had yet enjoyed. I had almost no clothes that fitted any more, so Tommy, who was about my size, told me to wear anything I wanted in his closets. Yes, I mean closets. He must have been the world's best-dressed man. There were easily fifty suits, all specially made for him and they fitted me perfectly. I spent the next few weeks being a social fop and trailing around with Nancy at parties with people I had heard of but never expected to meet, including the social, wealthy and famous from every walk of life.

Nancy was one of several heirs to a large fortune acquired by her father, a mining engineer. He had struck it rich in Canada after being ejected from a passenger train crossing the country. He didn't have a ticket because he couldn't afford it and had only just managed to escape the conductor by locking himself in the john. When he was apprehended and put off the train, he struck out cross-country and, during his trek, he found what turned out to be one of the world's most important gold deposits. The lucky accident made his fortune.

Nancy's wealth attracted many people and opened all the right doors for her, but it did not make her an especially happy person. She could not help viewing prospective suitors, or even friends, with a certain suspicion. Otherwise, she was a lovely person with a great diversity of interests, and we had a marvelous time together. However, it couldn't last for long because I started feeling like a total wastrel. I couldn't keep up my part of the cost of keeping up with her. I was becoming dependent on her even for little things. It would have been all too easy to let go, but, thank heaven, I didn't. We would have ended up making each other very unhappy.

SEVENTEEN

I took the train west from New York to Sun Valley where I planned to recover my old Pontiac. I had a few days before I needed to drive north to Missoula so I stayed with our old friends, Pappy and Tillie Arnold, in their new house on the hill in Ketchum, which Pappy had been busy finishing since his return from duty with the Air Force.

Snow conditions were fair and, although Sun Valley Lodge was still a Navy hospital, arrangements had been made through the management to open the lift on Rudd Mountain for the convenience of a few old VIP guests, namely Rocky and Gary Cooper and their friends, Ingrid Bergman and Peter Lindstrom, and Clark Gable, always referred to as "the King."

I borrowed some equipment and joined the illustrious party for a couple of days of skiing. The lift opening was justified for publicity purposes and Pappy and Til shot lots of footage for film and hundreds of stills.

Somehow the war seemed to have had a most egalitarian effect and I no longer suffered so much from the shyness I had always felt around celebrities and movie stars. Of course, Rocky and Coop made it easy for me with the others and there were few other people around, so no one felt the need to put on any sort of "act." Clark Gable was a real surprise. First of all I had always thought of him as a big, tall man and had even considered that he and Papa had similar physiques. Of course Cooper really was very tall so perhaps it was the contrast, but the King seemed to me short somehow and I would have gauged him at about five-eleven at most. He was warm and friendly but did not appear to me to have the range of interests that Coop had.

Ingrid Bergman and her husband, the surgeon Peter Lindstrom, were a fine couple, and she had that wonderful, healthy beauty so rare in star types. I thought them very happy, and they must have been at the time. Thus, it was hard for me later to visualize her leaving Peter for Italian director Roberto Rosselini. That was, of course, before I got to know any real Italians and learned to appreciate the charm that thousands of years of survival can bestow. Peter was sweet, well mannered and obviously kind but I suppose he may have suffered from the cool detachment of the Swedes. In any case those days spent together were pleasingly memorable for me.

Papa had left a lot of things in storage with the Arnolds and I found my sleeping bag and a fly rod of Papa's, which I prepared to put to use as soon as possible. The folks up at the Sun Valley garage were a bit dismayed that I was claiming my car back for the three hundred dollars they had agreed on before I left. I think they had forgotten all about our deal and had replaced the engine and put on new tires all around. My three-hundred-dollar car was now worth at least four times that amount and they hated to see it go.

After a send-off party with the Coopers and friends, I left for Missoula the following day. The journey from Sun Valley to Missoula is a long, hard drive now and was a lot worse then because the roads were miserable, mostly dirt, and a lot of it was washboard surface which bounced the old Pontiac sideways if I didn't slow down enough in certain places.

I picked up a rider somewhere outside of Salmon who wanted a hitch as far as Gibbonsville, a small stop on the way up the valley toward what is now called Lost Trail Pass. It started snowing heavily and I had to drive very slowly. The rider was strange-acting and seemed a bit like a punch-drunk fighter. He told me he had been with the Flying Tigers in China and was an ace. The way he told it led me to believe him. I think he must have been at it too long and the heavy drinking from the continual strain had got to him. He said he'd been in nothing but trouble since he got back to the States, and now he was headed home to visit the only relative he had left. I just hope he settled down. It looked pretty lonely at Gibbonsville when I let him out under the one light still on at the gas station with the snow falling heavily.

The University of Montana at Missoula was a far cry from Dartmouth but it was close to being paradise for me. Through the school I quickly found comfortable lodging with a nice couple who I'm afraid were a bit shocked by my rather free-wheeling ways. Nevertheless, the Coffees were kind and understanding and made me feel at home during my first days at the University. I found everything there to my liking. There was a year-round trout river flowing through the city of Missoula, and the campus abutted on it. There was even a clear stream, Rattlesnake Creek, which flowed into the river and kept a strip a few hundred yards long clear even during periods of muddy flows in the main river. Of course, it was also co-ed, something which wouldn't occur at Dartmouth for another thirty years. For that, and possibly other reasons, I settled into my studies rather uneasily.

I think I was still very much agog from a long period of over-excitation. I'm not really certain one ever truly returns to "normal" after combat duty in a war. I'm absolutely sure that veterans of long periods of combat in any war, and especially in such a personal one as Vietnam, for example, never truly recover. It takes a long time at best, and I believe the sudden emergence of the 'Nam veterans as a potent force in our society, fifteen or more years later, is testimony to how long the readjustment can take.

In any case, I was not ready for schooling on the old basis yet, though I took full advantage of the wonderful surroundings of Missoula, its fishing, the good friendships made there and, the best feeling in the world for me, the Mountain West. I made up my mind then and there that one day I would settle down in that part of the world and make it my permanent home. It was a plan which would take a long time and incalculable distances to fulfill.

I added to my fishing repertoire that spring, though I'm ashamed to admit I gave in to the newest thing in fishing at the time. Almost no one knew about it yet, save a few veterans who had seen it in Europe, or sophisticated-traveler fishing types who had already seen it eschewed on the chalk streams of Great Britain because of its incredible effectiveness. That, of course, was what attracted me to spinning in the first place. No one yet realized that it would completely revolutionize the sports fishing industry and the outdoor habits of the American fisherman. Nor did anyone realize that it would cause undue strain on the limited resources and would, in many cases, wipe those resources out until the cause was brought under control.

All I cared about then was that, with light spinning tackle it was possible to cast very small light lures farther than most bait casters could throw a heavy lure, which meant showing the small lures most attractive to trout in places where they had never been seen before. For the most part, these lures were spinners with a little weight or wobbling spoons whose flash resembled a minnow and could cause a large trout to strike. A new lure had just arrived on the scene, a small lightweight plug,

Hotelier and fly fisherman Charles Ritz understood
the sport and the tackle as few others ever have,
and was a long-time friend to Papa and me.

(Left) Casting on the picturesque Altier River in France's Cevennes region. *(Below)* We felt we should smile for the camera at the dedication of the Hemingway Memorial in Sun Valley in 1966. With Mary Hemingway and me are, from left, Don Anderson and *Atlantic Monthly* editor, Robert Manning.

Posed with my ancient black
buffalo, bagged on an East
African safari with Patrick,
Marty Gellhorn *(inset)* and other
family members.

(Above) Preparing to net the catch on England's Itchen River. *(Left)* A proud father with 12-year-old Mariel on the Itchen River. (Photo by Dermot Wilson)

That's the author, at left, in Paris' new version of the
Shakespeare & Co. bookstore, in 1977.
(Photo by Dan Callaghan)

(Below) I'm shown here with Dan Callaghan, fisherman, photographer and friend for many years. *(Right)* Posing with the youthful Margot (first name still unaltered) at a fashion show at Sun Valley Lodge.

(Above) The Hemingways at home in Sun Valley. From left, Muffet, Puck, Father Jack and Margot. Mariel was off, as usual, on filming location. (Photo by Tony Korody) *(Top Right)* Margot's Paris wedding brought out family, friends and scores of *paparazzi.* (Sipa-Press Photo) *(Bottom Right)* Fourteen-year-old Mariel was the flower girl at the 1975 wedding.

Our oldest daughter, Muffet, has all
the Hemingway-Whittlesey attributes.
She is the author of two books, an
expert shot and good fisherman, an
excellent cook, a skilled tennis player
and, not least, beautiful and charming.

Observing the style of river keeper
Frank Sawyer on Wiltshire's Avon.
Sawyer was possibly the greatest
nymph fisherman in the world. (Photo
by W. Eugene Rousey)

(Below) Doing what real fishermen do, with Lou Black in Chile, 1982. *(Right)* With my brother, Patrick, in Chile, 1982. (Photo by Carol Hemingway)

Living the good life in Sun Valley, Idaho,
with two of my friends and companions.

one model of which was being made for fly rods: the Helin flat-fish. It was a killer lure and, with a few split shot on the line ahead of it, it could be cast some distance and cover water with fiendish efficiency and deadliness.

I became a devotee of one or more of these lures and must confess that, in those early days when hardly anyone knew about the deadliness of spinning, I had a ball catching bigger fish than I had ever caught, and more of them. I admit to having used these ungodly things on the trout of a dozen of the finest fly fishing streams in America. I regret it now, but I suppose it was part of learning, and I did learn a lot from it — about where big fish lie in big water, and about the way fish take things they attack as opposed to the calm ingesting of foods coming to them with the natural drift of the river.

About midway through my first semester, I made a long weekend trip to Ketchum to visit the Arnolds, stopping along the way to detour west to the mouth of the middle fork of the Salmon River where I spent the night with an old-timer, Gus Peebles. Gus had been there since the depression and liked to have a bit of company in his run-down cabin. He showed me where to dig for the freshwater mussels we all used for steelhead bait in those days. With my spinning outfit, I landed two fine steelhead of over ten pounds which I took down to the Arnolds for some first-class eating. These fish had been in the river since early fall and were close to their spawning time; they didn't have nearly the fight or the elegant silver livery which they display when they first ascend the river from the sea.

Not long after my return, the Coffees found my errant ways a bit too much for them and I had to find new quarters. They were diplomatic about it and even helped me locate new digs with the Russell Smiths where I spent the balance of the term and the first part of the summer. Russell Smith was a young attorney, and I didn't see much of him until salmon fly time when the giant stone flies started buzzing the local rivers before mating and laying their eggs on the water. At that point, he decided lawyering needed a respite and kindly took me out to Rock Creek where he said the biggest fish were caught on one of the local floating salmon fly patterns. It was back to fly fishing, and about time.

The bunyon bug was the local fly of preference and it was fished on the surface but across and downstream like a wet fly. It was made of balsa wood with stiff horizontal wings of horsehair, and it floated and skittered along the surface bringing angry, slashing strikes from trout of all sizes who didn't want the big, juicy salmon flies to get away. I was so intrigued by the behavior of the fish with these flies that I acquired a number of them, and of their smaller counterparts. I wanted to try them in other spots during the summer when they might be used to fool trout feeding on dragon flies and damsel flies (the ones we used to call darning needles) or even grasshoppers. It turned out to be a great idea.

A marvelous summer lay ahead. Papa and Pauline had planned for me to do something useful during the break from college, and it happened to be something right up my alley. Mouse and Gigi would be out of school, and a good fishing trip with their older brother could do them no harm, they felt, and might even do them some good. It also made good sense for us to spend some time together and wander, more or less at will, around the best parts of the country in my old car.

The boys stopped first at their grandparents' house in Arkansas and were put on the train from there for Shoshone, Idaho, where I met them and we embarked on our odyssey. Our only injunction was to stay safe and healthy and to arrive before July first at an address in Seattle where Jay Allen and his wife were staying. Pauline would meet us there and further plans were to be agreed upon then. That left us a lot of leeway and a lot of rivers and lakes to explore and, in my case, to revisit. Papa hoped I would teach them something about fly fishing, and I suppose I did, although we all equipped ourselves with spinning tackle as well.

We headed first for Yellowstone country which I knew ought to be good already, even in early June, because of the clear streams and the warmer waters generated by the hot springs and geysers. In many respects, this was a repeat performance of the summer of '41, with the exception that my brothers were real neophytes, but their enthusiasm was boundless and they learned fast. They were handicapped by my haing got hold of the spinning tackle and, because of it, they did not come along as fast as my school chums. All of us used the spinning gear in many circumstances where it seemed appropriate but, had we not had it available, we would all have been learning a lot more about how to solve the problems which give fly fishing its particular endless charm.

Both boys did learn to cast well, and Gigi in particular

showed flashes of brilliance when we were dry fly fishing on the Firehole River. Unfortunately, that early part of the season was limited in obvious dry-fly opportunities. Had we known it, there would have been fabulous chances for us on the Henry's Fork of the Snake River just a few miles away, but for some reason, probably because writers on fishing in the park had neglected it, I had not learned about it yet. Still, we had some good days with the cutthroat trout of the Yellowstone River and the lake, and we pulled a couple of booboos which turned out to be very productive.

The first occurred when we decided to fish below Hebgen Dam. This was long before the famous earthquake changed the face of that bit of country forever. Where Quake Lake lies now there was a stretch of fine, heavy rapids below the dam which was known to be very productive of big rainbow trout. We had been told that bucktails or streamers were the ticket and all three of us were equipped with a good selection. We left West Yellowstone while it was still dark and drove to a point on the edge of the gorge below the dam at first light. We waded in our jeans and sneakers, since waders were still unavailable because of the diversion of all rubber production into the war effort. We spread out from the first current below the dam to maybe fifty yards below it. Within just a few minutes the two of us closest to the dam both had good-sized fish on the line, landed them, and, casting again, hooked others.

The fish were very long but were thin and snaky-looking and I suddenly felt that something was all wrong. The other brother down below us hadn't had a pull. I looked back toward the bank and could barely make out the shape of a sign but, in the poor light, I couldn't make it out. I sloshed back to shore and as I neared the sign the words "CLOSED TO ALL FISHING ABOVE THIS SIGN" became all too apparent. There is always a tendency for fish to accumulate below dams in unusually large numbers and, in this case, we were there so soon after the end of the rainbow spawning time that we had waded into the territory of a large number of lately-spawned fish, still skinny from losing all their eggs and milt, in the area above the sign. The fish below the sign had already been taken by the early-season fishermen, which accounted for the lack of action there.

The second blunder occurred in the area above Mammoth Hot Springs. There, a narrow road winds down from the high country above to the area where the park headquarters and the homes of many of the permanent personnel are located. We stopped on the road to look over the valley and spotted several small lakes down below us but still quite a way above the headquarters area. It looked like a tough enough climb down to keep most casual anglers out, so we clambered down and in one of the three little lakes we had some of the finest fishing for cutthroat and brookies I've ever seen. Every once in a while it's good for the soul to catch all the fish you want and we all did precisely that, keeping some to eat. They were delicious, and well they should have been. It turned out we were fishing in the water supply reservoir for the park headquarters, a fact which was clearly printed in the park fishing regulations which I guess we hadn't studied clearly enough. I hope the statute of limitations has run out!

After a visit to Livingston, Montana, where we visited the original Bailey's Fly Shop and watched the ladies turning out myriad fly patterns at a rate of dozens per hour, we fished our way north through the country around Missoula and then headed west through Spokane to Seattle.

When we arrived in Seattle, the Allens had a nice treat for us. They had arranged for all of us to go on a two-day cruise in Puget Sound on the motor yacht of a local beer baron. The baron himself couldn't come with us because of another commitment; however, he instructed his brand-new captain to take us out into the sound and up to the San Juan Islands where we would find good fishing for salmon. I didn't think it would be my kind of fishing but, however it turned out, it would be a pleasant change of scenery as well as a chance to see what Pacific Ocean salmon fishing was all about.

We started out late in the evening and the captain, a suspiciously young fellow who introduced himself as "Just call me Skipper," first exhibited his shortcomings by his near-inability to maneuver the yacht into position to go through the locks to get out of Lake Washington and into Puget Sound.

Jay Allen was Papa's old friend from the Spanish Civil War days who had spent a year in a Franco prison for his published views on the war despite the fact he was an accredited foreign correspondent. He regaled us with the story of Patton's landing in Sicily, which he had witnessed. He told us the landing was filmed some time after the assault waves had hit the beach. Patton wanted to look good when he waded ashore through the light surf but fell ignominiously several times, and, in each case, ordered the film destroyed and went back out to the assault craft to do it again until the cameraman got it right for posterity.

We went to sleep believing we were in competent hands and awakened to the information from the skipper that he was completely lost and had no idea where in Puget Sound we were. Of course, we were within sight of land, and there were obvious landmarks from which he could have taken sightings, and he had charts, but he was lost. Unbelievable as it was, the man was a total incompetent. We never reached any of the places we had expected to see. He just managed to get us into one fishing port where we saw some fresh salmon which had been caught by local sportsmen and they were, indeed, big and beautiful.

We tried trolling, but the "skipper" couldn't find a trolling speed at which the enormous flashers we were trying would even function properly. When we returned a day early, glad that we'd done so without mishap, we thanked our host profusely, but I believe Jay had in mind to inform him that he had been duped by a charlatan when he hired his new captain.

Jay was good enough to contact someone in the State Fish & Game Department to give the boys and me some accurate information on our best chances for getting in some good fly fishing for steelhead. As it turned out, their information was first-rate, for which I'll always be grateful. They told us the two best bets over the Fourth of July weekend would be either the Kalama River or the Wind, both of them in the southwest part of the state. Finding the Kalama literally changed my whole life, though when we got to the mouth of the river where the old highway crossed over, its appearance gave not the slightest indication of what we would find upstream.

We checked in at the motel just off the Columbia River Highway with the propitious name of "Camp Kalama: Home of the Steelhead." Its owner, Billy Cain, was a giant of a man with enormous arms and shoulders, and became a close friend of mine over the years. When we told him we were fly fishing, he sort of snorted, but told us anywhere above the falls would probably be okay, but that we should be sure to park well off the road because there might be logging trucks going by, despite the long weekend.

As we drove up the valley, we could see that it was a lovely little river, crystal clear with a great mix of pools, riffles, and chutes. There was a falls which we couldn't see from the road, but we knew the exact distance and, soon after, we saw the river again and parked at the first convenient turnout. We really had no idea what we were looking for, since the river didn't look at all like the North Umpqua where I had acquired my limited experience of summer-run steelhead. We all had reels with backing and the new nylon floating lines, heavy gut leaders, and a selection of Paul Stroud's squirrel tails. I was trying out a new type of no-click reel using a combination of leather and copper disks for a clutch-like drag, called the Arnold. It no longer exists, but was a predecessor of some of the modern clutch-brake, big game fly reels of today.

The spot we picked looked deceptively easy to get into and to fish. We looked down from the road into a stretch of water in the tail-end of a deep corner pool with a narrow, fast rapids extending well downstream into a series of shallow pools until it disappeared around a bend to the lip of the falls. The last slow part of the tail-out looked shallow and easy to wade. Our first difficulty was getting down to the river at all. The steep bank was a solid mass of blackberry creepers, each of which seemed determined to grab and hold us and, failing that, to tear through our clothing to bare skin. Being the most horse-like in appearance and build, I broke trail and the three of us inched down to the water's edge.

When we reached it, the water turned out to be much deeper than it had looked from above. What caused the deception was its extreme clarity. Also, the current at the tail-out was much heavier than anticipated. Neither Pat nor Greg was tall or heavy enough to try getting across. Consequently, they decided to work down along the shingle bordering the rapids and fish the shallow pools below. I decided to try to make it across the lip of the tail-out in what looked like the shallowest part before the current sped out into the river proper.

It was about 4:30 in the afternoon and the sun was still shining on the water when I got to the other side with a feeling of some relief. I had almost been swept away more than once on the way across and ended up down in the rapids. Now I was out of the water and I decided to work my way up as far as I could into the pool above so I could fish toward the steep bank we had come down. Farther up it was steeper yet and, from where I was, it looked like a natural holding area for fish to lie-in without having too much current to fight against after having ascended the rapids, but before entering the deeper part of the pool.

I decided to concentrate on this last hundred feet to the exclusion of all else. I had a deep conviction that if anything dramatic were to happen, it would be in this stretch or not at all. I started fishing it carefully, foot by foot, casting across, mending line to slow the drift as I had read in books on Atlantic salmon fishing. I went through the water I had chosen twice, thoroughly, while the sun was still on the water. Nothing. There might as well not have been a single fish anywhere in the river.

Suddenly the sun was gone below the ridge of fir trees and the whole world around me changed. I felt the river come alive and the very air seemed charged with expectancy. I was about a third of the way down the tail-out, opposite a six-inch-thick snag jutting out about six feet over the current. I was casting a long line with the fly landing lightly just above the snag. Because it was drying in the air on the long backcasts and floating when it landed, I jerked it to pull it under so it wouldn't drag along the surface. The fly slashed across about two feet of water before dipping under, then the surface erupted with an explosion which sounded and looked like a boulder being dropped from above.

My rod was bent and, after the fish came rocketing out of the water, somersaulting the while, line was speeding off my reel without the slightest sound except the singing whish of it as it cut through the water. My new clickless reel had eliminated the greatest cliché in fishing: the screaming reel! I was fast to a bright summer steelhead, one of the two finest freshwater gamefish a fly fisherman can encounter, the other being the Atlantic salmon.

After a series of jumps and long runs, each progressively shorter, the fish was ready to be led into the shallows on my side of the river with its head farther up the bank, I reached down with my left hand and grasped the wrist just above the tail and shoved in the same direction. When the steelhead was completely ashore, I put down my rod and almost jumped on the fish, I was so overcome with excitement and awe at its size and beauty. I had managed to stay relatively calm during the fight, though I was worried a couple of times the fish might be headed all the way down the rapid. Each time, though, it turned and came back into the pool. I knew I had been lucky at the start, not to be holding the line with my left hand trying to bring it in. If I had been holding the line at the start, I don't think I would have had the presence of mind to let go fast enough to let the fish get directly onto the line coming off the reel.

After knocking it on the head with a rock to make sure it was dead, I stuck my finger in the gill and carried it back to the edge of the trees where I hid it and covered it with ferns before returning to my spot. The next cast to almost the same spot brought a repeat performance, an almost identical fish, thirty-two inches long. It joined its twin under the ferns.

When I prepared to try once more, a steelhead jumped farther up in the deep part of the pool and a series of giant boils rolled in the stretch I had been fishing. My hands were shaking now and I returned to the fray, but this time the fly came around below me before it was taken with a great tug which took line right off the reel. This fish was a little larger than the other two and ended up in the rapid where I had to follow it and landed it in the first of the shallow pools below. Pat and Greg, who had been below all this time, witnessed this last battle, the third of three on three consecutive casts. I have never had such a thing happen with steelhead in all the years since. What a way to be introduced to summer steelhead on a fly!

By the time I gathered up my catch it was dark and we returned to the motel where I proudly showed the fish to Billy Cain. He just grunted and said we ought to try it in the winter when the big fish were in. His indifference was deflating to say the least.

After a fruitless try in the same place early the next morning, we headed down the coast, first for a visit in San Francisco with some cousins of Pauline's, then down to Los Angeles where we were put up in the studio cottage behind Jinny Pfeiffer's lovely house in the hills above Hollywood. Jinny, Pauline's younger sister, was a many-faceted lady who never married despite no shortage of beaus throughout her life. She had accompanied me on one of my early crossings from Europe to the U.S. and I remember admiring her ability as a skier in the early days of the sport, as well as her daring in being one of the first people to pilot an autogyro, the precursor of the helicopter.

Taller and slimmer than her sister, Jinny had a wealth of

friends all over the world and presently was sharing digs with a fine concert violinist, Laura Archera, a handsome Italian blonde who later married Aldous Huxley. Unfortunately, in those latter days they all became involved in Huxley's perennial fascination with mind-altering drugs which did nothing for their health, not to mention their longevity. To the extent that they helped lead the way for Timothy Leary, they were, in my view, precursors of a national tragedy of immense proportions.

After our enjoyable visit in Hollywood and the City of the Angels, it was time for the boys and me to be off to Idaho to spend some time with Papa.

EIGHTEEN

August of 1946 was a fine time to be in Idaho. Mouse, Gigi, and I arrived a few days before Papa and Mary and we settled in at the McDonalds' log cabin motel just south of town. Since Sun Valley was no longer comping the rooms so generously as they had before the war, Pappy and Tillie Arnold had organized rooms for us at the motel. Averell Harriman's departure from active participation in the Union Pacific for his spectacular diplomatic and political career had left the railroad, and the resort, in far more prosaic and less imaginative hands.

Averell, an athletic and ruggedly handsome young man who was invariably tanned as dark as boot leather in those days, loved the valley and knew its true value as a magnet for the world's skiing and outdoors-loving elite. He had really known how to run a resort, as well as a railroad! It had become a bottom-line operation as was apparent in the increased formality between employees and guests. Prior to the war, the employees, who were mostly local Idahonians, were encouraged to mingle freely with the guests, and their easy-going, natural Western good manners were a big plus, even among the many sophisticated guests from the Eastern establishment and the entertainment world who frequented the resort. But now all that was changing.

Tillie and I drove into Ketchum one morning soon after we arrived and stopped at the Alpine for a cup of coffee. On the way to the table, we paused to chat with Sepp Froehlich who was sitting with an auburn-haired woman and a breathtakingly beautiful, dark-haired creature with blue eyes whose name I didn't catch. I was so taken I just stared and forgot to listen when we were introduced. When we got to the table I asked Tillie the girl's name. Puck Whitlock, she told me, and I jotted it down in my file, permanently noted, especially after I saw her leave with her aunt and noticed the spectacular length of her legs.

When we got back to McDonald's cabins, there was a message to call Pappy Arnold at home. Papa had called from Casper where they had stopped for the night. It seemed that Mary had become gravely ill with what turned out to be a fallopian pregnancy. She had been near death but had come through okay after a crisis when Papa refused to accept the intern's verdict that he might as well give up on her, and resuscitated her himself. Papa wanted the three of us to come up to Casper on the bus and train and said to bring the fishing tackle since we would have to spend some time there while Mary recovered sufficiently to get on with the trip.

When we got to Wyoming we found that Papa was completely tied down to Mary and wasn't able to come out fishing with us. Because of the circumstances, he had arranged with a local railway engineer, named Blackie, to take us out to a stretch of the North Platte River below Black Canyon in an area now covered by Seminoe Reservoir. Blackie was a big-fish specialist and fished with copper and brass spoons, the backs of which he had painted in garish patterns of red, black, and brown with yellow spots. He used bait-casting tackle and was known locally for his expertise and the many big trout he brought home.

I paid the price for my cockiness after the three steelhead on the Kalama. Using the spinning outfit, Patrick caught by far the largest fish of the whole trip, a beautiful rainbow well over five pounds, while Greg and I made do with much smaller fare using flies. In those early days of spinning, there's little doubt that a lot of unusually big fish were caught simply because they had never been cast to before. Nowadays, they all get cast to and either learn to do a fair job of distinguishing the phony from the real or are eliminated from the rolls early in their lives.

There wasn't room in the Lincoln for all of us when Mary was well enough to travel, so Pat, Greg, and I headed back to Sun Valley the same way we'd come, except that Papa drove us to Green River in the old Continental. It was the last time I remember riding across a vast section of the West with Papa and it evoked memories of those great trips from Florida when we were little. We saw a spectacular pronghorn antelope buck between Rawlins and Green River and reminisced about the antelope hunts in Wyoming and Idaho before the war, when I had been the non-hunting fisherman. We remembered shooting the .22 Colt Woodsman at prairie dogs and other targets of opportunity, and we even recalled The Famous Bathroom.

By the time everyone got to Sun Valley, it was almost time for me to get back up to Missoula, but we had some good times, good food, and good fishing before I left. Papa was obviously proud of his sons and seemed to take special pleasure in our love of the outdoor sports he enjoyed so much, but, now that Mary was convalescing, his absorption with her was almost total and we weren't able to spend as much time with him, or enjoy the role of being his sons, as much as we would have liked. Mouse and Gigi didn't seem to feel it so much as I did, but being older I sensed acutely the distance that comes between fathers and sons, and realized that these days were precious. The hours we spent laughing with Papa and sharing experiences were to be important ones for all of us.

I had wanted to try the small bunyon-bug flies on Silver Creek and set out to do so both on Sun Valley Ranch and down by Point of Rocks. I found that it helped to coat the leader with glycerine to help sink it, and to grease the horsehair wings so they would float well longer. The method moved some fabulously big fish to the fly, but they weren't often hooked very well, due in part to an inherent weakness in the hooks. They were too narrow in the gap and too weak in the smaller sizes to hook and hold well. Years later, I made these flies myself in Europe with the right hook for the job and they worked to perfection.

That fall I had a new home in Missoula in the LeBarons' basement with a roommate who was a serious student and a forestry major. I saw little of him but remember his going out before dawn one morning and coming back at 8:00 a.m., having shot and dressed out his bull elk and hung it where he could get it that evening after classes. A place where such a thing was possible couldn't be all that bad.

I started going down to Sun Valley on weekends. That's over 600 miles round-trip: the sort of thing you can do in the West. Patrick was staying out of school for a year and Gregory had left for school back East, but my principal objective was to see that beautiful young widow, Puck Whitlock, who had moved up from Twin Falls in September to take a job as assistant to the purchasing agent at Sun Valley. She had dated George Saviers a few times and I ran into her while she was on a date with Bob Sherwood. I'd asked her to dance and got her to go out on a late date with me, and that was the beginning of my downfall. Within two weeks we were talking about marriage, and she even came up to Missoula with a friend for a football weekend.

For me it was a serious courtship, but I began to be hampered by two conditions beyond my control. One was her loyalty to the memory of her husband, a young lieutenant colonel in the 8th Air Force who was shot down in his B-17 over Kassel on his second tour of duty overseas. He had completed a tour in North Africa, serving under Killer Kane in support of the British Eighth Army, and later in the daring raids over the Ploesti oil fields in Rumania.

That was something about which I could do nothing but exercise patience, and hope for the best. The second impediment was the oncoming winter weather and the consequent heavy snowfalls which made it increasingly difficult to cross the two mountain passes separating me from Sun Valley. This was something over which I could exercise some control.

Papa, Mary, and Pat had left for New York to shoot at Gardiner's Island with Wolfie before heading home to Cuba. A storm had closed both Galena and Trail Creek summits for the balance of the winter, and Lost Trail Pass was temporarily closed. Furthermore, my old Pontiac had finally bit the dust with a thrown rod and it needed repairs which were way beyond my means. I got an offer for the car which was twice what I had paid for it and that would stake me for a while.

The lady in Sun Valley seemed much more important to me than an education, and I was damned if I was going to hang around Missoula all winter waiting for the passes to clear and then try to hitchhike down to visit the girl of my dreams. I did the only logical thing for a young man in love. I quit school, crammed all my belongings in a duffel bag, and took a bus the long way around, by way of DuBois, down to Idaho Falls, and over to Twin Falls, where I caught the Sun Valley Stage. I moved into McDonald's cabins where they gave me a good rate, then I started looking for a job.

Sun Valley was getting ready to open for its first season after the war. My first job was on a clean-up crew, running a floor polisher. The pay in those days was a pittance, since they had an oversupply of eager young college students who would take the winter season off to work at Sun Valley for practically nothing in return for a ski pass. I can't remember what that job paid, but it was less than the prevailing minimum wage and wouldn't begin to pay my rent at McDonald's cabins.

Puck's job included room and board at Sun Valley Inn, so I went to Win McCrea, the Lodge Manager, and asked if he had any job openings. He let me know a few days later that he could give me a job as a bellhop which, while the pay was only fifty a month plus room and board, presumably included a substantial income from tips. I jumped at the chance and started my infamous career only a few days before the official opening. I had to learn the location of all the rooms, the right way to treat people, and how to wait patiently until they realized they had forgotten something: the tip. I hadn't expected to go back in uniform so soon, but it was an experience to remember, if only for its lessons in human nature. Let me assure you, a bellhop becomes a pretty good judge of character and often gets insights into the seamier sides of his clients' personalities.

It soon became apparent that, while I was a proficient bellhop, I was not getting my share of the good tips. The reason was that I already knew a substantial portion of the better-known and wealthy guests on a first-name basis and, while they were happy to have me serve them, they were embarrassed to tip me. Believe me, carrying on a courtship on fifty-a-month and few tips was difficult at best. So as not to hamper my comrades' style, we arranged that I would disappear whenever one of the known big-tippers was due to arrive; that way the others could take care of the affluent patrons and get their tips and I would take all the secondary guests, and what we called "dimers."

The only thing that made the courtship possible was that Puck was so attractive that the local gambling casino owners, knowing she was a local, and knowing the fix I was in, would let us win more often than we should have, and would even point us toward the slot machines which were about to pay off.

McCrea finally came to the rescue and promoted me to desk clerk. The pay was now a hundred and fifteen a month with room and board, but no tips. Furthermore, I had to look presentable all the time, so Puck and her roommate came to the rescue and ironed shirts for me, I had come up in the world but was still in a form of limbo. The best thing about the job was that I was now privy to the infamous housekeeper's report which revealed, indirectly, who had slept in whose room and all sorts of tidbits of that nature. I could have done without it.

In those days, we workers ate in the employees' cafeteria, a run-down Quonset hut we walked to, sniffling and coughing from the occupational disease known as the Sun Valley crud, a lingering winter cold which wouldn't go away unless you were out in the sunshine on the mountain, something which was rare for most of us. Puck and her roommate shared a room with two single beds, but I continued to sleep in the Lodge basement in a room with hot water pipes running all through it. I was on a top bunk with a pipe right over me and would either sweat all night or freeze, depending on whether my pipe was turned on or not. I also had to sit up carefully or hit my head. Still, it was worth it.

Some time in March I got into trouble. I had had an argument with Puck over nothing and gone into town by myself where I proceeded to tie one on. Later, when I was well on my way, she showed up on the arm of one of my good friends. I went over to them in a totally illogical jealous rage and started swinging at her date until someone broke it up. Unfortunately, word got back to Sun Valley that I had been drunk and in a fight. McCrea, bless his little heart, was told to fire me and he assigned the job to his assistant, Morgan Heap, who took half an hour skirting the subject. Finally, I said, "Morgan, are you trying to fire me? If you are, why don't you say so?" He nodded his head and it was done without putting a black mark on my record.

Puck was pretty sore at me and I was at a loss about what to do. She had decided to leave Sun Valley at season's end to try to get a job as a stewardess with United Airlines. She already had an application pending and was waiting to hear from them.

Since my departure from yet another university hadn't exactly thrilled the family, I decided to patch things up with Papa and set off on the world's longest bus ride, all the way down to Key West. In Key West I drove the Crosley Pauline had bought for the boys. It was a tiny car, and about a week later they were both hurt in an accident in it. It hadn't appeared serious at first, but it turned out to have set off some serious medical problems for Pat, and, after I left, he and Greg went down for R&R in Havana.

My visit with Papa was a bit tense but he could always be counted on to come through with help. He remembered an old friend from the Spanish Civil War who lived in San Francisco and who might be contacted about arranging a job for me there. Ramon was in the import/export business, which interested me because I thought I might be able to use my language skills; however, it turned out he had just taken a new job with Gantner and Mattern, a textile and swimsuit company, as head of their foreign sales operation and there was nothing for me there. His wife, on the other hand, worked for the City of Paris department store and said she could get me work there until something more auspicious came along. All this planning was done by telephone and cable and ended up with my going to San Francisco, again by bus, where I stayed with Ramon and his wife, in their row house out by Ocean Beach. I took the streetcar in every morning to punch the clock at the City of Paris where I had the title of "assistant to the buyer" in the record department but was, actually, a plain old stock clerk.

Before it drove me up the wall, I actually learned to produce a running inventory using 4x5 cards, recording each purchase and preparing the necessary paperwork. The only saving grace of this otherwise tedious occupation was the discount I was given in the gourmet department which had a wonderful selection of fine wines and exotic foods. But, even with the discount, I couldn't afford it. In my correspondence with Puck, I learned that there was a chance she would be sent to San Francisco by United after she finished her training in Cheyenne. I knew the store was a dead end for me and started trying to think of something in the line of outdoor sports where I would have, at the very least, an intrinsic interest.

NINETEEN

I don't remember just how we met, but Peter Auer was a young man with the same fishing hunger that I had and, furthermore, he had ideas. A Marine Corps veteran, he was a native San Franciscan who had a small back-alley apartment on Telegraph Hill which he rented from his family for next to nothing. He was married, but not happily, and he wanted to get out of his store job with Roos Brothers, even though his job was at least in the fishing tackle department. He knew all the fly shops in town and had a wide acquaintance with sportsmen in the whole area through mutual interests and through his job. He thought that we could make a go of it tying trout flies for a living and selling them to the stores in the area, trying to build up our custom business over a period of time. The good money was, of course, in the custom work because the markups are high, and the price you could get from the stores was painfully low considering the time, skill, and effort involved in making flies of high quality.

I made the break with the City of Paris and, early that summer, with a small grubstake from Pauline, Peter Auer and I started our new partnership, Auer and Hemingway Flies. It was a crazy business which operated from his apartment. I had to leave periodically when his wife was out so he could have a rendezvous with his girlfriend. Going out meant going down the street to the Black Cat, a precursor of the many gay bars that now bedeck the area. My awareness of such things was not particularly well-developed at the time and it was some time before I caught on to the nature of the establishment. A friend of Pete's ran the place and they served great, thick, roast beef sandwiches between slices of sourdough French bread for next to nothing if you had a beer as well. When the bar was crowded you might have to put up with a little good-natured pawing, but mostly these people sensed where your interests lay and left you alone if you weren't interested in doing what they were interested in doing. Amusingly, one of the people I ran into there was Freddy, the black corporal from the 780th MP Battalion who had been to Oxford. He was temporarily between jobs as a movie actor.

Pete and I went fishing often, far too often for the business to become successful, as it turned out. Once, we went up to Fall River, a beautiful spring-fed stream which I desecrated with my spinning outfit. Another time, Pete, his girlfriend, and I took the bus up to St. Helena to fish a spot he knew in the upper Putah Creek Canyon called Hell's Half Acre. There was a pretty blonde girl on the bus who knew Pete and, first thing we knew, she was coming with us instead of going to spend the weekend in Little Switzerland, a resort on Clear Lake farther north, even though it was made eminently clear to her that we would all be camping out together. She turned out to be a free spirit and was good company, though she hadn't the slightest interest in fishing. Pete and I fished to our hearts' content, catching lively small-mouth bass in every pool, both spinning and fly fishing with streamers.

It didn't take long to find out where my blonde's interests lay. The location in the bake-oven-hot canyon called for frequent cooling swims, and it turned out, of course, that none of us had brought swimming suits. None were needed and the nearest other humans were miles away, across one of the most desolate pieces of country I had ever seen. The situation with Puck was uncertain and, in any case, it would likely be several months before I saw her again, and then only if I were lucky. Anyway, you know how it is, kids will be kids.

The fly-tying business was certainly going better than we had expected, and a new wrinkle came along in the form of some new steelhead fly patterns that Peter Schwab developed and wrote about in one of the outdoor magazines. The new tie attracted a lot of attention in the West Coast fishing fraternity. It was essentially a bucktail, but was tied with a copper, brass, or silver wire body both for the flash it provided and for the evenly-distributed extra weight which helped get the flies down to the level where steelhead were then thought to prefer having their meals presented to them. Actually, late in the season when the water becomes very cold and the fish less active, chances are better when you can put a fly right in front of their noses. At any rate, those flies became a very hot item and, since they were difficult to tie well, and most people didn't know where to get the right wire, we did quite well selling them on special order for a dollar apiece, and we could each turn out about six to eight an hour. For us, this was big money. The only catch was that it was a flash in the pan and didn't last.

What finally made the fly-tying business lose its allure for both of us was an order we received through an orthodontist friend of Puck's family in Twin Falls, Dr. George Grover, a fanatic fly fisherman who practiced in San Francisco and had given us some special-order business. His brother owned a chain of drugstores scattered through the Sierras, and George prevailed on him to give us all his fly business. The price was more than fair, but the problem was that the order was so large and the diversity of flies so small (100 gross of only three patterns in two sizes) that we almost died of the utter boredom which set in. In addition, the time by which they had to be delivered was so short we found ourselves tying twenty hours a day without ceasing. Our backs and eyes were giving us fits, and our mental attitude deteriorated by the day. Friends would come in bringing cases of beer and would party all around us while we slaved away.

Puck was at last assigned to San Francisco and had a new roommate, Cappy Jones, to share an apartment up on Sacramento Street. I hardly had a chance to see her during this period. By the deadline for delivery of the flies, we were able to deliver only about three-quarters of the order, but we were paid for it, and we continued to operate but our hearts were no longer really in it. We found out what can happen when you try to earn your living doing something you truly enjoy for its own sake but have to compromise your values in doing it. Our total earnings from the giant order had been around eight to nine hundred dollars apiece and we had taken two months to earn it. Meanwhile, we had lost a lot of the custom business which was the most lucrative and interesting. I could see that the best way to be in the fly-tying business would have been to have others tying for you in a situation which would allow you to have real quality control. Anyone doing so should have gone through something like we did just to learn materials and the true differences between a well-made fly and a piece of junk, just so he could then teach and supervise others.

That fall, Pauline came out, and so did Mary. They had become unlikely friends during Patrick's illness. When Pauline had gone to Havana from Key West to visit her ailing son, she and Mary had struck up, first an uneasy, then a quite comfortable friendship. Patrick was now at Stanford and we all got together for a Thanksgiving dinner at Puck and Cappy's apartment, substituting pheasants Mary had brought from Idaho for the traditional turkey.

That fall also saw Puck's first exposure to steelhead fishing when Peter, his girl, Puck and I drove up to the Klamath River while the weather was still warm. In those days the river fluctuated in level daily because of releases from the Copco Dam. I was on a bar fishing the far side of the river and asked Puck to go back to camp and fetch something I had forgotten, which she was pleased to do. When she got back she had to swim to get across the current to where I was wading. The river had come up without my realizing it, but she proved her grit. Crab-walking together, we managed to get back without a further dunking. She never complained about that, but she did express strong reservations about sharing our privacy with Peter and his paramour.

Puck had a short leave coming up during the Christmas holidays. She was too tall to be a stewardess and settled for becoming a reservation agent, but her talent soon led to her promotion to secretary to the chief of reservations for the region. When the vacation rolled around, we elected to drive back to Idaho to see family and friends and, for me, to spend Christmas with Papa.

Papa, Mary, a gaggle of friends, and not a few sycophants, were in Ketchum for the holidays. Some had been there through the fall as part of Papa's private hunting party. One of the visitors at this time was Lillian Ross, the writer, and *New Yorker* editor Harold Ross's daughter, who was there wrapping up her interview with Papa for her forthcoming profile of him in the *New Yorker*. The profile was not based on just this interview but on several more contacts, including a hectic day in New York. The New York interview, in particular, turned out to be a mistake of the first magnitude, not because Lillian Ross was untrustworthy, quite the contrary. After several meetings, Papa felt so at ease with her that he let down his guard and behaved in a manner that was usually reserved for family and close friends, using a sort of play-talk which varied with the seasons and from year to year. But Lillian had an ear like a tape recorder, and what came out on paper was so literally accurate it sounded completely phony. Literal transcriptions can utterly distort the essence of a personality. At any rate, the profile made him look ridiculous, and I am as certain as he was that such was not Miss Ross's intent.

Over the next few weeks, Puck and I discussed marriage further, and she was adamant that I must find something more substantial than what I was doing before we could make plans. It seems strange to recollect that the magic figure we reckoned added up to economic security was $300 a month. I agreed with her, but I simply didn't know what direction to follow. Papa came to the rescue once again and suggested that I come down to Havana where his friend, Charles Ritz, would be visiting in late March to fish for white marlin. Charley was the son of Cesar Ritz, the founder of the Ritz Hotel, and he had a shoe store to satisfy his mother who ran the hotel—and her family—with an iron hand; but the shoe store was really a front for a nearly full-time preoccupation with fishing, principally fly fishing. Charley had many friends in the fishing tackle business and was highly respected the world over as an authority on fly fishing; Papa thought he might be able to make some solid suggestions for solving my dilemma.

It was a good plan and it gave me time to put things in order in San Francisco and dissolve the partnership with Peter without rancor. While Puck and I were very much in love, she was a very level-headed girl and the conditions she laid down were only reasonable. In my view, she was such a prize that I didn't want to delay too long for fear of losing her. The same went for long periods of absence which, I was all too aware, didn't necessarily make the heart grow fonder.

The visit to Havana went well and I was delighted finally to meet Charley Ritz, who turned out to be a fiercely energetic, wiry little man who, once his enthusiasm was aroused, would stop at nothing to accomplish a goal. Since the problem being posed to him now involved his friendship for my father, he set about finding a solution with characteristic vigor. Within a week he had lined up a position for me as a sales trainee with the Ashaway Line Company in Ashaway, Rhode Island. It was a name known to everyone who fished at all and they had a fine reputation for quality. I was delighted at the prospect and was quickly bundled off to Ashaway, a tiny manufacturing hamlet just outside Westerly and only a few miles from the Connecticut state line.

The Crandall family were Ashaway in every sense. It was a

company town and the Crandalls were the local aristocracy. They were very kind to me and I started work in the office of their subsidiary sales office, Ashaway, Inc., where I was taught the ropes, from a cursory view of the line manufacturing processes to how the books were kept. I also learned about the structure of the sales organization, the products, prices, customers and how to deal with them.

In the process, there was some time for fishing for trout locally and a couple of times for striped bass in the Cape Cod Canal and the local surf. I never did catch a striper there, but I will never forget the sound of the frenzied feeding of a large school of bull stripers cutting through bait fish on the turning tide. The sound literally echoed off the stone embankments of the canal.

The best time we had, though, was a day of fly fishing for shad on a small stream between Providence and Fall River. It was my first encounter with shad. They weren't as strong as trout, but they were very fast and beautiful jumpers. Moreover, the roe were delicious when prepared fresh.

After a while, I was sent into the field with one of the young salesmen, Lloyd Riss, who had a territory which included part of Pennsylvania and upstate New York. His home was in Dubois, in West Central Pennsylvania, where he showed me some of the fine fly fishing which was just starting to recover after years of pollution from poisonous mine tailings that seeped into the local streams making them unfit for any living organism, including trout and the food on which they survived. At that time, some of the operations were cleaning up their act, but most had just gone out of business since the end of the year. The poisons just finally leached out. We visited the famous fisherman's paradise at State College, which was one of the few experiments in no-kill fishing, and where there were giant trout in the flume below the weir where the flow goes under a footbridge and on through the town. You could feed them and see them roll to chunks of hamburger or even bun.

In addition to calling on dealers and jobbers, we spent a week at the outdoor show in Buffalo where we did demonstration casting with the new slip-cast reel, a perversion of a spinning reel which Ashaway, Inc. was marketing. I was actually engaged in the spread of spinning in America. The show was interesting and I first met Joan Salvato there. She was already a champion bait caster while still in her teens and is now known as a great teacher of fly casting along with her husband, Lee Wulff, the iconoclast of fly fishing.

The firm finally decided I was ready to send out into the field. The job they sent me on was as ideal as a young man could ask for. I was to call on dealers from Southern California all the way up the coast to Washington and then cover the principal market areas in the interior parts of the West. Initially, the job was purely what is called in the trade "missionary work." Essentially it involved introducing and doing goodwill work with regard to the slip-cast reel. I was to report to a brother-in-law of Julian Crandall's who lived in the Los Angeles area.

The whole ideal would have been wonderful had it not been for a number of factors over which Ashaway had no control. The first of these was that I needed a car and, since funds were short, I had to settle for a used one, a fairly new Dodge. This is not meant to cast any aspersions on Lee Iacocca. This was way before his time, and this baby had been one of the first built after the war. The best I can say for it was that they did a sloppy job. It broke down halfway across the country and I had to wire the home office for money to effect the necessary repairs to the engine. That's not the best way to start a relationship with your employer.

Another problem is best illustrated by an incident that took place when I stopped by the North Umpqua to revisit the site of my first encounter with a steelhead. I was on my way north to Portland and, this time, drove up the river from Roseburg, Oregon. The road up the river from Glide was still terrible and unpaved. I arrived at the junction of Steamboat Creek late at night and, worn out from the drive, rolled into my sleeping bag and went to sleep, then awoke in the pre-dawn with a craving to fish.

I'm ashamed to admit that I was in the upper boat pool at first light using the spinning outfit and a small silver devon, an English spinning lure. I was in the process of landing a nice steelhead when one of the people from the camp across the river came out to fish. He was very excited about the fish and hollered over at me that he'd like me to drive across the bridge to the camp and bring the fish with me. I was pleased to do so but wondered a bit why.

Anyway, I got there ten minutes later. The fellow from the pool was there and introduced himself as Loren Grey. He introduced me to Clarence Gordon and his wife and the other guests who were just getting ready to have breakfast. I was invited to join them and they were delighted to see the fish, as it was the first to be taken from the camp water that season. I had read about the camp in Ray Bergman's book and was happy to accept their invitation to spend the rest of the weekend with them. Clarence took me aside and asked me if I knew anything about fly fishing, and when I said I did he went on to ask how in the hell I could stoop to fishing with that godawful spinning outfit.

I assured him I would never use one again, and I borrowed Clarence's outfit to fish the next couple of days. Clarence did me the great favor of taking me through all the camp water himself and showing me how he fished each stretch. Another day, one of the guests, a professor from Salem, was kind enough to take me down the trail with him and show me the many pools downstream. We each lost a fish on the first jump in Takahashi Riffle, a fastwater holding lie just above a steep chute and named after Loren Grey's father's Japanese cook, a man who was reputed to have caught many more North Umpqua steelhead than his employer, the famous writer Zane Grey.

You can imagine that it was less than comfortable to be traveling about in fishing circles promoting a type of spinning tackle in which I did not intrinsically believe. Its only real value was that the veriest duffer could become a dangerous fish killer using it. The trouble was that if everyone started to use it, a lot of damage was going to be done. What I didn't realize then was that this kind of tackle would convert literally millions of nonfishermen into fishermen-of-sorts by its ease. In some ways this was good but, until management methods could catch up to the new reality, the fishing resources of the country were going to take a hell of a beating, and I was contributing to the problem.

A further complication to the success of my new job was the fact that the central interest in my life was in San Francisco, in the form of one Puck Whitlock. An awful lot more of my time was spent in the Bay Area than was really justifiable, despite the fact that she encouraged me to get with it when I ought to be working.

By the end of the summer, I was driving down the coast when I stopped off in Carmel to see the Jay Allens. Their son, Michael, was a few years younger than I and wanted a ride down to Los Angeles. It was a presidential election year and one of the candidates was Henry Wallace. There was a rally of Youth For Wallace on the beach that night at Monterey. We decided to go and hear what they had to say. I never heard such rabble-rousing. These kids were not card-carrying Communists, but they were sure doing a job for the ones who were. I was less than impressed when, after the last speech, the young fellow who had been the loudest of the rabble-rousers came over to us and started talking. He seemed nice enough and it turned out he needed a ride south as well. We asked him to join us, and he did. We drove all night along the winding Coast Highway, and he never ran out of juice about how the masses had to rise and redistribute the wealth, and on and on, ad nauseam. When we came to Santa Barbara, he said we could leave him off in town, but we insisted on taking him all the way to his destination, which turned out to be one of the giant estates. That kid was just one of the series of people of his time who were assuming some sort of guilt for being brought up rich and wanted the rest of the world to pay for it.

Before I reported in to my immediate boss in Huntington Park, Michael Allen and I had a quick foray south of the border in Tijuana where, to use the vernacular, we had our ashes hauled. Michael turned into a fine man and his father would have been proud of him. When I last saw him, he was the pastor of a flock at St. John's Church in the Bowery in New York City and had a fine family. When I go to church and a man of God speaks to me about sin, I like to think that he knows what he's talking about.

My mission on the Coast was over and it was time for me to head back to Rhode Island to face the music. I got there in time for the annual company clambake. It was no secret that I was not the man Ashaway, Inc. had been waiting for to put them over the top in sales. The question was, would they break it to me gently or harshly? The picnic was an unqualified success and so was the drink that accompanied it, in which I participated freely. I had not received my marching orders but I suspected that it would be soon. I got a bit carried away and at some point I suggested that possibly the best thing that could be done with Ashaway lines would be to make tennis string out of them. I did not mean that as a creative idea but rather in a pejorative sense. I can only say that years later when I saw Julian Crandall again at the Ritz Hotel bar in Paris, he bore no ill will toward me and even sent me a selection of their newest lines to try. In the meantime, Ashaway junked the idea of a slip-cast reel and capitalized on the burgeoning tennis market with one of the first artificial racket strings to gain wide acceptance. I like to think that my remark that afternoon on the beach might have had something to do with it.

TWENTY

It was now the fall of 1948 and so far I had met only dismal failure in everything I had set out to do since the end of the war. I had found the right girl but I hadn't been able to find the right means to support her in the style to which I would have liked her to become accustomed. Further, I had already used up a lot of credit with my father and I was sure that he, too, was disappointed in me. First for failing to complete my education, and then for not sticking to any of the various projects he had helped line up for me. I was determined now to make my own way without help and to achieve my primary goal: making a living in a satisfying way and being able to support a wife and family while so doing. Just about the only thing for which I could give myself any credit was that I continued to be a perennial optimist and so remained cheerful despite circumstances that seemed to forbode a gloomy future.

Geographically, the two parts of the world that stirred my imagination were the Mountain West in the U.S.A., and Europe, especially France. Puck and I had pretty much eliminated the West because of the lack of opportunity for a person without capital resources. We both knew what it was like punching a time clock for a big employer and therein did not lie the answer. The logical course of action for me was to try to get back on active duty in the Army. It was, after all, the only trade for which I was suitably trained. My financial resources were limited but adequate for the purposes, so I decided to go to Washington, D.C. to mount a one-man campaign to get back in. It was a lousy time for it, since the Army wasn't especially anxious to increase its size, and congressional pressure was strong to reduce military spending dramatically despite the obviously increased importance of maintaining a strong stance against Soviet expansionism.

I had lost all touch with the old OSS people and my first tack after establishing residence at the Downtown YMCA was to contact Bob Thompson. Bob was living in Alexandria and told me he was occasionally involved with helping research some historical data about OSS but had lost track of most of our mutual friends. The intelligence business was undergoing multiple birth and growing pains at the time and a number of different agencies were vying for top spot in the territory. The CIA was just getting started under some other acronym, and it appeared that, for me at least, the best direction to go was the Army, where, with a bit of luck, I might even be able to return to active duty with my old rank of captain.

The trick, of course, was to avoid like the plague any assignment to occupation duty in Japan or Korea. I was able to make a few contacts through Helen Kirkpatrick and Bill Walton who put me in touch with a lady who was personal secretary to General Omar Bradley. She kindly promised to do all she could and I finally had my orders to return to active duty and to report at Fort Dix, New Jersey for reassignment to West Germany. I was elated and called Puck to tell her the good news. She was as pleased as I was and agreed to fly to New York for a farewell weekend together before my departure on December 10.

The weekend was a great success from my point of view in that Puck agreed definitely to come over the following summer to marry me. The only drawback was one of those storms of the century which brought the New York traffic to a total standstill. While walking to one of our destinations where we had planned to dance, Puck fell and sprained her ankle, so we had to make do with eating and drinking. Both the Jay Allens, who had a *pied-a-terre* in Manhattan, and Gerald and Sarah Murphy entertained us while we were in the City. Gerald even took me down to his company, Mark Cross, and gave me a very fancy Val-Pack case and presented Puck with a shoulder bag. When the visit was over, Puck and I said our sentimental farewells and she boarded her plane for the Coast while I headed south to New Jersey.

Fort Dix was a let-down. Being a bachelor officer, I was assigned to troop duty on the base before boarding the ship to Bremerhaven. It didn't take long to get back in the swing. I pulled duty on board ship, got back to spit and polish, and the Army way of doing things.

Though heavily influenced by its large U.S. Army population, the old city of Marburg was a lovely town and I took the opportunity to climb the steep footpath to the old castle where politico-religious history had been made in the 16th Century when it served as the site of a meeting between Philip of Hesse and Svingli, signalling the beginnings of the Reformation.

My assignment came through almost immediately, to my surprise. I was to report to the S2 Section at Berlin Military Post, an innocuous sounding title at best. S2 meant intelligence, but I had no idea yet that the job I was getting into was one of the Army's principal operations to try to get to the top of the heap in the intelligence game. In fact, for many years I didn't realize what a power struggle had been going on during this period for ascendancy in the intelligence field.

What I did find out very quickly was that the city was a hotbed of intelligence activity. The Berlin Blockade had been going on for some time and the airlift was in full swing. The tempo of supply flights into the various Allied airports in Berlin was frantic. Even coal was being hauled in by cargo plane, both to keep people warm and to try to maintain what rudiments of an industrial effort the West Berliners had been able to resurrect from the wreckage of their city. I learned that Berlin is a very special place and that Berliners are as different from other Germans as New Yorkers are from the rest of us. They have a special toughness of character, a sense of independence, and a sense of humor which is often lacking elsewhere. When John Kennedy went to Berlin years later and said, *"Ich bin ein Berliner,"* it meant a great deal more to them than was apparent on the surface.

My first job was as one of the security officers, which involved processing security clearances, establishing and overseeing security procedures for various installations and units under the jurisdiction of the Commandant of Berlin Military Post, and whatever else Lt. Col. Pretty, my boss, wanted me to do. I was billeted in a beautiful large villa in the best residential section of Berlin with a mish-mash of fellow officers and civilians, including one career State Department officer. We had a fine cook to prepare our meals and were issued rations from the commissary for the purpose. There was a powerful *Katrinka* who cleaned house and made our beds and a fireman to shovel coal into the furnace. There was also a plethora of clubs for officers and civilians in our immediate area and out at Wansee on the lake. In short, Berlin was pretty easy despite the blockade.

As my responsibilities multiplied and I became privy to more and more of the activities going on, life in Berlin also became more exciting. The city in those days always had about it a feeling of tenseness. Almost invariably at the many parties

the subject would come up of what one would do should the
Russians decide to take over Berlin or should it be overrun as
a part of an all-out Soviet invasion of Western Europe. These
fears were very real but you had to be there to feel them. All the
partying and drinking were more desperate in their underlying
tone than is common even in military circles. The fact of the
matter was that, living in Berlin, we were far more conscious,
all of us, that this was not peacetime as was believed by most
people at home, but that we were already engaged in a very real
war, albeit a "cold one."

My new duties included becoming the principal liaison officer with the French Forces in Berlin, with particular emphasis
on intelligence liaison. Unfortunately, there had grown among
the U.S. military hierarchy a deep distrust of the French, as it
was felt that the impermanent nature of their government,
which was changing frequently during this period, had permitted penetration of their military services by Communist sym-
pathizers. The strident voice of McCarthyism did nothing to
make them more trusting. If anything, suspicions were exacer-
bated by our own national fretfulness at home.

My own relations with the French were on a much more
practical level. My principal contact on a regular basis was one
of their counterintelligence chiefs. It had just worked out that
way because we both shared a deep love of fishing, as good a
basis for friendship and cooperation as any. He took me out on
numerous occasions in his boat to fish for pike on the Tegeler-
see in the French sector and showed me his favorite shore fishing spot in the wide moat around the Kronprinzenturm which
connected to the larger lake on one side.

Several times we did good business on these fishing forays.
The directives from the Department of the Army under which
we operated precluded such nasty bits of business as assassination and torture. Consequently, there occasionally arose situations where we became aware of ongoing treachery on the part
of agents in our employ. In one particular instance it became
apparent that one agent was selling the same information to
three Allied customers under three different identities, in
addition to which, it turned out, he was a double agent.

He was the sort who was well-enough known in his own circles that a message needed to be sent. At one of our fishing sessions the subject happened to crop up and the fact that we
Americans were not in a position to deal with him as effective-

ly as the situation warranted was made clear to my friend. "Worry not further about it," he told me, and we went back to casting our Voblex spinners along the reed beds.

Soon thereafter he showed me the clipping in the paper about the unidentified corpse found floating in the canal. Without elaborating further, he mentioned that the pike should grow larger in that stretch of the canal. One of the more gruesome fish stories in Berlin was to the effect that, in the last days of the Third Reich, the SS had driven a large crowd into a shelter located near one of the big canals and had then set off a charge which collapsed the wall of the shelter nearest the canal and the people had all drowned. The "joke" was that, ever since, the biggest pike in the city were to be found in that part of the canal.

I had hoped that being stationed in Germany would afford me lots of opportunities to fish some of the fine trout streams there. Now, here I was in the only place in Germany where this was not possible casually, such as on an off-duty weekend. Because of the blockade, everyone coming in or going out of Berlin had to do so under written duty orders, and space on the flights going in and out was at a premium. I could usually wangle a couple of days of delay en route (military for time off), which I used to good purpose with my fly rod, but it took a special occasion to give me the freedom I wanted on the trout streams.

On one occasion, I was assigned to a movie company as a technical advisor for a part of their film which involved dropping an agent behind enemy lines in Germany toward the end of the war. I was assigned to them for a week in Munich. When I arrived, the director called me in and asked me about my own experience and I explained that I understood that the methods used in occupied France were different than those used toward the end of the war, and that it was likely that something on the order of a Bristol Beaufighter would have been used for a night delivery. He said it didn't make any difference anyway because they had already decided to use a C-47, and wouldn't I like to join them all for drinks and dinner at the *Fier Jahre Zeiten?* I did and that evening met Eartha Kitt and Orson Welles, among others. They were quite a pair—a witch and a warlock. She was an enchanting witch, with her wit and hypnotic sensuality. He was a powerful warlock, whose mesmeric voice, you'd swear could "call up spirits from the vasty deep."

I was no longer needed as an advisor, so I spent the balance of my week attending the needs of a number of trout and grayling in the Ammer River above the Amersee and proved to my satisfaction that the bunyon bug, small version, was just as effective a deceiver of German salmonids as it was of the Western U.S. variety. I also discovered that the beer of Weilheim, the town where I was staying, in a small *Gasthoff,* was magnificent with a deep amber tint and a real kick, quite unlike the pale variety available to us in Berlin at the time. It was my first time off alone in a completely German community without the company of English or French-speaking friends. It felt strange but fascinating at the same time, and I think that I might very easily have acquired a facility in German had I been able to live there on that basis.

In the meantime, plans were being made for Puck's arrival in Europe in late June for our wedding. My mother and Paul had taken charge of the French end of things altogether. There was a fantastic amount of paperwork involved, especially so because of Puck's status as a widow which, in the French view of things, managed to complicate the issue unbelievably. Fortunately, Paul was a master of diplomacy and of the ways of French bureaucracy and managed to have everything organized for a late June wedding in Paris. Mamie was in charge of the guest list and the social amenities.

In Berlin, meanwhile, I had put in for married quarters and was assigned a nice two-story house within a couple of blocks of the officers' club, my office, and the Free University which was then just getting on its feet. My financial status had been on the debit side by a considerable amount when I arrived in Germany. Now I had a fairly substantial credit surplus, and I'll explain how.

One of the first things I found out after my arrival was that there was, literally, no funding as such for the intelligence operations our section was conducting. Agents, just like other folks, don't function for you in the name of love, patriotism, or any other ideal. It helps if they have that sort of idealogical motivation, but money of some kind is what makes the wheels turn. We were, in effect, forced to operate in the black market with the benign understanding of the Counter Intelligence Corps. (CIC), one of whose responsibilities was to try to curtail black market activity among the Armed Forces.

We were issued additional supplies of foodstuffs, coffee,

cocoa, sugar, tobacco, cigarettes, and whiskey, and expected to turn these into the cash we needed to operate. In many cases, of course, the people with whom we dealt preferred to receive the commodities directly and deal for themselves. Others preferred dollars or Occupation Marks. We had to be ready for anything. What we did have in plenty was the facility to establish safe houses at no cost and to maintain them with special funds. I don't believe I met one person during the period of the blockade and airlift who did not participate in the black market to some extent or other, and that includes the wives of both civilian and military personnel. The rumor around when Commanding General Lucius D. Clay and his wife left was that they had an entire freight car filled with the "spoils of war," not a small part of it in Meissen china.

I had just a small stake to start with, but since the mails were being used by everyone to order such items as one-pound bags of cocoa or coffee from mail-order houses which had gone into business purely for the purpose of filling the U.S. Army niche in the market, I started ordering those common items which were rare and valuable here. In the six months prior to Puck's arrival in Paris, I managed to pay off all my indebtedness and to have enough left over to pay for our honeymoon, and then some.

Two of my billet mates were in the Quartermaster Corps and their wedding present to me was two 100-pound sacks of coffee beans. When it came time for them to return to the States, both declined and volunteered to stay in Germany. I have little doubt that they laid the foundation for substantial personal fortunes during the immediate postwar years in Berlin.

*   *   *

June 25, 1949 was the wedding date. Two of my fellow officers in S2, Lieutenants Shankman and Kelly, came down with me to participate in the festivities. Because we were to be married first in the *Mairie* (local town hall) of the VIIth Arrondissement in a civil ceremony and two days later in the American Church, there were festivities before the first ceremony and in the intervening days as well. Puck looked absolutely wonderful and had a beautiful tan acquired at home before her departure. Because Mamie knew Puck was tall, she had made a point of getting hold of her friend, Julia Child, to be the matron of honor. Julia is over six feet tall. She and her husband were both ex-OSSers, and Paul Child was now working in Paris for the Marshall Plan. Her sister Dort (for Dorothy) is six-five and Bob Shankman squired her around during the festivities. He was about five-feet-six, and when the two of them got out of her little MG TC and stood up, crowds would gather and stare in awe at the wonderful mismatch.

Both weddings took place as scheduled and the only problems were my mother's in trying to keep Puck and me apart during the two-day interim between the civil and the church ceremonies.

We received a number of congratulatory cables including one from Papa and Mary in Havana where he was working hard on his new novel, Across the River and into the Trees.

The reception was held at Mamie and Paul's apartment, only a short walk around the block from the church. David Bruce, the U.S. Ambassador and former chief of OSS, Europe, honored us with his presence, as did many of Mamie and Paul's old friends, some of whom I remembered and some not. But the hit of the reception was Alice B. Toklas. I remembered her as one of the two giant women gargoyles of my childhood. Now she had turned into a chattering little bird who moved without cease and came through the reception line three times, pouring out an endless cacophony and sparkling conversation laced with questions she never gave either of us time to answer. Moreover, she brought a lovely gift of an antique silver chalice. It had not been that long since Gertrude Stein's death, but Alice B. seemed to be doing just fine.

There seemed to be no end to the flow of champagne. It turned out Mamie had wisely chosen Dick Meier, an old friend who bought champagne for a living, as one of the first invitees. But whether it was the champagne or just my delight in finally bringing my lovely bride to the altar, spirits were high and it seemed to be as fine a wedding as any man and woman could ever want. And since we still feel that magic together all these years later, it must have been a charmed affair.

We all drove out to Crécy in the early afternoon and, after a few photographs had been taken of us by the garden wall by Paul Child, Puck and I started off on our honeymoon in Paul and Mamie's late-model Pontiac sedan, alighting the first night at a tiny country inn on the west side of the Loing River just above an ancient stone bridge. The scenery and almost everything else was lost on us. The champagne and the pernods we had at our table in the back garden beside the river did us in.

I think Puck first began to realize what she had gotten herself into when the rumor of possible fly fishing for Atlantic salmon reached us at our honeymoon hotel in Gavarnie, high in the western Pyrenees above Lourdes where Paul had reserved a room for us. My immediate reaction was to decamp from the beautiful alpine valley where the local trout seemed only interested in maggots and seldom exceeded six inches in length. We headed for Oloron-Sainte Marie where the Gave d'Aspe and the Gave d'Ossau join to form the Gave d'Oloron, the only obstacle-free tributary of the Gave de Pau and the Adour River, and where our native informant claimed the salmon were running.

We found an inexpensive hotel in town on the river which then had a Michelin star. I set about making inquiries in the local tackle shop about a possible salmon guide. We were directed to a young man who was anyone's dream of a guide. He was a full *chef de cuisine* in Chamonix during the winter season and returned home to Oloron every year for the spring and summer to fish for salmon professionally. French salmon fishing at that time suffered from an ailment inflicted on it during the Napoleonic period when, in an effort to achieve some semblance of naval superiority, salmon netting rights were given out in perpetuity to those who would sign up for a life-long naval career. These *inscrits maritimes* were limited in the amount of time they could extend their nets but there were excesses and the salmon resources suffered greatly.

The Gave d'Oloron was one of the few rivers where there was still a viable run of salmon and, along with the Allier in the North, provided most of the domestic table salmon for French kitchens. The netting season closed before June and the price of salmon rose sharply then in the marketplace, along with the sudden decrease in supply.

Enter our guide, Jean Terens, who, with his sixteen-foot-long Calcutta two-handed fly rod and giant antique brass reel with oiled silk fly line almost as thick in the mid-section as a lady's little finger, was a first-rate classic wet-fly fisherman and knew the river well enough to average two fish a day for the balance of the season. These smaller summer fish averaged around fifteen pounds and the going price was then the equivalent of $3.50 a pound. That came to very big money then and, fortunately, Jean was the only one around who consistently did that well. The beauty of it was that the water was low and clear and the salmon absolutely refused the lures constantly being presented to them by the spin fishermen. Flies presented near the surface were the ticket.

We had several wonderful picnic days with Jean and his wife and their four-year-old boy who took a shine to Puck and kept kissing her in the ear, much to her consternation. Watching the two women trying to converse with everything from sign language to sand drawings was a sight, but the picnics were delicious. I never caught a salmon but enjoyed watching Jean land several on the giant rod. Puck and I went several times alone but were warned by Jean not to leave anything around on the shore while we were fishing. There was a local character called *l'Américain* who would steal anything, including a fish, if you left it on the beach. He had gotten his name because he had once traveled to America and never ceased speaking of its marvels.

At the conclusion of our honeymoon, I took Puck with me back to Berlin to set up our house and start our new life together. Despite the lifting of the blockade during our stay, life in Berlin was a bit of a culture shock for her, but she adjusted quickly and was well accepted by my group of friends and associates. And apparently something else had taken root, and she soon showed signs of impending motherhood.

TWENTY-ONE

We stayed in Berlin for another year and a half. My involvement both in nefarious and multifarious activities expanded to include a fascinating job as a member, as well as an interpreter, on an allied planning staff where we dealt with the harsh realities of what might be done in the event of a Soviet takeover or the overrunning of Berlin. The only problem with the job was our mid-day meal at the British A mess, where luncheon was preceded by Guinness stout, accompanied by claret or hock, and followed by port. Needless to say, afternoons were most unproductive.

We used up our leave time in travel and fishing expeditions to the Zone, as we called the rest of occupied Germany, or to Paris where we met Papa and Mary on one occasion and enjoyed some fine days at the races and visits to Harry's Bar. They stayed at the Ritz but we made do with more modest accommodations at the nearby St. James and Albany. Papa appeared to be in good form generally but I thought he looked overweight and more jowly than I remembered. Drinking in the room, in Bertain's little bar, at George's big bar, as well as at Harry's went on apace, but I must admit I thought little about its significance in those days and only do so now in retrospect. One thing I did notice then, however, was that Papa had entirely given up driving cars himself, probably as an after effect of the accident in Havana.

Puck and I tried to get them to come to Berlin for a visit but they showed no interest. Paul and Mamie had gone home to retire in New Hampshire, but we were favored with a wonderful visit from Pauline, who showed no aversion to coming to Berlin where she stayed with us for a week, the high point of which was our gluttonous consumption of the kilo can of caviar and the Russian vodka she and Puck had purchased at the Intourist store in East Berlin. Being classified as "sensitive personnel," I wasn't even allowed in the East sector. Puck and I were moved that Pauline should be, with just one distant exception, the only member of our family to brave the dangers of the flight to Berlin to come visit us. That was the last time we ever saw her; she died of a previously undiagnosed ailment in the fall of 1951 before our return home.

The other exception was a distant cousin of Puck's who came to Berlin for a short visit from London where he was attending the London School of Economics. His visit created a most awkward situation. The three of us had sat around drinking after dinner in our house on Ihnestrasse. Her cousin had a sharp tongue and, at some point, vented his spleen in no uncertain fashion about some family matter, which infuriated Puck to the point that she picked up her heavy glass tumbler and threw it at him. She missed him completely except for the contents of the glass, but the tumbler hit me square in the forehead causing a bloody gash and a lump of no great consequence but for its extreme visibility. The evening's entertainment ended without further ado, but the following morning was another matter altogether.

I had to make an appearance at General Maxwell Taylor's office to see the Secretary of the General Staff (SGS). As I entered, he gave my bandage a quick look and told me the General wanted to see me for a minute. I went in and reported and General Taylor asked me if I had seen the *Taglishe Rundschau* yet. I hadn't been to the S2 office yet and hadn't scanned the translated German news summary put together from various papers published on both sides of the iron curtain. I had been the subject of a couple of scurrilous and totally apocryphal stories in the East sector papers wherein I was referred to as the evil or villainous Captain Hemingway who was known for torturing innocent citizens of the East Zone in the basement of my home. General Taylor, who was a talented linguist, read me the day's latest report in free translation from the German text. It said that I had taken a taxi the night before and, being in my usual inebriated condition, not only refused to pay the poor-but-honest driver but had also beaten him up, although the driver had succeeded in inflicting a wound on my forehead in self-defense. The whole time the General was giving an occasional glance at my bandage and, when he had finished, asked me what the hell had really happened. Rather shamefaced, I told him the exact truth and he laughed. If he hadn't believed me I would have been in serious trouble. I immediately requested a change in maid-cook and fireman.

On the 5th day of May 1950, Puck gave birth to our first

daughter, Joan Whittlesey Hemingway, at the American Hospital in Paris, where she had spent the previous month in a hotel alone awaiting the birth. She was so tall and regal-looking that the taxi driver who was called to fetch her to the hospital refused to believe that there was any impending childbirth. She scarcely showed at all except for that wonderful skin quality and ripeness of breast with which expectant mothers in good health are endowed. We both had been determined that our first child should not be born in Germany but in France which I loved so much. There had been May day riots in Berlin and I was obliged to stay throughout the high-risk period in which all Allied personnel were on full alert, but I left as soon as I could on the train through the Russian zone of occupation with a good connection to arrive in Paris early the next morning.

The morning of Muffet's birth—for that's what we started calling her—I got off the train at the *Gare de l'Est* and took the first taxi in line. I recognized the driver; I had spoken to him the last trip to Paris when making arrangements for her at the hotel, the hospital, and with the obstetrician, Dr. Ravina. At that time I had been in civilian clothes and the driver conversed with me freely, but now that I was in my U.S. Army uniform, it didn't matter how clearly I spoke, he wasn't capable of understanding a word I said. There must have been a built-in mechanism within him that said, "He's American, therefore he can't speak French, therefore I can't understand him."

Puck looked great and so did the baby. For some reason, one's own babies look great while other people's always seem kind of shriveled up. Puck was breast-feeding her fine the first couple of days but then developed a staph infection and had to switch to formula. In those days in France, they still kept mothers in the hospital for a full ten days following childbirth, so Dr. Ravina told me to bring my wife a bottle of champagne (the French cure-all) and some nylon hose for her nurse and take off for a few days. I was doing more harm than good, he said, hanging around aimlessly.

With that news, Charley Ritz invited me to join him for a couple of days' fishing on one of the famous French chalk streams, the Risle, in Normandy, which flows through the same zone of solid chalk downs which runs across the south of England. A close friend of his had spent years acquiring bits and pieces of the river and at this time owned outright about five kilometers of the most productive and beautiful water. There was a lovely Norman country house with the typical outside beams, Tudor style. There was also a a guest cottage with a thatched roof. The weather was cool and blustery and, so far, there had been no sign of any emergence of the famous mayfly which is known for bringing even the largest old brown trout out of hiding to feed on the surface. The large size and vast numbers of mayflies in the spring constitute a sufficiently filling meal to attract even the old hook-jawed males who spend most of their time feeding on minnows and even others of their kind.

Each guest was assigned a specific beat, or stretch of water, for the morning fishing and then another in the afternoon. Along each beat there were little posts which marked the location of a live-fish basket into which you were expected to release your catch. Twice a day the keeper would come along and either release the fish or kill a few if some were needed for the kitchen at the manor house.

It was all terribly well organized, but what struck me most was how dressed up everyone was. I felt quite ridiculous and out of place in my old jeans, borrowed boots, and my old plaid shirt and sweater. These people all wore plus-four knickers or riding trousers and never took off their hacking jacket and tie, or the wool hats and caps which have only recently become fashionable here in the States. Each also carried a red bandana fastened to his belt at one corner; its purpose was to wipe off any fish slime which might inadvertently get on the hands during the handling of fish. Wading was not permitted because it was felt it could damage the aquatic vegetation, so you knelt to keep your silhouette low and out of sight of the fish.

Well, I must say, despite all their chi-chi getup, most of those folks were damned fine fishermen, and the fish they were going after were as difficult as you could find anywhere, with a sprinkling of very large fish.

The Norman chalk streams, like their English counterparts, are rich in aquatic insect life and they are clear and slow moving. Because of this, the fish get a good look at any fly you put over them and they become finicky in the extreme so you have to know what you're doing to succeed in catching them regularly. It was a great treat for me and I especially appreciated Charley's guidance and the generosity with which he shared his special knowledge. He showed me some nymphing techniques for catching these trout when there was no apparent hatch of flies coming off the water. We did get a hatch of a smaller species of mayfly and I did well on my own when that happened.

After the two days, I was ready to return to Paris and see my family. Robert Capa was in town, so he and Noel Howard, the actor whom I had met on the movie advisory job, showed me around the hot spots and I had a chance to see Magnum Photos' first working office and the system they had set up for selecting the best pictures from among the many thousands that the brothers Robert and Cornell Capa and the other photographers in their early troop were constantly shooting all over the world. Capa explained to me that taking good pictures wasn't the problem, but rather, selecting the great ones that told the story you were after constituted the real art of photojournalism. Although Capa's taste in clothes was suspect in my mind after Papa had entrusted him with outfitting me properly at Abercrombie & Fitch during my prep school days and I ended up in a bright green Harris tweed, he was without a doubt a true master photojournalist.

That turned out to be my last visit with Capa. The last time we'd seen each other before that was in Hollywood where he was doing a stint as an assistant director, just after the war. He was being paid a ridiculously large stipend but wasn't allowed to do anything, so he spent the whole time at the racetrack trying to win back the money he'd lost to his producer who forced him to play, then cheated openly at gin rummy.

Capa's wife had been killed in combat during the Spanish Civil War, crushed between two loyalist tanks she was photographing when they ran together during an attack. Capa was later killed, himself, taking photos in combat during the French war in Indochina. I can't help but come to the conclusion that combat photographers deserve a great deal of respect, and they have mine.

We settled into Berlin life with the baby in fine fashion except for a small error on my part which cost Muffet a small share of her early growth. Dr. Ravina had given me a formula and I fouled up in my translation of grams into ounces which led to the baby's not gaining any weight at all for about a month before we discovered the error. As soon as it was rectified, she more than made up for the initial slowdown.

During the year that followed, we suffered a serious setback which affected our thinking about continuing on in Berlin.

Puck became pregnant again but appeared to be having some trouble and was regularly under a doctor's care. We weren't overly concerned until one night when she started hemorrhaging badly and I rushed her to the hospital where, despite all efforts, she lost the baby which was taken from her by Caesarean section, almost four months premature. We were told that a special kind of surgical instrument which was not available in Berlin at the time would have saved the infant's life. It had been a male child and Puck was broken up about the loss, especially, I believe, because she thought I had badly wanted a boy. It took a long time to persuade her that my feelings were quite the opposite and that I had no particular desire to share my hegemony over the household with another male.

Nevertheless, Berlin had lost its attraction for Puck, and I started trying to wangle a transfer, either to the Zone or to one of the U.S. commands in France. It was not that simple since the manpower situation had become critical with the advent of the war in Korea which had started on that May day just before Muffet's birth. There simply weren't that many staff-level interpreters around and I couldn't be replaced that quickly.

Meanwhile, we had become friends with an American Overseas Airline pilot, Everett Wood, who was an ardent fly fisherman. When returning to Berlin from a flight to the Zone, the Swedish stewardess, Barbro Tholerus, spotted my rod case and told me her boyfriend was also a fly fisherman, and after she had introduced us, Woody, who spoke perfect German, acquainted us with some of the interesting German restaurants in Berlin as well as with the German wines on which he was an authority.

Bob Shankman was being rotated to the States, though he still had a dream of starting a French canal barge tour some day. He had a wonderful, matronly housekeeper who babied him shamelessly and he arranged for her to come to us. Her name was Meta Zielinsky. She had been an assistant to the chef at two different embassies, had been widowed by the war, and had sound motherly instincts. It was love at first sight between her and Puck and the baby, and we immediately became her family.

When Muffet's first birthday rolled around, on May 5, 1951, the three of us had driven to Paris in our first car, a tiny Renault, crossing the Russian Zone from Berlin to Helmsted with some trepidation, and paying our respects at the military cemetery outside of Liège, Belgium where George Whitlock was buried on the edge of the Ardennes Forest. The baby was in a basket which Meta had fixed up for us with a lovely lining and we celebrated Muffet's birthday in Paris at the little Ritz Bar with Bertain Azimont in charge, and after a few of his fresh raspberry and champagne specials we pledged with some new-found friends to foregather in Albi in Southern France for the purpose of avenging the Albigensian Massacre before proceeding on to our vacation destination in Guetary on the Basque Coast. The new friends never showed in Albi so we continued on our way.

When we got back to Paris there was news for me. A message had been left for us at our hotel advising me to telephone the Military Attache's office at the U.S. Embassy. The news was good. Orders had come through for me to transfer from Berlin to 7th Army Headquarters in Stuttgart. I had to act immediately so I left Puck and little Muffet with our delightful friend, Jane Mason, whom I had known from the early days in Havana. I had been with her and her children in her car in 1934 when a *Guagua* bus forced us off the road over a forty-foot embankment and, as we tumbled through the air, Jane had had the presence of mind to turn off the ignition. Despite the trauma of such an accident, we all escaped with only minor bruises, thanks to Jane's quick thinking and a little luck. Now that she was temporarily remarried for a third time to the European bureau chief for *Life* magazine, and living in Neuilly near Paris, she made room for Puck and Muffet until I could return from our new station to pick them up.

Puck told me later she had had a fine time with Jane, being driven around Paris in her chauffeured Phantom III Rolls Royce. On one occasion they went to dinner at Prunier's, the famous seafood restaurant. Her dinner partner had been a young senator from California named Richard Nixon who left an indelible impression, principally for his ridiculous request for California wine and for his fascinating account of the details of the Alger Hiss/Whittaker Chambers affair in the denouement of which he played a critical role.

When I was briefed on my new mission by the G2 and G3 officers (Intelligence and Operations) of both 7th Army and VII Corps in Mohringen, outside Stuttgart, I couldn't believe my good fortune. I was to be liaison officer representing 7th Army and VII Corps with the French I Corps in Freiburg im

Breisgau in the Black Forest. It was a dream assignment in one of the most beautiful parts of Germany, working with the French Army, which suited me perfectly. It was especially challenging at this time because relations between the two armies, while outwardly cordial, were in reality lukewarm at best. This was not only because of reasons mentioned earlier but because the French were extremely sensitive about their stature which had lost much of its luster during WWII and, furthermore, they were already bitterly engaged in a desperate conflict in Indochina which was bleeding the flower of their officer corps and regular army enlisted troops, for which they were getting nothing but criticism both at home and worldwide. Public opinion was already being manipulated against the enemies of Communism by a calculated program of disinformation. The actual level of training among regular army units of the French Army was as good or better than anyone's, although their draftee units were of low caliber. French law would not permit conscripts to be used in any war zone so the professionals were bearing the brunt of the war in Indochina and later would do the same in Algeria. It was little wonder their pride took a beating when American soldiers and officers tended to treat them as inferiors.

My job was to coordinate contingency plans between American units and I Corps, the southernmost of the French Corps in Germany, and to do the same with regard to the annual European Command Maneuvers which were held for a month each fall. Captain John Stockton, a West Pointer who became one of my best friends, was already engaged in similar work with the French II Corps in Coblenz. He was invaluable to me in helping me to get organized properly. On the other hand, I rendered him valuable service and advice on suitable fishing tackle and where the best fishing was to be found, as well as on French wines and other such niceties of life as are not taught at West Point. I was finally getting around to finding out that everyone is good at something.

The hardest part of the move to our new post was getting Meta to leave Berlin where her furniture, all that she owned in the world, was stored somewhere in the East sector. Even though she couldn't take it out, it pleased her to know that at least it was nearby. Her loyalty to us finally overcame her sentiment and we got everything packed for shipment to Freiburg.

Little did we know how long it would be before we would be able to unpack.

Shortly after we left Berlin there was a tragic occurrence within the ranks of my friends in the S2 section. We had actively participated in the smuggling out of scientists from the East to work on Army projects. While awaiting specific arrangements for their new identities and documentation for their families who would join them later, these scientists were often kept for varying periods of time in safe houses scattered throughout our sector of Berlin. Some of our officers worked almost exclusively undercover and, being specialists in the languages of those they worked with, spent most of their time based out of safe houses for their own security and the security of the people they were handling. One of these houses was penetrated by an enemy agent. When I was told about it later, I remembered the man who had been a jack-of-all-trades who was used for odd jobs and repairs around the place. He apparently waited for a particularly important scientist to pass through then executed his plan. He poisoned everyone in the house including all the staff, the scientist, and the American lieutenant who had been in charge of the operation. The young officer was a highly decorated veteran married to a lovely German girl and had done an outstanding job for his country in nearly total obscurity. I was aware that there was a big flap of some sort when I was leaving Berlin, but it wasn't until much later that I discovered what had actually taken place.

Puck was overjoyed when I came back to fetch her and the baby. We soon moved into our temporary quarters in a charming hotel in Freiburg where I had already installed Meta. We had two adjoining rooms with a connecting bath and it would have been perfect if we hadn't had to wait almost three months for permanent quarters. Apparently someone in authority in Heidelberg had kept a French officer waiting unduly long for quarters and, due to the games being played by U.S. and French headquarters, we were forced to endure the same insult. I was assured that everything would be ironed out as soon as the Frenchman was properly quartered, but the two rooms had become incredibly confining during the wait.

General Malaguti, who commanded French I Corps, was a fascinating man. A confirmed bachelor, he determined to make our stay pleasurable despite the difficulties he was being forced to create by higher headquarters. We were frequently invited to meals at his residence where he kept a marvelous staff of servants, including an outstanding *chef de cuisine.* The General liked living well and he enjoyed sharing his lust for life with those about him. He insisted he was a dyed-in-the-wool sportsman, and I was aware of his interest in racing cars and in mountain climbing, but one day he said he also loved to hunt. I knew perfectly well he showed no great interest in it, and his Secretary of the General Staff (SGS) who was a noted big game hunter, had specifically told me the General did not care for blood sports. Nevertheless, he invited Puck and me to join him for *"une partie de chasse."* When we met him at his residence, he personally handed us our equipment for the hunt: a linen-lined basket to carry into the field. He smiled cheerfully and explained that this was the only type of hunting which pleased him: *"la chasse aux escargots."*

We went to some vineyards on the Kaiserstuhl, a hillocky formation which rose in the flat of the Rhine plain not far from Freiburg, and most of the staff and their wives proceeded gaily down the rows of vines picking off snails of a suitable size for a feast to be held a few days later. The wife of the Assistant G2 instructed Puck in the manner of cleaning the snails in a series of cold-water baths before finally snipping out their tiny intestines prior to cooking.

Those first three months in the Freiburg hotel were frustrating because it was impossible for us to take advantage of Meta's fine cooking either for ourselves or to reciprocate the many kind invitations we were receiving from our new friends. It was a beautiful summer there in 1951, and the one way we were able to take advantage of Meta's talents was to go on picnics. She and Puck would go shopping in the German markets and then supplement their selections with delicacies from the French Army Economat, their commissary, where they were able to purchase unbelievably cheap good wines in every quality as well as a broad selection of regional specialties. Meta and Puck would put together picnic baskets to make your mouth water, and off we would go into the highlands of the *Schwarzwald,* the great Black Forest, to any of a wide range of beautiful trout streams.

Once the perfect spot had been selected, Meta would rig a little hammock between a couple of trees for Muffet's little pillow-lined basket. Under French occupation regulations, no stream or river was closed to us and only Allied personnel were permitted to fish. We literally had one of the most beautiful parts of Germany almost entirely to ourselves, except on holidays. Our favorite was the Brigach, one of two small streams which join their minor currents with the flow of a large spring in the town of Donaueschingen to form the source of the east-flowing Danube River. The Brigach was the perfect size for Puck and me to fish together, one on each side, working slowly upstream casting small high-floating dry flies along the edges above us and catching handsomely spotted brown trout up to fifteen or sixteen inches, and nice fat grayling of the same size. Puck was fishing beautifully and could cast very accurately to any spot I suggested to her. She hadn't yet learned to read the water and relied on me for guidance, but she had the natural gift of timing and tightening up on the fish without hitting too hard and pulling the fly out of the fish's mouth, so often a failing among beginners. Sometimes Meta would prepare our catch at the picnic, but mostly we took them back to the hotel kitchen where they were prepared for us in a variety of ways.

My mornings were spent in the office where it was either very busy with reports and documents to be translated, or it was so calm that I would bring out my fly-tying materials and concoct some patterns for the local streams. I had to drive once a week across the mountains and north to Stuttgart to report to my superiors, and eventually I was assigned a German driver and a Mercedes sedan for the job and was able to save my own little bug for our exclusive use. During the course of the summer I managed to organize and schedule several plans conferences between my American generals and the French generals and their staffs. By ironing out points of friction and disagreement in advance and wheedling concessions from both sides, I was able to set up meetings which functioned smoothly and in which both parties started to develop feelings of mutual respect. Eventually, an atmosphere of real friendship and understanding which had not existed before my arrival began to emerge, which gave me a warm feeling of accomplishment.

On one of the weekly trips, I returned by a different route, taking the autobahn to Ulm then leaving it in favor of back roads southeast through the upper Danube basin. I wanted to have a go at a chalk stream I had heard about, the Blau, which flows east and south through docile meadow country from its spring sources to end up in the Danube. The tiny town of

Blaubeuren is headquarters, and when I arrived the air was filled with big mayflies, some of which, when the wind gusted, skimmed the water's surface like fleets of tiny Arab dhows.

This was the first place I had fished in Germany where I saw German fly fishermen plying their art. Although the mayflies had been coming out for some time, and the biggest fish were sated, I had a marvelous time catching some good trout up to two pounds on dry flies of my own tying. I was pleased to note that the German fly fishers I observed, and later met at the little inn, were proficient casters and fished with well-balanced tackle and well-tied flies. The common bond of fly fishing easily overcame the awkwardness of feelings I generally felt toward the Germans in those days.

The SGS, a major whose skills as a staff officer were only matched by his abilities in the hunting field, took me under his wing to make a hunter out of me. Once, he even had Puck and me sitting in a *hochsitz,* a well-disguised tree stand, where we remained for several long hours, from dusk to dark, neither uttering a sound nor even smoking while waiting for wild boars to come out of the woods to a baited area below us along the edge of the woods. We heard the boars in the undergrowth beneath us, but they sensed something wrong or were made nervous by a change in the weather and refused to leave the shelter of the woods to approach the pile of corn cobs. However, the wait was not without its rewards, and we were fascinated by being able to witness one of nature's minor dramas as we watched a fox stalk a hare feeding in the open field, nearly succeeding in the capture.

On several occasions I was invited on organized *battues,* or drives, for wild boar where large groups of the local peasants formed a line and used everything from old pans and spoons to horns and sticks to drive all the wild game in the area toward the line of hunters awaiting them. The hunters were placed about twenty yards apart and could expect anything from roe deer and hares to wild boars to come exploding from the dense cover toward them. Wild boars are courageous and smart, so, when the drive was specifically for boars, we refrained from shooting at anything else and were often treated to the sight of red deer and roe deer halting in front of us, totally oblivious to our presence while they stared in the direction of the oncoming cacophony of the beaters.

I never had the good fortune to have a boar break out on my

stand during one of those drives, but I heard them coming out nearby on several occasions and heard the shots and the hit by other guns and rushed over to witness the death of the savage beasts. Wild boars are one of the few big game animals which inspire no sympathy. They look like the very personification of evil, and their features are those used since earliest times to inspire fear and loathing, in art as in ancient tales of wickedness and lycanthropic transformations. In the art of the Middle Ages, the faces of evil, a wolf's mask, or that of a wild boar are virtually synonymous. It would be impossible to portray them as sweet innocents with Bambi-like eyes and long lashes; therefore, I actually enjoyed hunting them, and to top it all, they are a gastronomic delight when properly prepared. They were hunted year-round but still managed to keep up their numbers and were a plague to the small farmers whose row crops were often ruined by these *Wildschwein,* as they were called.

The most exciting hunt for wild boars I ever participated in was a truly international affair. The French SGS, a German *Jaegermeister* (professional hunter), and I managed to fake a drive when a local farmer called in with a depredation complaint in a wild part of the Black Forest not far from Freiburg near the village of St. Peter. The terrain was precipitous and there was a long ridge, like an *arête,* with one side wooded along its length and the other a cornfield where the boars uprooted the young shoots. The *Jaeger* knew the place and he positioned the SGS and me inside the hundred-yard-wide strip of wood, with me above near the crest and my French friend halfway between me and the lower edge of the woods. He then proceeded by a long, roundabout route to the farm in a hollow just under the top of the ridge where, along with the farmer, he started shouting and making loud noises, barking like a dog, and then loosed his Dachshund who joined in the noisy fray. The SGS and I kept the silence of the dead during the long wait and concentrated our attention on the spacings between the trees ahead of us. All the noise being made came from a kilometer away, but within a minute or two at most we could hear the approaching boars as the galloping sound of their cloven hooves and the stirring of the underbrush grew louder.

Suddenly, there they were, no farther than thirty yards in front of me and coming fast in single file with a rolling, stiff-legged gallop, four of them led by what seemed to me, in that indelible instant of excitement and fear, to be a monstrous big old tusker. I stood up directly in their path and aimed my rifle at the shoulder of the lead boar. Sighting me, they veered off to the right and kept on going. Altogether, I fired four times as quickly as I could work the bolt. To my knowledge, only one of the boars fell. The SGS got in his licks as they darted across in front of him.

We checked the ground and, with some difficulty, found the boar I had knocked down. It was one of the smaller ones but already weighed nearly 200 pounds and had razor-sharp tusks burgeoning from its lower jaw, and was quite able to kill a man if wounded and cornered. There was blood spoor everywhere. The SGS had shot at all three that passed him and said all three were hit but not fatally. When the *Jaeger* arrived with his dog, we found another one, then followed the dog about seven or eight hundred paces to the third, which was dead. But the big one was still out there and after two or three kilometers, with the blood spoor varying from heavy to finally nothing, we gave up and went back to retrieve and clean the first three, all of them about the same size. The dog refused to come to the hunter's call and the *Jaeger* said he thought it would stick to the trail until either it found the wounded boar or the scent disappeared. He felt certain the boar would be reported and that we would receive word before too long. As for me, I had seen more action in a short space of time than on all the previous drives put together.

The next day we found out the final outcome. The dog, one of the unbelievably courageous large Dachshunds, had tracked the boar all the way out of the *Kreis* (county) and had cornered it and stayed with it until found by the *Jaeger* from the next *Kreis* who, quite properly under the local ground rules, claimed it for his own then returned the dog who had been seriously but not fatally wounded. I don't recall the exact weight of the big boar, but it was twice the size of the others. The straight-line distance it had travelled, wounded with the dog on its trail, was over fifteen kilometers from where we had shot it.

The SGS had a part of the ham prepared for each of us, then we had a feast of civet made from the smaller boars and gave the rest away to the sergeants' mess. The previous year, the SGS had shot the post-war record boar for the Black Forest, a monster weighing in at over 300 kilos, or 660 pounds, and not an ounce of fat.

When we finally moved into our permanent quarters, Puck and I were greatly relieved and were able to expand our circle of friends, including a number of Germans, with some of whom we still keep in touch. We also became close with a British couple, John and Bobby Kell. He was the civilian liaison to the French High Commissioner. John was full of stories of government intrigue, but I didn't find out until much later that his father had been one of the most highly respected of Britain's chiefs of secret intelligence.

Aside from the annual Eucom Maneuvers, when I was in the field for almost a month, we had a wonderful autumn in Freiburg. On one particularly memorable day, I accompanied Senator Henry Cabot Lodge on a tour of French forces and was pleasantly surprised to find that he was one senator who spoke perfect French and had no need of my services as an interpreter. But the last day of the giant inter-Allied exercises was particularly stressful for me. Alphonse Juin, now elevated to Maréchal of the French Armies, was no admirer of the U.S. military, and he may have had his reasons. At any rate, at the joint Allied critique, which was held in a large hall with the senior staffs of all three armies in attendance along with several smaller Allied groups, Maréchal Juin embarked on a ten-minute harangue, including some brutal criticism of the U.S. forces and their leadership.

I think it was his belief that there was no adequate American interpreter capable of correctly conveying his candid remarks and he never paused in his delivery, as was the custom when an interpreter was being used. I was the interpreter and, fortunately, I was able to make notes as he went along. When he ended with an angry look in his eye, I stood up and delivered a verbatim translation of his remarks which, fortunately, drew a few smiles from the American leaders who realized the Maréchal had not expected to be translated so accurately and was now obviously somewhat embarrassed. When the meeting broke up, the Maréchal was good enough to send for me and to congratulate me with a twinkle in his eye as he conceded that perhaps the Americans weren't as helpless as he had intimated. It was a highlight in my duty with the French forces and was followed by a fine letter of commendation from General Malaguti to my superiors. Still, while I was doing it I was scared witless from dread of the possible consequences.

There was excellent bird shooting on the Rhine plain and the

French officers' hunting association had over thirty thousand hectares set aside for their exclusive hunting use. I took full advantage of the hunting there and was joined on several occasions by our friend, Woody, and another pilot, John Brons, a midwesterner turned Floridian, whose wife, Penny, was the only woman I ever met who made it unnecessary to have a bird dog along. She had an extraordinary ability to hear pheasants hiding in thickets and would even go in and flush them for us if rewarded properly at the end of the day with her full quota of refreshment.

I had no hunting dog then and it is a tribute to the vast amount of game available that we did as well as we did. Our family dog, a miniature poodle called Bumby, so-named in the hope that, hearing of it, Papa would allow me to grow out of that nickname, came with me once but bolted at the first shot and reappeared only hours later cowering under the car. Since, in addition to pheasant, there were plenty of grey partridge, woodcock, snipe, and waterfowl in the area, I very much wanted a shooting dog, but a tragic event put me off the idea for a long time thereafter.

Puck and I had driven up to Coblenz for a visit with John Stockton, the liaison officer with French II Corps, to do a bit of duck shooting. One evening John and I were to meet with one of the French hunting fraternity at the shooting grounds along a stretch of the Rhine where there was excellent duck flighting and where it was possible to shoot at night against the light of the full moon where there were ducks passing or coming in to alight on a slow stretch of the reed-flanked current. The French officer had a dog, a curly-coated pointer who retrieved well, and he had promised to bring it along. But when John and I arrived at the appointed place and time, our French friend hadn't shown up, and after a full hour wait we decided to go down to the river's edge and station ourselves well apart in such a way that we could see the birds against the newly risen moon just above the horizon to the east.

From up above we had heard wingbeats most of the time we'd been waiting. We agreed that once we were both sure we were in position we could shoot. It was amazing. Every once in a while you could actually see one of the ducks outlined against the moon and you had to swing on it and pull the trigger ahead of where you imagined the duck would be on impact. I dry-fired a couple of times to get the feel of it then shot and heard the bird hit the water out in front of me. I heard it thrashing about in the water and, assuming it was only wounded, I fired again at the spot on the water lit by the moon's shimmering glow where I could just see some splashing. To my horror I heard the pained yelping of a dog. Apparently, our French friend had arrived late and was just sneaking down the bank to join us when the shot was fired, and his dog broke for the water to retrieve the bird. I was standing in the reeds in water up to my knees and never heard a thing. I waded out in the shallow water with the Frenchman at my heels to find his dog, dead, and the duck floating right next to him. It cost me many a sleepless night and almost a month's pay to replace the dog which, unfortunately, had been the family pet as well as a hunting companion.

Among our German friends was a family called Gutterman who owned a thread factory in the little town of Gutach where I sometimes fished the Elz River above the town. The water there was clean and trouty. Frau Gutterman's father was a Scotsman who had been personal physician to the Sultan of Zanzibar in times past and had died before the war. She spoke perfect English but was almost equaled by her internationalist husband whose family operated thread factories in scattered places around the world. I wish I had been able to take him up on his invitation to be initiated in the rite of shooting *Auerhahn,* the capercailzie of Scotland, known for its size and the rarity of its plumage. The *Auerhahn* is supposedly the largest grouse in the world. The hunt is a matter of serious tradition in Germany and is followed by an initiation ceremony dating from Medieval times.

I had an amazing experience while fishing a border stream on the way to the hunting property I had leased that season. I had paid one hundred dollars for the lease but was amply repaid by the sale of the game shot on the only drive I held there. The stream, named the Wutach, is the border between Germany and that part of Switzerland known as the Schaffhausen Enclave for much of its course. What happened there is, I'm certain, nothing more than a trick my mind played on me, but at the time it seemed absolutely real.

I had been fishing one not-very-attractive stretch of the stream where the brush and woods had been cleared on both sides because of its function as a frontier. The stream, however, was productive and I caught several fine trout in the two-pound range when my concentration waned and I visualized this very place as a spot I had been in during my prisoner-of-war time. I clearly saw in my mind the narrow footway crossing above the weir and the attack dog the three of us had killed when he assaulted us as we tried to cross over. The stream had been in spate and we were afraid to wade it because the current looked so deep and powerful, but now I saw that we could have made it across anywhere, no matter what the water level. I know that the vision was only a trick of the mind, but I've tried to explain it to myself by logic and reason and I simply can't. It was like a feeling I'd had as a child in Brittany wandering around the ruins of a Trappist monastery in which sheep were grazing. Within those ancient walls, open to the sky, I had a strong sense of having been there before, perhaps in a past life. Half-formed memories crowded into my mind, too vivid to dismiss. But the vision of events along the Wutach was totally distinct and clear and went considerably further than I am revealing here.

This brings me back to the matter of memory. Many years later, on returning to the sites of some of my wartime experiences, I discovered that certain events I'd have sworn were real had apparently been pure fantasy, and some of the things I thought might easily have been imaginary, were verified in complete detail by other witnesses. The only thing that appears certain in all this is the possibility of the existence of greater dimensions of the mind than those in which we are accustomed to thinking.

TWENTY-TWO

It was the early spring of 1952 and nearly time for rotation back to the U.S.A. During the years we spent in Germany we had taken leave several times to France and, on one occasion, went to Venice with Puck's former sister-in-law, Lynn Whitlock. Papa had told me about the many friends he had there, but I didn't know their names or how to get in touch with them. I remembered that he had stayed at the Gritti Palace so we stayed there although it turned out to be a place not meant for people on an Army captain's pay. Lynn had to help hold up our end as well as her own.

We had wanted very much to go to Spain which was reputed to be very pleasant and cheap, especially if one spoke the language. Because of Papa's well-known convictions about the Spanish Civil War I asked him what he thought about the idea of our going there on leave. He was strong in his opposition and stated that it would be wrong for anyone in the family to travel in Spain since it might be construed as a tacit approval of the Franco regime. I concurred with his opinion and we gave up any further plans to go there despite the strong temptation posed by tales of first class trout and salmon fishing. Because of the dictator's personal interest in fishing, the government had apparently imposed severe restrictions on poaching and salmon netting in Spanish rivers and, as a result, the fishing had improved dramatically. While it was too expensive for most Spaniards at the time, the cost in dollars would have been more reasonable for us than comparable salmon fishing anywhere else in the world. That information was filed away for some future time when the situation in Spain might change.

My orders finally came for our return to the States. After a suitable delay en route, I was to report to a Military Intelligence Group at Fort Bragg, North Carolina. But the first order of business was to show off our two-year-old daughter to three different sets of grandparents in three widely scattered parts of the country. The closest to our point of arrival in New York, where we debarked from the giant troop ship, was Mamie and Paul's house in New Hampshire. Our household goods would be a long time in arriving at Fort Bragg, but we had ordered a brand new Nash Rambler while we were overseas, when it was still possible to get a special deal on American cars, so Puck, Muffet, and I drove directly to Chocorua, New Hampshire for a pleasant visit. Little Miss Muffet was the center of much admiration, love, and attention. Paul took me fishing with him on Tim Pond over in Maine where we caught many fine brook trout, and on our return we hit a couple of small, secret lakes off the beaten path which boasted sizable populations of land-locked salmon, a few of which we caught.

After bidding farewell to Mamie and Paul, we headed on the long drive west to Twin Falls, Idaho for a visit with Puck's parents, By and Horace Whittlesey. They were pleased as punch with their first grandchild and welcomed me into the family in wonderful style. I enjoyed a few days of fishing in some fresh places shown to me by a new friend, Ruel Stayner, who had a good fly tackle shop in Twin. He knew better than anyone what was going on in the fishing scene. After a pleasant visit, it was time to get back to North Carolina. Since our furniture still hadn't arrived from Germany and we didn't know yet what sort of housing we would have at Fort Bragg, we decided that Puck and Muffet should stay with the folks in Twin Falls until those things were settled.

Since there were no interstate highways at the time, the drive from the Northwest to the Southeast was long and arduous. Northwest to South Mid-Atlantic was a morass with interminable stretches of slow, winding roads which seemed to go on forever through the Ozarks, then the Appalachians, on what had appeared on the map to be the most direct route. The only break in the trip was a day-long stopover in Piggott, Arkansas, where Patrick and his new bride were having a try at tenant farming some of his grandfather Pfeiffer's cotton land nearby, although they were already making plans to go to East Africa. After trying that stretch of highway, I decided to take a different route later that summer when I returned for the family, going east then south.

We had hoped to arrange for Meta to come over later on but, despite her attachment to us and little Muffet, she could not bear to live so far from her precious furniture, her only connection with a happier past. Our friend Woody tried his best to get her through the maze of bureaucratic impediments, but she melted under the glare of the uniformed German functionary who asked if she really wanted to go to the United States. "Why would a good German want to do such a thing?" he asked, and she said she'd changed her mind. We deeply regretted losing her; we felt she had truly become a member of the family.

Bragg was much like many other big Army posts and the MI Group to which I was assigned was full of the unlikely people one finds in Army Intelligence. They are truly a breed apart and are often scoffed at by the regulars and "professional soldiers" because the soldierly qualities so admired by the regulars are frequently lacking in Intelligence types. MI people are generally linguists, artists, photo interpretation experts, document analysts, or even economists, and are apt to be casual in appearance, though they know how to get the job done.

My new job turned out to be in Group Headquarters where the S3 was a friend from Berlin who took me in as his assistant. The job involved teaching, training, and setting up training schedules for the unit which was really an intelligence pool for assigning people to jobs worldwide. I was staying in the Bachelor Officers Quarters (BOQ) until family quarters were assigned and there was a long waiting period for the Wherry housing on post. I started spending my evenings at the main officer's club and there I met Major Don Hopper, one of the plans officers for XVIIIth Airborne Corps which was headquartered at Bragg. We became friends right away and he encouraged me to transfer to his organization where I could be on jump status and earn an extra $100 a month, a significant amount in those days. Also, if I were going to make the Army a lifetime career, which seemed likely at the time, staff duty with the XVIIIth was a much better credential. Over the long term, intelligence work tended to be a dead end.

The formalities of my transfer were arranged conveniently so that when I returned from the leave to pick up my family in Idaho, I could start my duties at Corps Headquarters without interruption. I decided to make a quick pilgrimage on the trip west but I didn't want to upset Puck by arriving late so I drove straight through to the Kalama River in Southwest Washington with the aid of some stay-awake pills and a couple of short naps in the car and arrived late at night, slept in the car, then fished early the next morning with two steelhead on the fly to my credit. Then I set out for Twin Falls and again drove straight through before finally collapsing from complete exhaustion at the Whittleseys.

Since we had decided to postpone our visit to Havana to see

Papa until the following spring, I took advantage of our extra time in Idaho to learn even more about the local fishing from Ruel Stayner and, in the process, started an innovation in fishing which was to become a major trend in lake and reservoir fishing throughout the West. Years before, my father had rigged up an inner tube with a seat in it for use in some of the high mountain lakes near the L-T Ranch in Wyoming. The only problem with the device was that there was no effective means of propulsion. Kicking the feet under water created a lot of commotion but little motion. Papa had jokingly called his creation "Christ pants" because they enabled the fisherman to walk on the water, in a manner of speaking.

Now that the war had created the new phenomenon of Army-Navy Surplus stores, I was able to get a cheap one-man life raft and "Pops" Whittlesey, a man with every tool in the world in his basement workshop, rigged up a specially shaped plywood bottom which allowed me to dangle my legs. With the addition of a pair of the newly available swim fins, I was soon fishing circles around the shore and boat fishermen on the many reservoirs in the region. It was a perfect way to fly-fish because you were low in the water and invisible to the fish and could get very close without disturbing them. I could cover literally miles of shoreline while moving along slowly; in those days it elicited some funny looks and comments from the bank fisherman who couldn't figure out how the devil I was able to move around so freely without paddles. Within a few years I started meeting other fishermen using similar systems with the sophisticated float tubes, now the lake fisherman's bread and butter.

After the dry hot days and cool nights in Idaho, the change to our tract house (actually half of a duplex) in the damp, August heat of North Carolina's coastal plains was not easy on any of us, and Muffet immediately started suffering from prickly heat and chiggers. Some fine neighbors, the Eisens, and our new friends, Don and Joan Hopper, soon came to the rescue with advice on dealing with the heat and family morale started to improve even before the cooler fall weather set in. Still, the heat was overwhelming, and some of our best Venetian glasses simply shattered on the shelf from the intense heat and humidity.

My job at XVIIIth Airborne Corps was interesting but dull

once I'd gotten into the routine. I began hearing about a new type of unit that was starting to take shape at Fort Bragg. Despite Don Hopper's warning that, whatever it was, it couldn't improve my prospects for a long-term military career, I started taking a closer look. In the meantime I had to prepare for parachute status by jumping at least once, and then every three months to get my jump pay benefits. I was qualified by virtue of my combat jump in France, but I hadn't the vaguest idea of what to do under normal military conditions, jumping out the door of a C-46 or out the rear of a C-180 flying boxcar. Don, a veteran of more jumps than he cared to remember, took me in hand and put me through a rigorous series of preparatory exercises and practice jumps from a mock-up as well as instructing me in all the basic commands for jumping in a "stick" (the line of men jumping out the door in a straight line, one after the other). The dangers, I learned, were considerably greater than jumping individually or in small groups such as I had done during the war because of the high risk of collision and tangling whenever a large number of people jumped as close together as possible.

My first stick jump was a pay-qualifying jump with other members of the Corp Headquarters staff. I was toward the back of the line and the jump went without a hitch, though the opening shock of the T-7 chute used by the Army was greater than what I had experienced with the British chute used by OSS. While I was at Bragg, the Army changed to the new T-10 chutes which were developed from the British model.

Eventually, word came down that volunteers were needed for the new unit I had been hearing about and I put my name on the list, despite the old Army maxim about never volunteering for anything. I soon heard from Colonel Aaron Banks that he wanted to interview me and, with my commanding officer's permission, I found myself involved with the new 10th Special Forces Group and was quickly assigned to the first class set up for new members at the Psychological Warfare Center already in operation at Fort Bragg.

Since those early beginnings, the Special Forces have become part of the military lore of this country and it's hardly necessary to explain what they were all about. But what I couldn't understand was how the military had managed to go so long without such units, since their effectiveness in special operations had been proven time and again by another entity: the OSS. Perhaps that was the reason. Like any other bureaucracy, the military doesn't easily accede to competition. Once the war was ended and the OSS was terminated, the Army was slow to apply what it should have learned from "Oh, So Social."

At any rate, the school set up for our first Special Forces class was tough, grueling and challenging in the extreme, as it was meant to be. Puck took the changes with characteristic good cheer, but she showed some concern about the possibility of greater danger should I end up with another overseas assignment with the new unit. As it turned out, my performance in the first class was creditable and I was asked to remain with the Psy-War Center to become part of the Special Forces School staff. I would have a chance to help develop some new courses and participate in the drafting of new policies which could be instrumental in shaping the course of events in the future. Since the assignment meant exemption from overseas duty for the foreseeable future, Puck was pleased.

When Christmas leave rolled around, we asked one of my classmates, Lt. Ike Williams, to come to Twin Falls with us for the holidays. Puck and Muffet went by commercial airline while Ike and I hitched rides on military aircraft without too much trouble. The three of us went up to Sun Valley for a day, and a night on the town at the Christiania Club where we were able to renew some of our old friendships, but we spent Christmas and New Year's with the family. On New Year's Day, Ike and I got caught up in some fast and furious pigeon shooting along the rim of the Snake River Canyon, then stopped off for hamburgers on the way home, having forgotten that a big New Year's Day dinner was planned. We didn't dare let on that we'd forgotten, and managed to fake our appetites for the sumptuous repast, but Ike was clearly suffering and Puck, who was in on the secret, kidded the heck out of him.

When I started working with the Special Forces School, Ike stayed on with the original 10th Special Forces Group and later served with them in Germany. Some time later, he left the service and went on to become a highly-regarded mercenary in various parts of Africa, sending us cards over the years with imaginative pseudonyms. When he finally left that adventure-filled life, he settled down to become a successful Florida businessman.

In the spring of 1953 we finally took our leave to visit Papa in Havana. We stopped on the way for a little celebration with the Hoppers who drove down as far as Savannah with us, then we went on to Miami for a short visit with John and Penny Brons and a day of fly fishing for baby tarpon in the canals and lagoons of Everglades National Park. We were fascinated by the house they had built in South Miami with its enclosed swimming pool. That visit started us thinking hard about alternatives to Army life; I was a bit jealous that I wasn't qualified to be a Pan Am captain like John.

The Easter visit with Papa and Mary was exciting because Papa was so pleased with the recent success of *The Old Man and the Sea*. He was in generally good spirits, though I had the vague impression that he wasn't quite so delighted with his new role as a grandfather. Mary, on the other hand, could not have been more forthcoming and she and Puck seemed to enjoy each other's company. Before the arrival of Leland Hayward and Spencer Tracy to discuss the making of a film from the book, we all had a wonderful picnic along the river's edge on the road to Matanzas after which Papa fell asleep from the wine while I fished and Muffet played by the stream under the watchful eyes of Puck and Mary, who talked the whole time.

After Hayward and Tracy's arrival, there were long serious talks about the project and a couple of evenings at the Floridita and a small restaurant just off the Prado where we all had our pictures taken.

At the dinner table of the small restaurant we were all drinking red wine with our food. Papa, Mary, Puck, Roberto, Leland Hayward and Spencer Tracy and I were seated on all sides of a fair sized rectangular table in the rear of the place. There were hurricane lamps around the candles on the table. Leland said, "Ernest, do you really believe it can all be shot here?"

"I know it can Lee. It would be dead wrong to shoot it anywhere else."

"But what about the chance of not getting a really big fish? I know we could get you one off Cabo Blanco."

"It wouldn't be the same but we might have to do that—but we still ought to shoot most of it here for it to be right—maybe for fish though—"

The rest of us were silent throughout this talk. Tracy was polite, pleasant and reserved. On the way home in the station wagon Papa said to Mary, "What did you think, Kitner?

Didn't you think he behaved well?"

"Not a solitary sign of rummyhood," she replied.

"I think maybe this time it will work and if I see to it they get the right fish stuff—"

The hope for a successful shoot turned out in vain as did the conviction that Spencer Tracy was a paragon of sobriety. His arrival for the filming was delayed by a long drinking bout in Miami with production costs soaring because of time lost directly due to his prolonged incapacities from excessive drinking, and his friend Katherine Hepburn kindly came down to use her influence to get him to straighten out. It may very well have been that he was nervous about the role with its extensive scenes of soliloquizing in the boat. But it is to his credit that he did come up with a magnificent performance, despite the difficulties.

My old pal, Joe Dryer, was in Cuba working on a pet agricultural project at the time and we had a nice reunion with him. He had become a good friend of Papa's. Papa took kindly to anyone who was not a phony and was especially attracted to people who had taken part in legitimate combat. Joe used to come out to the Finca for a swim and he had a set of horrifying scars which had been hard-won in an assault landing in the Pacific campaign where he had served as a Marine lieutenant and a platoon leader—easily the best sort of qualifications for Papa's friendship.

Before leaving, we had one fine day of fishing on the *Pilar* along the edge of the Gulf Stream, Papa's great blue river, a day only slightly marred when he grew somewhat testy at one point after drinking because his not quite three-year-old granddaughter didn't respond with sufficient alacrity to one of his captain-of-the-ship commands. I didn't realize until after our visit was over that at no point had I been able to spend time with Papa alone, and I don't believe it was the result of any reluctance on his part. Unfortunately, I would not have a chance to see him again for almost two years.

Shortly after we got back to Fort Bragg, I received in the mail the check awarded to him for the Pulitzer Prize. It was for $500 and Papa had endorsed it to me. Before cashing it, I had a photocopy made. It was the equivalent of five months' jump pay and was much appreciated.

During the course of the summer and fall that year, a serious schism developed between the instructors at the Special

Forces School and the leaders responsible for planning future
policy. Essentially, it involved differences of opinion over
whether our emphasis should be on developing men who were
intellectually qualified to conduct operations behind enemy
lines using indigenous personnel or on training U.S. Army personnel to accomplish missions of a paramilitary nature themselves. Of course, that is an oversimplification, but it reflected
a basic difference in the philosophical approach to our whole
training program. It was the eggheads versus the gung-hos, and
it became a *cause célèbre* which stirred a great deal of bitterness. Those of us who favored the intellectual approach found
ourselves in the middle of a nasty investigation instigated by
members of the faculty who felt we were conducting some sort
of mutiny. After much soul-searching and conferring with my
friends and with Puck, I decided to request relief from active
duty, the equivalent of resigning in protest, and I clearly stated
my reasons for it. The request was granted with regret and was
to become effective in January 1954, but my accumulated
leave time permitted us to pack and leave in late November.
The last words I heard at the school fell from the lips of a career
reserve lieutenant colonel who could not believe that anyone
would risk losing the holy grail of Army retirement with only
nine or ten years to go. As I went out the door he said, "You'll
be back." He was dead wrong.

We headed west in our newly paid-for Nash Ambassador
with high hopes but with little upon which to base them. My
father-in-law was the distributor for Schlitz, Canada Dry, and
Olympia Beer in South Central Idaho at the time and, I must
confess, I secretly entertained the possibility that he might take
me in with him. At any rate, we headed for Idaho and got
across the high country before any major snowstorms made
the roads difficult. We stopped to see Puck's aunts in Pocatel-
lo, on the way to Twin Falls, and were welcomed as usual and
invited for the holidays, along with the offer to have Puck and
Muffet stay over while I went off in search of work.

I took advantage of the visit to spend some time with my
father-in-law down at his warehouse and to try to feel him out
about my going to work for him. He was a very wise man and
he told me of his personal experience early in life when he had
worked for his own father-in-law. He said it was the worst thing
that ever happened to him and that it was a situation that
couldn't work out well. He didn't want our relationship to sour

and he generously offered whatever help I might need to find a civilian career, short of a job. Among the many things he did to help was to introduce me to his friends in a wide diversity of businesses in the Twins Falls area. These men really went to bat for me, and through them I learned a great deal about business in general. From one in particular I developed a greater than passing interest in the possibilities for someone in my position, without a college degree, to make a mark in the investment field. Then and there I started reading from a list of books and other materials he recommended in order to try to learn as much about investments as I could.

I also went to Ruel Stayner for advice, not about business, but about our common interest in fly fishing. I remembered having read in *Field & Stream,* before the war, about trophy rainbow trout winning prizes in the annual *F&S* fishing contest in the "Western Fly-Caught Trout" category, from the waters below the American Falls Dam on the Snake River. A check with Ruel revealed that it was, indeed, a big trout spot and that those fish had been caught during the Christmas holidays. He told me the fishing was done in the forebay but, assuming I wasn't a dolt, he didn't bother to tell me what a forebay was. He did mention that there was a good spot where a current came into the forebay from the side, so that seemed a good enough clue.

Well before dawn of a mid-December day, I headed for American Falls. It was cold but not quite freezing and I made the ninety-mile run in good time. I drove across the road on the top of the dam and followed the first path I came to that went down into the canyon. It was still quite misty, but I could just make out the power company building below me and I headed for the nearest spot which resembled Ruel's description. About halfway down I could barely make out a current flowing out of a wide pipe into a small stream channel and into the side of the pool. That had to be the place. I started fishing with an old worn silk line without any floatant dressing on it so it would sink well, and I used a big streamer to imitate a minnow like the ones I could see schooling in the current where it entered the pool. I noticed the water steaming in the cold air and stuck my hand in it to discover that it was luke warm, which must have been what attracted the schools of minnows from the icy waters of the larger pool. On my very first cast I had a heavy tug on the line and was fastened solidly to a very strong, heavy fish which fought well but didn't jump at all.

When it finally rested on its side, defeated, I was amazed to see that it was an unbelievably fat brown trout, a species I didn't even know existed in the Snake. It was only about twenty-two inches long but weighed 7½ pounds. It was stuffed, absolutely jam-packed full of minnows. I caught no more browns, but I did catch several beautiful silvery Snake River cutthroats, all of them in marvelous condition and running to five pounds. I released them and when I got home I told Ruel and Mr. Tooffelmeir, the editor of the local paper and also a fly fisherman, about my good fortune. I was shocked to learn that I had been fishing below the forebay, which explained why I was alone the whole time. That stretch was supposed to be closed until the regular fishing season. I recalled having seen a crowd of fishermen in another area altogether as I drove home. That had apparently been the place I was looking for. I learned soon enough that there aren't many places where it's legal to fish where big fish come as easily as those did. From that time on, whenever things seemed to be going too well, I made it a point to double-check the regulations and, when possible, to ask around to be sure I was doing the right thing.

Soon after the holidays, armed with a list of securities dealers in the Northwest and some letters of introduction to a few of them, I left the family in Twin Falls and headed west by way of Walla Walla to drop off Puck's younger sister, Bee, at Whitman College. From there I headed through Portland to the lower end of the Willamette Valley in Eugene where I started my search. I should admit that this search included a fair amount of research into the fishing potential of the areas I was considering and was not strictly limited to employment opportunities.

Eugene had the advantage of being a university town with excellent fishing nearby, but there were no openings for me in any of the local securities firms. The same applied to the other valley towns heading north to Portland, the place where I had the best chances and the best contacts. When I got to Portland, I installed myself at the Congress Hotel at a favorable monthly rate and made a devoted search in both areas of interest and hit pay dirt in each. The firm of Zilka Smither & Co. was willing to give me a period of training and pay me a modest salary until

I was prepared to take my test and become licensed and bonded as a registered representative. At that point I would receive a minimal guarantee plus commissions.

It all sounded great and I started with them while keeping up my fishing research which included the building of a wide acquaintanceship in local fishing circles. The Congress Hotel itself was a hotbed of traveling men among whom were a number of fishing fanatics. I soon found myself a member of the Izaak Walton League and, within a week, was suckered into going along with being railroaded into the position of secretary-treasurer. Jim Zilka thought that would be good for my business contacts, but all I developed from it was a talent for licking envelopes and hand-addressing club mailings.

I wanted to bring Puck and Muffet out as soon as possible but wanted to have a home lined up before their arrival. While houses in Portland were relatively inexpensive, the cost of buying one was prohibitive to me so I was on the lookout for a reasonable rental until I could put aside enough for a down-payment. By this time it was late in the winter.

I was driving back from an afternoon's fishing on the Toutle River when I got an unexpected bit of news. I had just caught my first winter steelhead on a fly while fishing upstream in pocket water on the edge of a rapid. I had used a floating line and a fluorescent yarn fly with a split brass bead head. It had been very exciting because it was just like fishing with a weighted nymph upstream and I clearly saw the line stop and I lifted and tightened into a silvery torpedo who gave a good account of himself and weighted 13½ pounds on the hotel scales that night—my largest fish to a fly yet.

I had the radio on in the car and was swilling a bottle of beer, totally contented with myself, when the news came on and there was an excited announcement that Ernest Hemingway was reported lost in a plane crash in the vicinity of Murchison Falls on the Victoria Nile in the center of darkest Africa. No sign of the wreckage had been sighted, the announcer said, but it could only be assumed that all aboard had been lost, which included the noted author, his wife, and the pilot. I'd already been through all this in North Africa so, while stunned, I maintained my composure and a more skeptical attitude.

The following few days were hectic as news came of the rescue of the crash victims from an island in the river by an excursion boat taking tourists to view the falls. This was followed shortly by the news that they had crashed again on take-off but without serious injury, a prognosis which proved to be far from accurate. Papa and Mary were inundated with telegrams of congratulations on their miraculous survival from the two consecutive plane crashes, including my own expressing relief and gratitude.

There had already been a Hemingway song, by Noel Coward I believe, that came out before the war and whose tune I can still hum. It was called "Please, Mr. Hemingway," and it is best left to rot in the graveyard of failed music. The crashes, and the subsequent report that Papa had come out of the jungle holding a bunch of bananas in one hand and half-empty bottle of gin in the other, gave birth to a new short-lived recording by Jose Ferrer called "A Bunch of Bananas and a Bottle of Gin." I'm not certain if they had charts then, but if they did, the song might have been on it for a couple of weeks before fading into well-deserved obscurity.

I finally found a good little rental house off Canyon Road and brought Puck and Muffet to the Congress Hotel for the week I had left on my month's rent while we unpacked our household belongings and settled into our new ninety-dollar-a-month abode, approximately one-third of my guaranteed minimum salary.

With one glaring exception, very little that was earth-shaking took place during the three years we lived in Portland, except that we loved the city and its people and still have many good friends there. The exception was that in July of 1954 it became clear that Puck was pregnant again. This time excellent medical care and the foreknowledge that we had incompatible Rh factors and blood types enabled Puck to get through the pregnancy without any recurrence of the Berlin tragedy. At about 1:00 a.m. on February 16, 1955, Puck went into labor, woke me, and I drove her to Good Samaritan Hospital where she gave birth to a healthy female child for whom we chose the name Margot Byra. Margot was the Medieval French queen and a favorite of Papa's whose name he borrowed for use in his story, "The Short Happy Life of Francis Macomber." Byra was for her maternal grandmother, a sweet woman who had come over from Idaho to help with Muffet while Puck was in the hospital and to be available if any difficulty should occur.

We got used to the rain in Portland and I fished a lot more than I should have. What clients I had were almost all people

I had met on rivers. I discovered something I should have known before, and that was that I was a very negative cold-call salesman. I shrank from calling strangers on the telephone, or even calling on them in person, to try to talk to them about their finances. When you're new in a city and trying to get started in the investment business, calling on strangers is one of the things you simply have to do. I even tried to remedy this failing by taking a Dale Carnegie course, but it eventually became evident that I was not going to be able to earn much more than my guarantee, and that was obviously not enough for a family of four. I left Zilka with regret and made a couple of half-hearted attempts in other fields but found myself deeply depressed and badly in need of two things: a boost in morale and a financial shot in the arm.

One of the projects in which I had become involved was a foundation started by a clever fellow Dartmouth alumnus who had me working for the group with high hopes and no remuneration. It looked at some point as if there might be some advantage in bringing the foundation to the attention of my friend, Joe Dryer, whose North Atlantic Kenaf Corporation was starting to get off the ground in Cuba with a special decorticator developed for them by Krupp. Joe was starting to grow Kenaf fiber, from which jute-like material could be woven to make bags for Cuba's sugar crop, once the Krupp machine had solved the problem of removing the worthlex cortex from the usable fiber. It made sense for me to use this excuse to visit Cuba and see Papa for the first time in two years. I had the promise of a paying job with George Patten, an independent investment broker with a fine reputation who had a small one-man operation and was interested in taking on a youngster to help him service his growing clientele. Nevertheless, I wanted badly to discuss the question of my future with Papa with complete candor and possibly to find a totally new and more rewarding direction. Although Puck was holding up well under the circumstances, her spirits were only kept from flagging by Muffet's obvious brightness in her first school at St. Helen's Hall, and little Margot's alertness and charm. To make matters worse, I had to borrow to pay for my airline ticket to Havana.

When I got to Havana, preceded by a cablegram, it was some time in March 1955. Mary was back from seeing her mother and making arrangements for her after her father's recent death, but Papa didn't look at all well and was obviously badly overweight. He did seem pleased, however, to hear about the trouble-free birth of his second grandchild and was especially glad about her name.

I couldn't get around to the object of my visit right away and shied away from it for several days, during which time I made contact with Joe Dryer and his brother, Peter, who was sharing digs with him in an apartment near the Malecón on the edge of old Havana. Their project sounded interesting but there was no place in it for me, and the idea having to do with the foundation turned out not to have been appropriate. It had really just been an excuse for me to come down anyway.

Papa had recently been awarded the Nobel Prize and he complained often about the greatly-increased loss of privacy it entailed. "Privacy," he said, "is the most valuable thing a man can have and an absolute necessity for a man to be able to write. Now every son-of-a-bitch in the world thinks he has the right to steal it from me." I did not express aloud my own opinion that Mary's love of the limelight and entertaining did little to aid in meeting that need, despite the protective shell she erected around him to keep him from being disturbed unnecessarily. The trouble was that I felt strongly that I was one of those she was keeping out, and that feeling remained in full force as long as he was alive.

There was little doubt in my mind that Papa had undergone drastic changes from the man I had viewed all my life as my number one hero. He could still be as gentle and warm as ever, but it was more and more infrequent, and his mood generally seemed to me plaintive, occasionally truculent, often so with Mary, and with an underlying bitterness. Of course I knew nothing about Adriana Ivancich except that he had written about how much I would like Venice and what a fine girl she was, along with a number of other friends there. Anything else I could only surmise from the tenor of the conversation when the subject had been mentioned during our first visit to Havana with Muffet two years before.

This, then, was the setting for our "man to man" discussion, as I came to think of it. We had all three had the usual mid-day preprandial martini, despite his supposedly having given them up, and I took this moment to ask for a private pow-wow.

"Papa, can I speak to you alone?"

"Of course, Schatz," he replied. "Let's go in the living

room." I received what can only be described as a hard look from Mary who then said, "I think I'll go have a nap, lamb," and closed the door to her room none too gently.

Papa settled into his big armchair and I sat down nervously on the couch opposite with only the big woven reed mat on the floor separating us.

"How are things really going?" He made it easy for me, but it still wasn't easy.

"I don't know why, Papa. I just can't seem to make a decent living. Not enough to support my family. Whatever I've tried just hasn't worked for me."

"You were a damned fine soldier."

"I probably never should have left the army. It's just that it was no life for a family, always unsettled, and it was actually getting so Puck would know when I was jumping the next day, even though I never told her. I was twitching in my sleep and she could tell."

"Goddamnit, Schatz, you're going to have to stick with one thing. If you keep switching jobs much longer, you're going to find yourself unemployable."

That hurt. I was thirty-three years old and already faced dismal failure.

"Papa, it isn't that I don't try. I know I should have finished school but right after the war I just wasn't ready for school. I'd already been in real life and school wasn't real any more. Anyway I didn't finish and now there just isn't that big a choice of jobs. The sales field is the only area I have any chance of making real money in but I just can't seem to cut it."

"Look, Bum, you're in a good place, a place you chose. You'll just have to stick with it. I'll help all I can with monies but you're going to have to stay with one job in one business until you learn to make a living."

"I'd give anything not to need money help but God knows I do need it." I broke down almost completely, "Sometimes I get down so bad I wonder if it's worth going on living . . ."

I believe this shook him for he cut in, "Schatz, listen to me. I know how bad it can seem. There have been times when I felt the same way. Christ, if you had any idea of the shit I live with all the time." He went on through a litany of problems, including Mary and his lawyer, which made mine pale into insignificance. Then he reminded me about what a mistake it had been for Grandfather to shoot himself as it had turned out that his financial worries would have solved themselves. At that point he elicited a promise from me I shall never forget. He said, "Schatz, the one thing you must promise me you will never do, and I will promise you the same, is that neither one of us will ever shoot himself, like Grandfather. Promise me and then I'll promise you."

So I promised. And then he promised.

After that we talked some more and he pledged some financial aid until I should become better established, although he said it was difficult for him because he had so many expenses with Mary's parents' hospital bills, Greg's continued schooling, Mary's insatiable appetite for expensive things, taxes, and so forth and so on.

He was happiest about how well Patrick was doing in Africa and bitter about his relations with Greg, which had deteriorated badly after Pauline's death, when each, in turn, blamed the other for the circumstances which might have been a contributing factor. He then went on to tell me that I need have no worries about the long-term future because he had made a will which would take care of the three of us boys.

Because Pat and Greg had inherited substantially from their mother, he said he had provided in the will that I was to receive half of what he left and that each of them was to receive one-half of the balance. There was no mention of Mary and I presumed that he had thought only in terms of their both going together. Since I had not initiated this turn in the conversation, I did not question any of it nor ask him further about it. I would not have brought the subject up on my own under any circumstances.

According to Carlos Baker, author of the "official" biography, my father wrote his will and had it witnessed on September 17 of that same year, six months after my visit. In the same account, Baker states that I visited Havana for two weeks in October of that year as well, and that is patently inaccurate by six months, but then he probably relied on Mary's memory for his information, much as he relied on information supplied by Toby Bruce about events in Key West which also were way off the mark.

In fairness to Baker, I have to say that I did not cooperate with him as I probably should have at the time he requested information from me; my own affairs required the full devotion of my time and I was somewhat embittered about the whole business for reasons which become apparent later, and I wished to have as little to do with it as possible.

That night there were guests for dinner, as was often the case, but Papa arranged for us to have a tiñosa (buzzards or turkey vultures which we jokingly referred to as *enemigos,* or enemies) shoot the following day. He had René get hold of a dead carcass to put on the roof of the Finca to attract our quarry within range. The tower Mary had had built since her tenure as chatelaine would provide an ideal platform on its parapeted roof for our shooting, and I looking forward to another chance to be alone with Papa—truly alone this time since Mary's room would not abut on our meeting place as it had that afternoon in the living room.

The occasion of the *tiñosa* shoot is one of the most memorable moments of my lifelong relationship with my father. It was the single time in my life when Papa and I were alone together since my adulthood when no holds were barred and we both let down all our defenses. It started at about eleven in the morning when Papa and I climbed up the outside spiral iron staircase to the top of the tower above his new workroom. We used only one side-by-side shotgun, the Duke of Alba gun I think, and we had plenty of boxes of twelve-gauge shells.

Papa set forth the rules: "We'll just use the one gun. Each of us gets two shots. Then we trade off. The one not shooting is observer-fire controller. you know, like, incomer on your right about two o'clock high . . . air force style."

As senior officer present he got first go. One of the big black buzzards who had shifted their flight away from our hill when Papa and I arrived on the tower slanted down an air current towards the dead goat on the red tile roof below us. I called out, "Incomer, ten o'clock, range 75 yards. Fire at will."

Papa let the big ugly bird swoop within 20 yards, led him perfectly and crumpled him just over the edge of the roof and he crashed into the mango trees and hit the ground with a thump. Another one had dropped in from the right and I called, "Enemigo in range three o'clock low." But Papa had already fired his second barrel at him and he crashed on the front terrace. He had a double and, pleased, yelled for René to bring up a pitcher of martinis and two glasses. Meanwhile the ripeness of the goat seemed to be having an hypnotic effect on the giant carrion eaters, bringing them swooping toward our hilltop from miles around. The shooting didn't put them off for long and before the martinis arrived Papa had called one for me which I needed to pump both barrels into to collapse him.

They were no easy target. As any goose hunter can tell you, the flight of big birds is deceptive in the extreme and a bird can appear to be going very slowly while actually traveling at high rates of speed, particularly when there's a strong wind. The fact that the *tiñosas* were mostly soaring made their air speed that much more difficult to gauge accurately, and we had variable winds.

It was a never-to-be-forgotten shoot, and after a while we yelled down for René to bring up yet another pitcher. By the time we had expended all our shells, well over two hours had gone by and we were drunk as coots. Mary kept coming out onto the patio beneath the tower calling for us to "stop this at once" and "come down and eat lunch right now," but we just kept on drinking and shooting and laughing and shouting after the third pitcher, which René had the good sense to accompany with some sandwiches.

Papa finally growled, "Cease fire." Then René's volunteers, youngsters from his family or friends from the town, started the big cleanup which we likened to the graves registration unit going onto the battlefield after a big firefight and both Papa and I directed them from our vantage point on the tower. I have forgotten how many of the big stink-ugly birds were picked up but I hasten to explain that *tiñosas*, while protected at home, were not protected then in Cuba. And since we never made a habit of shooting them, the minor diminution in their numbers inflicted on that memorable occasion cannot have had any serious effect on the ecological balance. Furthermore, nobody had yet used the word "ecology" in public.

We climbed down the spiral staircase very carefully and headed into the living room.

"Let's watch Casablanca, Mister Bum."

"Wonderful, Papa. Can we see it okay with the light?"

"Sure. The bulb's strong and René can rig up some blankets over the windows. Help me set up the projector."

We were in no shape to set up the projector properly, especially not to thread the film. René finished the job as we settled into the two big easy chairs with the screen set up in front of the couch and the projector behind us near the capehart record player.

"René, traiga una botella de tinto, haga el favor!"

"*Sí, Rene y con dos vasos!*", I chimed in too loudly, bringing Mary to her door behind the screen to the right where she took one long glaring look at us, then went back into her room, slamming the door hard. She was furious and stayed that way until my departure.

I can't really blame her for being angry at the moment, but she needn't have stayed that way, mean, angry and silent. Anyway the film came on. Papa shrugged and the two of us were swept up in it as always, perhaps, more so because of all the alcohol.

It was a bit like going to a movie in a college town. Neither of us could keep quiet though we kept shushing each other.

"Isn't the Swede beautiful? I mean truly, really beautiful. . . beautiful."

"Yeah, Papa beautiful. She's really, truly, truly beautiful."

"So beautiful, so, so beautiful."

This went on and we started crying and repeating over and over how beautiful she really was. We were overwhelmed by her beauty.

It was totally maudlin and wonderfully close and human all at once, and I'll always be grateful that it happened.

I never had another chance to be that close to him again. Much later, I wondered if, during that time, he had already foreseen the onset of his ruin. The signs were there for others to see, but I must confess I hadn't the wit to see it for myself. Either that, or I didn't want to.

TWENTY-THREE

I managed to struggle on in Portland with some fine moments for our family, some great fishing, a wonderful visit from Paul and Mamie, and finally, in early 1956, I had the good fortune to meet Ned Ball, then the new manager of the Portland office of Merrill, Lynch, Pierce, Fenner & Beane. As with all my other contacts, I met Ned through fishing and, first thing I knew, he offered me a job. He explained that Merrill, as the firm is called on the street, trained its account executives thoroughly first in the home office where they would be working and then in a special training school in New York, I would have to work in the Portland office for six months doing every possible kind of job in order to gain experience in all facets of the business and then attend the three-month training school. The starting salary was low but an improvement over what I had been making, and Ned stressed that there would not be the same kind of pressure to produce business right away that I had seen in other firms. He painted a pretty idealistic picture, but I think he believed it all himself and that he was expressing his own high personal standards. I'm not sure I ever met another office manager whose view of the brokerage business was as unsullied as his. It was going to be a treat working for Ned Ball.

The six months of training in the office went by quickly, and just before September I was off to New York for phe training school. They housed me in the dim upper reaches of the now-defunct St. George Hotel in Brooklyn along with the other trainees who had come without their families. The expense of bringing Puck and the two children would have been more than I could afford, but I noticed that a surprising number of the younger trainees did bring their wives and children and it impressed on me that it helps to have money when one is starting in the investment field. It's a bit like borrowing from a bank: if you appear to need the money they won't lend it to you, but if you have no pressing need for it you can borrow all you want.

Training school was not physically tough unless you went out on the town at night which, I must admit, I did on several occasions, though feeling a bit guilty about Puck's being at home in Portland with the responsibility of the children. I suppose it was some relief that Muffet was proving to be a good helper and loved to help take care of her little sister.

I took advantage of Papa's friendship with Toots Shor to get tickets for both the tennis finals at Forest Hills (young Ken Rosewall's first U.S. Championship title) and two World Series games, including the famous Bobby Thomson bases-loaded homer game. He got me enough tickets to take several of my pals as well. Another incident of note was going for cocktails at the Harvey Breits' where I had the good luck to meet William Faulkner a mild-mannered courtly gentle man in tweeds, and was able to tell him how much my father had praised his writing on several occasions. He seemed pleased and told me how much it would mean to him to meet Papa. As it turned out, they never were to meet.

During the training course, I happened to meet one of the Merrill Lynch partners, "Ruby" Rubezanin, a lusty fellow who had made a name for himself as one of the major innovators in educating and selling stock to the so-called "little man." Our friendship resulted in my making possibly the worst move I ever made. Ruby thought it would be a hell of an idea for me to go down to Havana as an account executive rather than return to Portland as planned. Unfortunately, I went along with the idea and agreed to it without first consulting Puck. She went along with the idea reluctantly and only after the persuasive argument that Havana was one town where I did have an entrée with all the wealthy, and the chances of making a great deal of money were excellent.

There was one factor, however, that none of us took into consideration: being sent down there by one of the partners to work for an office manager who had had no say in my selection and hiring, a procedure which was in direct contravention of the Merrill Lynch way of doing things. We should have foreseen the deep resentment that Ken Crosby felt at my being shoved in on him and the steps he took thereafter to impede any possible progress on my part. I was kept as an assistant to his two highest producing account executives for more than a year, nine months longer than the norm, and only permitted to go into production for myself after Ruby came down and forced him to do so.

It was a nightmarish eighteen months in which we started

out living at the Finca, while Papa and Mary were away in Europe. When they returned we moved to an apartment on the street side of a building overlooking the ocean near the mouth of the Almendares River. Since my total paycheck was barely $300 a month, the exact amount of the rent, Papa had to help with expenses. Muffet went to Ruston Academy, the only bilingual school, another necessary expense. Mary would come to visit Puck or take her to concerts but avoided asking us out to the Finca except on very special occasions; still, we were hearing from our friends about their frequent visits there. In the whole time we were there, Papa came to visit us only once but stayed in the car and wouldn't come upstairs to see the apartment which Puck had made a special effort to have ready for him. We felt very much estranged and I never felt that Papa was his old self, but then again, it would have been hard for me to judge since we had so little opportunity to see him.

In the background the whole time was the tense revolutionary current in Cuba. Sentiment was growing stronger against the Batista government by the day and, while most of us sympathized with the mood of the people, Batista was forced to intensify his reign of terror in order to stay in power. Revolutionists' bombs exploded in cafes, theaters, and public buildings almost daily, and the verified tales of murder and torture by Batista's secret police grew into the tens of thousands.

The end of my career in Havana came only a few months after Ken Crosby had been forced to put me on production. With the help of my closest friend in the office, Luis Toroella, a young Dartmouth graduate born and raised in Havana, I started right off proving how wrong Crosby had been. The only problem was that many customers who had been with other account executives asked to transfer their accounts to me, which resulted in no net gain of business for the office. Then I came down with a serious case of hepatitis which laid me up for a long spell. By the time I was back on my feet, conditions were worsening so rapidly that we decided to go for a recuperative visit to Chocorua with Paul and Mother. It turned out to be a propitious departure, as it preceded the overthrow of Batista and the installation of Fidel Castro by only a few months and, needless to say, the business climate for American stockbrokers did not improve.

While we were in New Hampshire, Puck came down with

hepatitis as well and we were even further delayed. In the meantime we heard from friends in San Francisco. Don and Joan Hopper had gone there to start a graphics business after leaving the Army but had been forced to give it up; now Don was a research analyst with a local securities firm. He volunteered to recommend me if I would come to be interviewed.

So we drove first to Idaho where I left Puck and the girls with the Whittleseys and then I drove down to San Francisco and stayed with Don and Joan in their comfortable North Marin County hilltop house. Don had things pretty well lined up for me with his firm but, on the basis that I already had good credit with Merrill and the prospect that I would be luckier here than I had been in Cuba, I went to see the head of the local Merrill office, Ken Rearwin. He was delighted to give me a chance; the office was doing very well and the firm was even considering expanding their San Francisco operations. I was hired, this time by a manager who had not had me shoved down his throat and in a city where no revolutions were going on. Of course, it meant starting new all over again, but the outlook was good and I knew Puck would love being back in the Bay Area where we had such fine friends as the Hoppers and where she still had friends from her days there with United Airlines.

After one false move on my part in finding a house which Puck couldn't stand, we moved into one of the prettiest rental houses imaginable in Mill Valley overlooking Richardson Bay. We stayed there a year before finding a permanent home close to the tennis club on a spur of Mt. Tamalpais. The nine years we spent in Mill Valley were, on the whole, happy ones and semi-prosperous. I commuted to the city during the odd hours dictated by West Coast trading on the New York stock Exchange, and when the traffic was easy. I never became a ball of fire as a securities salesman, though I must admit that there were times when I found it very exciting. I had a basic problem which can't be all that uncommon: I was happy as a bedbug when my customers were doing well but I suffered abject misery when they didn't. My friends all told me that, since the customer always took credit for those decisions when they profited and blamed the broker for those which led to a loss, there was no reason to be so sensitive about their feelings. If you wanted to survive and stay happy in the securities business, that is certainly the attitude I should have developed, but, try as I might, I could not change those feelings.

The best times in Mill Valley had to do with fishing for steelhead on trips up the coast to Northern California streams and rivers in the winter. In the summer we drove up to the North Umpqua, and even started going there regularly. There was a wonderful shad run both in the Feather River, which flows into the Sacramento, and in the Russian River, which enters the Pacific at Jenner-by-the-Sea, north of San Francisco. Shad run in the springtime and one Sunday I went up there with Margot in tow while Puck and Muffet were busy with something else. We ran into Doug and Angic Merrick, old friends from the Winston Rod Company, who showed me a few tricks for hooking shad more often than I had been. Margot, who was about four years old, called out to me as I was wading deep in the current. "Daddy, can you come and help me? I gotta go."

There was a fair crowd along the river and I was in the hot spot and wanted to postpone getting out as long as I could, so I answered that I would be with her in just a minute.

A few minutes later she repeated her request, and again I postponed for "Just one more cast, honey." A few more minutes went by, and guiltily, I started backing out of the pool to come to her rescue when I and everyone else heard a loud sob. "It's okay, Daddy. You can stay. It's too late now." The crowd roared with laughter, much to the embarrassment of both of us.

We took an Easter vacation by tacking weekends on both ends of a short week in the spring of 1961 and took the kids, both of whom loved to ski, up to Sun Valley. Margot went into ski school, as Muffet also did part of the time, but most of the time the big sister skied on Baldy (the big mountain) with me, and she was starting to develop good confidence in a diversity of snow conditions.

Puck visited with Mary and other friends, but we saw little of Papa except on one evening when we were invited to join them for dinner at the Christiania: Papa's favorite. Papa was totally subdued and appeared to have lost an excessive amount of weight. He had that gaunt look of someone who has lost too much weight too fast. I thought he looked pitiful, and that is a word I can't imagine ever having applied to him before. He had new, smaller clothes, yet even they hung loosely on him. He barely spoke, and when he did it was so low you could hardly hear him. I saw only one hint of a smile and that was when, after Mary had made a pronouncement, I contradicted her with the facts, and I had the distinct feeling he derived a measure of enjoyment from seeing her corrected.

I tried to find out what was going on but was only reassured that Papa was coming along fine and now had his blood pressure under control and was only weak from complications which had built up since the air crashes six years before. Unfortunately, I didn't contact George Saviers, Papa's local doctor, who would have set me straight. Mary did not choose to level with me about what was going on or what had already been done. George would have sought me out to brief me himself had he had an inkling that Mary had not filled me in.

I had sent Papa a check for a substantial amount shortly before coming up to Sun Valley, to repay a loan he had made to me when we needed help with the down payment on our Mill Valley house. I didn't bring the subject up, but I was a bit dismayed that Papa made no mention of it. That was very uncharacteristic of him; it had always been his way to give full credit whenever and wherever it was due. We left for home refreshed from our fine vacation, but I felt an overhanging gloom I couldn't explain.

Our main holiday that year was a planned two-week stay at Steamboat Inn on the North Umpqua. We liked to go early, a week before the Fourth of July crowds would flock to the river. While the chances of steelhead weren't as good, we at least had the river mostly to ourselves and didn't have to struggle to find an unoccupied stretch of good water.

It had been a year with unusually warm weather and very little runoff, and the river was as low as it would normally be in August. Plenty of fish could be spotted in those pools where they usually show, but the best fishing had been even earlier, and firstclass fly fishermen were coming in after long days on the water without even a tale of a strike or the bulge a big fish makes behind the fly. It was years before I discovered how effective the dry fly can be under such conditions.

The day we arrived we met up with Frank Moore, whom we call "the ledge" behind his back because he is a legend in his own time. Frank took Puck out in the camp water to fish the lower Kitchen Pool, a treacherous wade for anyone unfamiliar with it, and showed her where to cast. It was late in the evening and she hooked and landed a magnificent summer steelhead of some seven pounds, although with considerable help from Frank. On the way out of the pool, where I have slipped a hundred times over the years on the wax-slick runnels, Frank let go of Puck and inflicted her ritual dunking for a first-time steelhead on a fly. They came in wet but happy, though Puck was a little concerned about taking such a dunking when she was early in a new pregnancy.

During the next few days, Puck's steelhead loomed even larger as the only fish taken by anyone, and she took great pleasure in behaving insufferably toward all and sundry who gave her half a chance. One day she asked an old-timer, normally a sweet-tempered gentleman with impeccable manners, "Would you like to know what fly I got MINE on?" and he snapped, "Shut up, goddamit!" If the truth be told, his reaction reflected exactly the feelings of all us "experts" who were being thrust even further into ignominious shame with each successive fishless day.

About a month after our return home from Sun Valley we had received one panic-stricken letter from Mary in which she had revealed part of the situation with Papa and expressed the hope that I would agree with her decision to take him for treatment to the Mayo Clinic. She felt that taking him to some place like the Menninger Clinic, which specialized in psychiatric disorders, would tarnish his image if it ever came out publicly. She did not tell us that he had already been to Mayo and had already attempted to kill himself, but only that it appeared that suicide was a risk. I telephoned to express my complete support for whatever action she deemed appropriate, but I must confess that the subsequent days on the river temporarily removed the problem from my thoughts. That is, after all, one of the greatest benefits of fishing. But the problem returned to all of our thoughts the morning after Puck's admonishment by the old-timer.

I came in from the early morning's fishing having had my first glimmer of a take in the fast water just above the rapid at Wright Creek. A fish came short but refused to come again. Even so, the nearmiss bucked up my spirits and I came back into camp full of hope and with a big appetite. Puck was down at the cabin when Frank came up to me and said, "Jack, I think it's bad news. You're supposed to call this number in Ketchum." I recognized the number. It was Papa's, at the house he'd bought overlooking the Big Wood River just outside town; the house he had bought from his friend Dan Topping's brother, Bob, which had never really become home because he hadn't yet been there for all the seasons of a year; the house where he had shot himself early that morning, as Mary told me when she answered the insistent ringing.

Frank Moore came to the rescue again, as he had done so many times on the river, by volunteering to fly us from Roseburg to Ketchum. We landed on the short strip just north of town by the dump (now a nine-hole golf course flanked by expensive homes), and half a mile north of the cemetery. The flight was over hot, black desert, the air rough, and Puck and the girls got sick. I was tense and miserable. We had called Puck's folks in Twin and they had driven up to take Puck and the girls home with them until time for the funeral a few days later. Mary had checked into the hospital where she was under sedation and the press were starting to home in like wasps at a barbecue. The phone never stopped ringing and it was a madhouse only made bearable by the yeoman duty being performed by Papa's friends, the Arnolds, the Andersons, the Atkinsons, George Saviers, Duke McMullen, and George Brown, who had traveled west with Papa and Mary from the Mayo Clinic.

I was thoroughly briefed between phone calls and was shocked to learn how long the problem had been going on but my priority was taking care of the details and coordinating the funeral arrangements with Patrick's arrival from East Africa. When Mary was able to face the onslaught again, most of the arrangements had been made, but she assigned me one of the worst jobs I have ever had to do. We had received a telegram from Marlene Dietrich saying that she was coming right away to attend the funeral. Since the day I had been too shy to approach her in Regensburg, I had met her and talked with her when Puck and I went backstage following a show in San Francisco. She had been kind and generous with her time with us. But Mary was furious at the idea that Marlene should even consider coming to the funeral, and she ordered me to telephone her immediately and tell her that we were having no outsiders because it was going to be a simple, family-only funeral. I was never more ashamed and, of course, I couched my call in more diplomatic terms, but I could sense the hurt at the other end of the line.

I slept in Papa's room until Puck and the family came back for the funeral. The night before Patrick's scheduled arrival, other family members and close friends were already in town and staying at the Christiania Motor Lodge. Mary was starting to regain her form but continued to be adamant in her insistence to the press that Papa had shot himself accidentally. I suppose the possibility that someone might conclude that Papa had willingly left a life in which she played so large a part was anathema to her. Before retiring that night we had a long talk in which she recounted the whole history of Papa's illness, how pathetic had been his last attempts at making love to her, and how difficult it had all been for her. We both had had quite a lot to drink and I found myself being sympathetic to her position. She even thanked me for sending Papa the check and said she hadn't had a chance to show it to him so she hoped I would understand when it was returned endorsed by her. It would go a long way to help defray all the expenses that had piled up.

She told me that Alfred Rice, Papa's lawyer, would be arriving and that he would get us all together after the funeral to discuss the future. She also thanked me for taking over during her stay in the hospital, an exaggeration since Papa's friends had rallied to do all the legwork. I had only helped make the hard decisions, and some of those had been made for me. As it turned out, my role was completed and, like an actor killed off in an early scene, there was really no further need for me.

Patrick arrived and he, Greg, and I spent some time together before the funeral. The grey eminence of our lives made his lawyerly appearance and, once the funeral was over, convoked Mary and the three of us upstairs and laid the chill hand of our father's will upon us in a short summation to the effect that Papa had left everything to Mary and that no provisions of any kind had been made for anyone else. Weeks later we saw part of the holographic will published in *Life* magazine before having seen a copy ourselves. I never saw a copy until years later when I had my attorney get a copy made from the probate records.

The other family members totally ignored, my two brothers and I and our families dispersed to our widely separated homes while Mary got started in her new career, alone except for the man who now had only one client named Hemingway.

My primary concern in the following months had to do with the health of Puck and our imminent new arrival. In a situation such as ours, where the parents' blood types and Rh factors are incompatible, each successive pregnancy harbors a greater risk unless special measures are taken. Puck's health was delicate throughout the latter stages of her pregnancy with Mariel but, despite an extended period of hospitalization prior to her premature birth on November 22, 1961, everything turned out for the best for both mother and child. As usually happens in such circumstances, the youngest member of the household soon became the focus of everyone's attention.

Aside from the ebb and flow of fortune in the business world, my own life was unfolding with a new interest: Muffet's entry into the world of competitive tennis. There being no other males in the family, I had never become a little league parent. Instead, I became a tennis mother.

TWENTY-FOUR

During the years following my father's death until 1967 when we moved to Idaho to stay, everything was tinged to some extent by that event in one way or another, and we were far from being the only ones affected by it. The French have a saying that to know people one should see them inherit. I would add that seeing them fail to inherit can also be revealing.

In my own case, I was too numbed by events to react quickly and plausibly, but Mother and Paul did so for me and, as a consequence, my two half-brothers as well. Hadley and Paul perceived that a great injustice had been done and took steps to rectify it with special emphasis on the recovery of Mother's painting, Miro's *Farm*. I had been brought up with that painting which Papa had given her on her birthday. When it was never returned after the five-year loan to Papa, its absence left a sort of vacuum in her home. My mother, a trusting woman, took Papa at his word and did not take the precaution of keeping the letter he had sent her asking to borrow the painting, but in the voluminous correspondence which Carlos Baker read to research his biography of my father he apparently found a letter confirming all of this. At my request Baker kindly tried to locate it for me but it turned up missing. It had been returned along with all the other correspondence to Mary then failed to reappear in the collection given by her to the Kennedy Library.

Through their attorneys, Paul and Hadley took action to recover the property which Mary, on her counsel's advice, claimed as her own. Prior to that I had written her suggesting that, in view of the fact that Papa had not followed prudent procedures common to estate planning, there was no reason to compound the error by failing to take steps in her lifetime to avoid decimation of the estate by unwarranted and unnecessary inheritance taxes. She took my suggestion as a direct attack on her and she let me know it in no uncertain terms.

Paul and Mother's course of action, however, awakened Mary and Alfred Rice to the great risk involved in doing absolutely nothing in my brothers' and my behalf. Consequently, they set up a trust, the corpus of which was the foreign rights on all of Papa's works and the income derived therefrom. Mary was the grantor and she was one of the four beneficiaries as well as the recipient of whatever tax benefits might accrue from the depreciation of the properties. So, in one act of generosity on her part, we were taken care of but, as it turned out, the act was considerably more generous than she or Alfred Rice had imagined it would be.

When I questioned Rice about the prospective income at the time of its inception, he suggested that it might come to around ten thousand dollars to each of us per annum but that, in all likelihood, the amount would decrease over a period of years since that is the pattern which normally occurs after the death of a well-known author. In this instance, it did not decrease but has grown steadily except in those periods of great strength in the dollar when it has managed to more or less hold its own. Alfred Rice is the sole trustee as well as agent for the properties and, since the advent of Mary's nearly total incapacity a few years ago, he has been most reluctant to divulge cogent and necessary information to my brothers and me, although we hope he may presently be changing his ideas in this regard.

Years after the creation of the foreign rights trust, Greg, while researching with his attorney the possibility of selling some rights, came across a recent United States Supreme Court decision which found that true heirs, even when not inheritors of copyrighted property, could not be denied their fair and legitimate share of those copyrights once they had gone into the copyright renewal period. After considerable negotiation, we were able to get Alfred Rice to comply with the intent of this finding, and that has had a most favorable and growing impact on the incomes of all three of us sons.

Such an explanation of the tangles we had been through may help to explain how it was possible for me to become a tennis mother. The fact is that once the trust was established I had the luxury of choice for the first time in my life and, believe me, I took advantage of it.

In 1965 I decided to exercise that choice by completing my education at Sonoma State College, then a brand new campus housed in a group of low-rent duplex apartments forty miles north of Mill Valley in Rohnert Park, a bedroom community of Santa Rosa. I had in mind to prepare myself to become a teacher, but I found that there were great gaps in my educational background which needed filling badly. At forty-one years of age, I was finally sufficiently mature to benefit fully from a liberal arts education.

I was fortunate in having some excellent teachers at Sonoma. Yvette Fallandy made French literature and history come to life for her students, and every day was an adventure. My daughters benefited indirectly because I became a reliable source of help with homework. With my usual tendency toward procrastination, I put off some of the courses required for graduation until the last year—courses I had missed early on because of my off-schedule start at Dartmouth during the war. It was an error I later regretted.

The science and math I had so long avoided were introductory in nature and conceptual in approach, so that instead of getting bogged down by the mechanical drudgery of experiments and mechanical computation, I was being exposed to ideas and concepts which were made exciting by teachers who knew how to teach and loved their subject. I was able to grasp the ideas without having to be embroiled in the minutiae, and the result was thoroughly stimulating.

This led me to seek source materials in the library dealing with the particular science which elicited my greatest interest: that is, anything to do with fish and fishing, and especially trout and their environment. The discovery of the science of limnology changed my work habits at college. I started spending more and more of my free time reading everything I could find in the library. In sum, I educated myself in a field for which I was unqualified except by virtue of a consuming interest, and I sensed that the day would come when I would be able to use what I had learned to accomplish something of value.

The return to finish my formal schooling had inadvertently given me a great deal more than a solid overview of our history and culture. It had given me the greatest gift of all: the key to unlocking all the recorded knowledge about the things that truly interested me most. Learning to find what one needs to know is a key which remains yours for the rest of your life. That may be the best thing college can do for you.

I enjoy doing many things, some of them active and many of them passive. Among the active things I like to do are a number of sports, and in that period of time before we left Mill Valley I was able to indulge in some of them on a competitive basis. My first love in sports had been fencing, which I hadn't been able to do since Berlin where I fenced regularly at the

Olympische Stadion with Wolfgang Neumann. Neumann allowed me to help him in the initial training of the first post-war German olympians who were then preparing for the "one touch épée" part of the modern pentathlon. In San Francisco, I now took advantage of a well-organized fencing establishment organized around several excellent *salles d'armes.* I took lessons and competed, then later at Sonoma State I started a fencing team and coached it. There were some wonderful people in fencing there and they had blossomed under the tutelage of the members of the Hungarian Olympic Team which defected *en masse* during the Melbourne Olympic games in 1956 when their country was overrun in an act of brutal savagery by the Armed Forces of the Soviet Union.

I had played tennis in bits and snatches all my life but had never stayed with the game or learned to play it well. While in Mill Valley, we joined a tennis club and I tried to learn to play properly. To this day, I'm still trying and make some small improvement every year.

My greatest fun with tennis, though, was watching Muffet's beginnings and her progress through the ranks of competitive junior tennis in Northern California. To be quite honest, her tennis became my obsession and she was forced to shoulder it until she was burned out at the tender age of sixteen when she had her most successful year of competition. Because my time had become so frequently my own, I often ended up taking Muffet and friends to the various tournaments in the Northern California section of the U.S. Lawn Tennis Association. There were something like twenty six sanctioned events in any given season, and since the ones in the summer often lasted several days, if she played well, it was a lot of fierce competition. I still find it hard to believe just how fierce girls can become in competition, even little girls. I fully realized that I had become a tennis mother on the day I found myself exchanging catty remarks with another tennis mother about her daughter's sloppy backhand after she had dismissed Muffet's win as luck.

As children will, Muffet let us know in her own way when I had gone too far. She did the logical thing and it made me furious at the time. She revolted and did so with sufficiently damaging effect to bring me to my senses and teach me not to become overly involved in trying to run my children's lives for them, a policy I have learned to follow with Margot and Mariel.

Muffet gave up the game for several years and now competes only for fun. After the hiatus, she did casually walk onto a court one day in Idaho for the first time in more than two years to join in some mixed doubles. Her pickup partner asked her to accompany him to the State Championships in Boise to play mixed with him the following weekend. They were out in the second round but Muffet entered the singles on her own and won the Women's Division of the State Championship to everyone's, and her own, surprise and delight. I was off fishing at the time. I had learned my lesson well.

In the winter of 1966 we all went to Sun Valley for the holidays, though we spent much of it in Twin Falls at the Whittlesey house. I started then looking for a place to build a house. We had found a contractor in Mill Valley who had built a room onto an unused section of our deck. His work was good and fairly priced, and he got us thinking about finally making the move we had wanted to make for so many years. On top of that, disturbing trends at that time in the behavior of the very young, and the not so young, seemed to pose the real threat of peer pressure and induced exposure to dangerous new substances which were ruining lives all around us. Those trends added emphasis to our desire for a healthy change. Furthermore, it was a move which would be welcome to the girls, all of whom loved Idaho.

New developments in building materials and techniques now made it possible to live comfortably and well in a climate which would have been unbearable for us during long winters in the past. Houses could be built to withstand enormous snow loads on less sharply pitched roofs, eliminating one of the worst bugaboos of a long, snowy winter: cabin fever engendered by having snow from off the roof covering the space in front of the windows. There were also double-thermopane sealed windows and improved insulation which, if installed in double thickness, could make electricity, the cheapest heat in Idaho, efficient. New machines for removing snow, and a community organized for winter with new and more efficient materials for winter clothing, had made the outdoors into a usable paradise the year around.

After much searching, I found the perfect place, and on a return visit in February I made a down payment on the property. Through friends who would become neighbors, I lined up a contractor who would be building two other houses near ours the same summer. I found a floor plan that more than met our needs and even fulfilled most of our dreams. It was easily buildable and the bank estimated we could pay for it eventually, so we were in business.

That summer we lived in a small rented house in Ketchum and I spent every day out with the crew, though I played some hooky on the nearby stream. Puck provided the most valuable service a wife can give while a house is being built for her: she stayed away from it and made not one suggestion for a change here or there. As a result, the costs stayed within sight of our estimates and by early October, before my birthday, we moved in. Muffet and Margot were in school, and Mariel, who was just under age for first grade, went to the playschool run by Judy Odmark. They all skied on weekends once the snow started to fall. Puck's mother loved the new house and came up often from Twin falls; unfortunately, Puck's father, Horace, hadn't lived long enough to see it.

Later that fall, I went through another life crisis which took us all by complete surprise and made me reevaluate a lot of things, but especially how to supplement my income. I was taking advantage of all that Idaho had to offer in the fall like a pig in a puddle of slop: hunting, fishing and sometimes both, every day. After one especially hectic day of snipe hunting for hours, ankle-deep in bogs, followed by a few chores at home then another session of fruitless searching for grouse up a nearby mountain, I returned home for dinner and ate and drank much too heavily. After I had gone back out again to haul a pickup load of building debris and miscellaneous junk to the dump, I found myself feeling very bad indeed. I went downstairs to my den and lay down on the couch waiting to feel better. Instead, I started feeling a lot of chest pain.

At first I thought I was passing another kidney stone, but it was different somehow and there was numbness in my arms, especially the left. Suddenly I realized the pain was not in the same place but higher, much higher, and I got scared. I guess I yelled because Puck came down to see how I was doing and immediately called our friend, Dr. George Saviers, who told her to bring me straight to the hospital.

It was a full-blown myocardial infarction, a heart attack, and it took a lot longer than the weeks I spent in the hospital to recover fully from its effects. To try to sum it up, a heart attack is more than just a serious illness: it is an event which seems to issue a challenge to the man in you. It seems to say that you're no longer the man you used to be and that you won't be able to do the things you like to do, maybe never again. It scares the hell out of you, and it can demoralize the hell out of you too.

I'm grateful that George Saviers was one of those doctors who already felt that it was sound to try to exercise lightly as soon as you could, and within weeks I had started to walk a little more each day. Within two months I was walking almost four miles but resting whenever I felt slightly winded. If I had had the good sense to stay off smoking when I had that chance in the hospital—the easiest place to quit if you really want to—I might have avoided my later struggles to do so which, when unsuccessful, almost led to another heart attack and frightened me sufficiently to keep me off them ever since.

That year and the next I worked part-time on the Sun Valley sports desk for our old friend, Don Anderson. One summer I even guided fishermen for him, but I found myself feeling too much like a whore to be able to deal in that way with what I like to do best. The only occasion I remember being glad I was guiding a novice fisherman was occasioned by taking out a fisherman who was totally blind. I thought the whole thing would be a disaster but, instead, found him enthusiastic and full of healthy curiosity. A pianist, he had excellent manual dexterity and, after I had rigged his fly rod for him and gotten him into a pair of waders, we waded into an easy stretch of lower Silver Creek where there were some uncautious small trout which might be relied on to hit a dragging wet fly. He managed to get some line out, following instructions well, and soon hooked a small rainbow and brought it in close enough for me to land. he felt the fish in the mesh of the net with his fingers then asked me to release it. We worked down a little farther and he caught a couple more before wading back to the bank where we sat with our feet in the water and smoked a couple of cigarettes. On the way back to the Valley I asked him how he liked the fishing. He said it had been one of the best experiences of his life but what he enjoyed most was wading and feeling the current pressing against his legs through the waders. He had never waded in water before, except for sitting in a bathtub or a pool.

Although most of my experiences as a guide were somewhat more disillusioning, I understand the need for good guides and have used their services on many occasions. What I object to most about guide trips is trying to teach fundamentals to complete novices who really have no long-term interest in the sport. They're looking for a simple victory instead of making an effort to prepare themselves in advance by reading good books and learning to cast with such instructional aids as the video tapes now commonly available on the subject. There are already enough people crowding streams without trying to recruit more simply because they have the ability to pay. Good trout streams are a finite resource, and casual sportsmen are better off on the golf course or the tennis courts. In fact, I have adopted a new motto: "A kid on the tennis courts is a kid off the stream."

In addition to my work on the sports desk, I was persuaded to write a weekly column for the local paper by the publisher who skipped town two years later owing me a year's pay. I wasn't alone as it turned out. None of the other columnists had been paid either and had, like me, subsisted on the empty promise of a penny a word. Insult was added to injury by the fact that I also wrote, for the same publisher, a column for her monthly paper.

My progress from amateur to professional writer was the result of a wonderful invitation from Patrick to come out to East Africa. Puck and I had seen a lot of him when he came to Berkeley with his wife and daughter to work on a doctorate in zoology. Unfortunately, his wife's untimely death precluded his completing the work and he went back to Africa with his small daughter. He got the job he had been training for anyway at the East African College of Wildlife Management on the south slopes of Mt. Kilimanjaro in the north of Tanzania. It was a good job, and perhaps best of all, his salary was tax exempt. He kindly shared his bounty with us by extending an invitation for Puck and me to come out at his expense and go on safari. We were also to get in some fishing out of his weekend bungalow on the coast of the Indian Ocean at Pangani, where he kept a small fishing boat.

After we had made our travel plans, I arranged to meet with Arnold Gingrich in New York. Gingrich had been a close friend of Papa's for years during the time Papa was writing for *Esquire,* but since his recent marriage to Jane Mason, who had once been a flame of Papa's (or perhaps I should say that she was more like a beautiful moth attracted by Papa's flame),

Gingrich's view of Papa had somehow changed. Be that as it may, he was a lovely man with every goodly grace, and he was a dedicated fly fisherman and a member of Charles Ritz' magic circle, the International Fario Club. Gingrich and I had become friends through fishing and I approached him with the idea of my doing a piece for him on the forthcoming African trip. The safari part was to be with a white hunter named Clary Palmer Wilson who had been a young apprentice with the Kudu hunter in Papa's *Green Hills of Africa.* The young Wilson had once visited Papa's and Charles Thompson's camp with a Kudu trophy that turned poor Papa green with envy.

The story idea caught Gingrich's attention and he arranged for me to spend some time with Harold Hayes. Hayes was late for the meeting but spared me enough time to tell me to keep the story as personal as possible and then had a thousand dollar advance issued to me. I still owe that story to *Esquire* and they never wrote to goose me along, so I can only assume Gingrich absorbed the loss himself. He's gone now but I still owe him one, and I'll repay it one day.

While in New York, I also contacted Clare Conley who was then editor-in-chief of *Field & Stream* and we talked about my doing some fishing pieces for him and arranged to get together again when I returned from Africa.

The African trip was unforgettable. The beauty of Tanzania was so different from anything Puck or I had ever seen. We were continually amazed by the color combinations in birds, plants, and animals. The birds were the most striking of all and we never ceased to marvel at the gem-bright colors of the bee eaters and the uncounted species of eagles and other birds of prey. I shot very little, and not especially well when I did, with one of the school-issue .375s Patrick brought along for me. Patrick showed us lots of country in the wilds of the Selous Game Reserve, and the Palmer Wilson camp was delightful, with wonderful food, especially when we had wild game to eat.

Martha Gellhorn spent part of every year in Africa and was with us on the safari at Patrick's invitation. She kept wondering aloud how Patrick could possibly have brought us to this god-awful, hot, unbearably humid pest hole full of bilharzia and heaven-knows-what other dread diseases. Puck loved the beauty and the animals but she suffered from the heat and the humidity which never let up day or night. Marty and Puck left camp a week early, and Puck had a chance to spend some time in Dar-es-Salaam at the Twiga Hotel where there were ceiling fans and even air cooling, plus a roof-garden restaurant, which made waiting for Pat and me to come out of the bush rather more enjoyable.

Pat wanted me to try for a lion but it was so hot the beasts wouldn't come out in the daytime. My best shooting remained the old bull Cape buffalo I had shot before Puck and Marty's departure. Pat had made me challenge him to make him charge, which he did, and I had to shoot four times, the last to put him out of pain after he was down. Pat said it was also important to be sure he was dead since they are the most dangerous of animals when wounded. He was not a great trophy. This part of Africa was not an area for big trophies but, rather, a place where there was an unbelievable multitude of game, and without a doubt the impala capital of the world.

After a beautiful drive from Dar to Pangani, we spent a week at Pat's seaside bungalow with fresh spiny lobster whenever we wanted it and a wide selection of marvelous fish. Patrick loves deep-sea fishing so I kept a fly trolling behind the boat on my fly rod and we had to keep stopping so I could land the fish I caught. Altogether, while trolling and casting from shore and around a small atoll on the edge of the Pemba Channel, I caught twenty-seven different species of fish on the fly, including everything from small, brightly-colored reef species to dolphin in the blue water, and I had one big shark for a short while which had swallowed a tuna I was fighting.

*   *   *

I did a piece that year after getting back home for *Field & Stream* on North Umpqua steelhead and another for *National Wildlife* magazine on steelhead and the problems besetting the species at the time. The *Field & Stream* connection got me a chance to meet and hunt chukar partridge with Ted Trueblood, the most distinguished sportsman in Idaho and a great conservationist who clearly understood the relationship which allows a man to hunt and fish for a prey he loves, a relationship that eventually leads him to give his best efforts toward preserving intact the natural habitats those species need to survive. I was then put on the *Field & Stream* payroll as Northwest Field Editor, which meant contributing an annual roundup of fishing prospects in my region and any other pieces I could produce that might fit.

One day, sometime later, I received a call from Denis Brian who was putting together a book which was eventually titled *Murderers and Other Friendly People.* It was mainly a book of interviews with interviewers, except for one part called "The Hemingway Hunters" in which he included separate interviews with Mary and me. When I saw the book, I was struck by how similar our answers had been to the questions put to us by Brian; but he hit a mark with me in his last question, which was, "Do you think about your father a lot?" My answer was that I did not, as a habit, but that I kept thinking what a wonderful old man he would have made if he had learned how, and further, I didn't think he'd ever faced up to becoming old. Offered the same question now, I would add the feeling I felt that night when Mary and I had stayed up late talking things out before the funeral: "Poor Papa . . . Poor old Papa."

*   *   *

All of a sudden it was 1970 and not only was it a gubernatorial election year but there were some hot environmental issues dividing opinion in our state. This was early on, and environmentalists had had few successes, particularly in those states whose orientation was more rural than urban. In Idaho there were two issues that loomed large and in which the outcome meant much to me personally. The first was the possibility of a giant molybdenum mining operation in the White Cloud Mountains close to where we lived which would badly pollute a primary salmon and steelhead spawning stream as well as ruin a giant piece of completely pristine country used by thousands every year to find the magnificent solace only wilderness can give to those who approach it with respect.

The threatened area was a place where Muffet, Margot, and I had hiked years before on the day after Muffet's first beer bust. The hard hike and overnight campout helped instill in her a healthy respect for the aftereffects of abusing drink. The proposed mine was an issue which the incumbent Governor, widely known as "Dumb Don", stood four-square behind, and the conventional wisdom was that he would win reelection and the mining issue would in no way hinder him. It was an issue, however, which could swing an election if enough of the general public could be made aware of what was really being stolen from them should the mine project go through as envisoned.

The second issue was not quite as immediate but was just as

surely sinister in its implications. It involved the building of a giant impassable dam at a location called High Mountain Sheep on the lower end of what remained of the Hell's Canyon of the Snake River after previous dams in the upper and middle reaches had effectively blocked all upstream migration of salmon and steelhead to the historically important spawning streams above the canyon. Although a program had been initiated to transfer all the fish that still ran up the Middle Snake to a hatchery operation in the Salmon River drainage, it was no substitute for the real thing. The proposed dam would also have flooded an area which has since proved itself to be a valuable and irreplaceable national treasure.

The governor's challenger took the risky stand of supporting the protection of Idaho's natural resources, and with a lot of letter-writing and speaking around the state, he and his supporters, who included me, managed to win over public support on these issues, as well as the election. I was, and am, a Republican, and I formed a Republicans-for-Andrus group which may or may not have been helpful. The new governor apparently thought so and he appointed me to the most challenging, gratifying, and exciting job I have ever had; I became a member of the Idaho Fish & Game Commission.

It was a six-year appointment and it was filled with controversy from the very beginning. For a while it even looked dicey as to whether or not my appointment would be ratified by the State Senate, which was heavily weighted with strongly rural elements who viewed environmentalists as the new evil in the world sent by the devil to deprive them of their God-given rights to do any damn thing they wanted to their own land. Somehow or other, the older and very valid concept of stewardship of the land had been lost along the way, yet I know that most Idahonians really feel a sense of stewardship when their dander isn't up. I was finally able to convince them I wasn't a Socialist or a Communist and that I truly did believe in private property and, despite a delegation of disgruntled sportsmen from my own area whose chief honcho felt he had been overlooked for the commissioner's job, I was confirmed with only one dissenting vote.

The following six years was a period of education, exercising of opportunities, and a personal campaign to change some prevailing points of view about fisheries management in particular, where I could at least pretend a little theoretical expertise.

A marvelous coincidence had created a situation which was extremely helpful to me in keeping a step ahead, so to speak. My best friend, a fly-fishing attorney *cum* wildlife photographer named Dan Callaghan, and Frank Moore, my friend from Steamboat on the North Umpqua, were both serving as fish and game commissioners in Oregon and kept me current on all the new developments there. Dan and I first met at Steamboat in 1962, the year after my father's death, when I arrived in camp from Mill Valley with a beautiful eleven-pound steelhead I caught along the way and brought to show to Frank Moore. Frank said he wanted me to meet somebody and suggested I bring the fish along to the guy's cabin.

It seemed this fellow had a bad case of flu and was lying in bed, miserable. We went down and Frank introduced me to the pitiful figure of one Dan Callaghan, obviously suffering from the tortures of the damned, eyes and nose swollen. I shoved the steelhead in front of him and a remarkable transformation took place. Within minutes he was up, clear-eyed, and ready to go fishing. It turned out, however, that nothing could be done about his nose. That's the way it always was, I found out later. We became fishing partners then and there and we both learned from each other and shared all new knowledge, as friends will, and over the years we've fished so many places together we've lost count.

Dan and I had met a young biologist named Dick Vincent up in Montana. He was conducting some experiments in the effects of stocking hatchery trout on the populations of wild trout and he was doing it in different water types but all in streams and rivers. His findings, we learned, were conclusive and indicated that areas where there was no stocking of adult hatchery trout had much better populations of wild trout. The survival rate for hatchery trout through the severe winters was negligible, but their very presence in streams where they were put caused abnormal conditions for the wild fish. Wild fish were driven out by the hatchery stock much the way Indians were driven out by settlers or the way farmers flee from developers.

The stocking of so-called catchable trout had become a way of life in Idaho and a commissioner who was against it would appear to be a threat to jobs and careers built around stocking. Anyway, I was able to persuade my fellow commissioners that it was something that would bear looking into and that we should do something about it. Finally we did, and we did it without jeopardizing any of the hatchery jobs because we determined where their efforts could be most effective. The process was very intricate and much more complicated than it appears, and it took years, but during the course of my six-year term we were able to bring about some of the most forward-looking fisheries policies anywhere in the world, including the institution of vast areas of catch-and-release fishing in waters which otherwise could not withstand the heavy burden put upon them by the ever-increasing number of sport-hungry anglers. The amazing part was that home folks started accepting these new policies because our plans had included something for everybody.

For all the catch-and-release fisheries on first-rate streams lost to the meat fishermen, there were increased opportunities in reservoirs and lakes where the bulk of the hatchery fish were being put in as youngsters, and where the vast quantities of feed allowed them to grow into fat fare for the table. I felt that a new atittude toward sportsmanship was emerging and a greater acceptance of sport for its own sake was taking hold, to the point that *macho* no longer meant a long string of dead fish. I personally encourage the policy that one should always believe any fisherman who tells you about the huge number of giant fish he has caught and released, no matter what a dedicated liar you know him to be. Otherwise, he will feel constrained to kill what fish he catches to prove his superior skill.

They were a wonderful six years and by the time they came to an end—when I refused the new governor's suggestion that I accept reappointment—I had seen great changes take place and the beginnings of even greater changes to come. I suppose I made a few enemies, but most of the people I came in contact with were men and women with whom I felt a strong bond. My fellow commissioners, who came from every walk of life, all of whom arrived on the scene with their own deeply-entrenched points of view, did what they felt was best for the resources with which we had been entrusted and for the people whose careers and futures were our responsibility for a short period of time. The professionals in the department proved their dedication time and again for relatively low pay and a lot of public scorn. They are the real heroes of the ongoing fight to preserve our natural heritage for generations to come.

The Federation of Fly Fishermen was organized in the late sixties to represent the interests of fly fishermen, first in America, and then around the world. I attended the first of its conclaves with Dan Callaghan in Jackson Hole, Wyoming, and, believe it or not, we took our wives along. It was a wonderful experience because it was close to outstanding fishing and because we were able to meet some of the greats of fly fishing. While there, we were also able to help influence the choice of Sun Valley as a site for one of the next annual conclaves. In view of the fame of Silver Creek and the resort itself, it wasn't so difficult a feat.

The first conclave at Sun Valley was a special treat for me for two reasons. I had a chance to renew my friendship with Roderick Haig-Brown, whom I first met on his own stretch of the Campbell River in British Columbia in 1955. There he had generously turned into reality the wonders I had read about so avidly in his fine books. No finer writer about nature's wonders, as viewed by a fisherman, ever lived. Rod and his loving wife, Ann, joined us for the conclave and for a few days thereafter when he found one of the tributaries of Silver Creek an evocative reminder of his beloved Frome in Wiltshire, the English chalk stream where he'd learned to fish as a boy.

One evening we had a picnic there. After we'd all had more than a few nips of the stuff that killed Dr. McWalsey, one of my friends, Jim Davies, crept to a place in the willows just above the spot where Rod was making a few farewell casts in the fading light. He sneakily threw several of the abundant meadow muffins (or cattle droppings) into the water near the bushes about a minute apart, convincing Rod there was a gigantic trout feeding in the dark shadows above him. We dared not disabuse him, and I hope he always carried with him the memory of that big gulper in the meadow.

Some of my most exciting fishing adventures I owe to another friend I met at a Sun Valley conclave, Ernie Schwiebert. Ernie is as good a fishing author as there is and his works had guided me well long before I met him. Because of him I had my first chance to fish in Chile, where I have returned year after year to turn late winter into early fall. Ernie took me first just before Christmas and my appetite was permanently whetted for the lovely country near Lago Ranco, where Adrian Dufflocq runs a great lodge for visiting fly fishermen.

It was also through Ernie that Ed Rice made an Alaskan dream trip possible for me, to Kulik and later to Enchanted Lake. I was supposed to be substituting as Ernie's photographer, since Dan Callaghan couldn't make it because of prior business. Poor Ernie! When he needed me to take photos of the enormous rainbows he was hooking and playing with the casual skill of a true master, I was so busy with my own fish that I refused to move from the hot spot I had found where I was taking the biggest rainbows I had ever seen. Result? No pictures, save a few of the gang and of the scenery; not the stuff a writer needs to illustrate the pages of his stories.

A conclave friendship led to a memorable test of Western steelheaders against the masters of the Atlantic salmon on the famed Grand Cascapedia as guests of Nathaniel Reed, then Assistant Secretary of the Interior for Fish, Wildlife, and Parks. What a lineup it was: Reed, Grant, and Schwiebert *versus* Moore, Callaghan, and Hemingway. The home team won, but it was close. Ernie lost a great fish and felt worse about it than I would have thought it warranted. He explained that he needed that fish for the hungry maws of those outdoors magazines which insist on perpetual success and not the reality of oft-confronted failure, the stuff of learning. But such failures couldn't hold down a man of Ernie's caliber for long; he was the man who taught me that "Anything worth doing at all is worth doing to excess!"

I owe my brother Pat for the great George River of Ungava and the continuing friendships with Lou and Tom Black, and that little Italian comedian who needs two ordinary men to balance the other end of the canoe, Dick Lumenello, known to his friends as "Captain Salmon." The pals one makes in the course of a lifetime of fishing are irreplaceable. Though I prefer to fish and hunt alone, a large part of the wealth I have is in the friends who shared the camps and the evening fellowship and never ceased to plan the ultimate trip.

While all my fishing expeditions were going on, those three girls of ours wouldn't stop growing and getting themselves involved in wondrous things. Puck and I tried to keep a modicum of control over the directions they might take, but all of them seemed to have popped into the world intent on making it their oyster.

Muffet fell in love, then fell in love again, then helped write a novel, co-authorized a fine cookbook on gourmet picnics which still sells very well, then fell in love and married, and then, for reasons which are no one's business but their own, divorced and returned to Sun Valley which, in our case, is not too bad a place to be, for all of us.

Margot and a pal took charge of press relations for the Evel Knevil Snake River Canyon Jump as seventeen- and eighteen-year-old impresarios, and the multitudes of photographers who shot her picture agreed that it was impossible to take a bad one of her, which led to her leaving without our blessing to make her fortune in New York. Before I could stop fishing long enough to rescue her, she was on the cover of *Time* with the most lucrative modeling contract ever awarded until then. What can I say? Now she's learning how to keep a little of what she makes and, though she's had her rough times, her spirit is undaunted.

Mariel was thrust into the limelight at thirteen when, the most gifted ski racer of the three, she took a part in Margot's first movie and, unwittingly, stole the show, and she hasn't stopped for long any time since. She's bright and talented and has the makings of a great actress. She's just taken on a lifetime partner and her future is without limit. Throughout a bad time in Puck's life, when the odds looked long and gloomy, Mariel was the catalyst who made her mother fight to live and win.

I have been quoted as saying that I spent the first fifty years of my life being the son of a famous father and am now spending the last fifty as the father of famous children. There's a lot of truth in that. The only waves I have made have been in the currents of trout and salmon streams, and now that our fledglings are all out of the nest, that's where I propose to continue to make waves.

I did once, however, find out that I was a public figure. It started with an incident of what my friend, Mike Burke, called "Outrageous Good Fortune." I had bought a ticket in a fund-raising raffle and won. I won a Mercedes 280 SEL, and one man, seated at the table with us, said nothing but seemed visibly resentful. He was the editor/publisher of one of the valley newspapers and is now long-gone. Soon thereafter, having inherited a sum of money when Paul Mowrer died, I bought a piece of worthless land down in the lava desert south of us. I bought it because it had a marginal trout stream flowing through it which intrigued me with its potential under proper management. I did not know at the time that the Fish & Game

Commission had once considered it for purchase; no such proposal had ever come before me while I had been a commissioner.

Nevertheless, there appeared in that editor/publisher's newspaper a signed piece by a regular contributor accusing me of purchasing the land fraudulently with a view to reselling it at a huge profit based on inside knowledge I had acquired as a Fish & Game Commissioner. It was a patently false accusation but, like all such things, it hit me right in the gut and I took legal action. That's when the court declared that I was, in fact, a public figure, and if I could not prove malice on the part of the writer, the editor, or the paper (which refused to publish a retraction), I simply had no further recourse under the law. The lower court's view was upheld in the Idaho Supreme Court, but at least the facts had been brought into the open.

I loved that piece of land out in the middle of nowhere, and one year I actually spent a part of at least 200 days fishing on it and doing such things as planting willow shoots and reed canary grass for bank cover. I picked up old cans left from the original homestead which had gone broke in the depression when the folks there had sold their best water rights for enough cash to try to make a start somewhere else. The only rights left were the use of excess high water during runoff, not enough at the right time to be able to farm the small bits of arable land scattered between the lava hummocks. There had been an old half-ruined house there, but vandals had burned it down, and vandals acting after the first libel was published, no doubt thinking they were doing the "right thing" to that uppity dude from Sun Valley, set fire to the land as well and burned vast acreages of public land as well as mine.

I had hoped someday to build a small, rustic shelter on a lava dome next to a favorite pool for family picnics after a day of fishing. I had even entertained the thought of a second home there, but the cost of bringing in electricity, and a deep well to be drilled through solid rock, were prohibitive. I decided the best way to enforce my wish that it be kept a place for fly fishermen exclusively (that stretch made up only a tiny percentage of the total stream's length and all the rest was open to any kind of fishing) was to give it to the Idaho Parks Foundation with the proviso that they assure that it be made exclusively available for catch-and-release fly fishing in perpetuity.

The Idaho Parks Foundation was glad to accept these conditions and they reached a management agreement with the Fish & Game Department for their enforcement. The area is named for Papa's best friend in Idaho, Taylor "Bear Tracks" Williams, and it has a sign stating that it was a gift to the people of Idaho from John H. and Byra L. Hemingway. Through the introduction of brown trout and the elimination of grazing, that area has become one of the finest pieces of desert fishing water anywhere, and there are some giant surprises lurking there, including rattlesnakes.

I still find signs of poaching by bait fishermen who can't resist what obviously has become better fishing because of the stricter management. The "Fly Fishing Catch and Release Only" sign will be the finest epitaph that I can have in that far-off time when I will have fished for my last trout and fired my last shell.

I still have many untold tales of fishing and hunting, which I will spare you. I'm reserving them for those among my kindred spirits who, like me, dream the closed season long of the shooting of swift birds in flight, and of the dogs, all good, some great, who point and fetch; and for those as well who, like me, dream of unfished streams yet to explore and of those small past triumphs we all so magnify in our winter thoughts.

AFTERWORD

My mother followed Paul in death in 1979 after a severe deterioration of her health. The news of her final illness caught me driving east with a load of household goods for Mariel who had just moved to New York. I was fortunate to be able to be with her during her last few days. She was eighty-nine years old and had been lovingly cared for by my cousin, Fonchen, and her husband, Bill Lord, in Lakeland, Florida. Her biography, *Hadley,* had been written some years before by Alice Sokoloff, steering clear of some of the revelations she had frankly made to Alice on tape. Alice kindly made those tapes available to me which dealt with her relationship with Papa. In them, Mother expressed the same view that Pauline had held, to the effect that Papa was such an unusual and special person that one should forgive him his very human failings. I have long held with the same point of view, but I would like to point out that, in my opinion, those failings, while real enough, were neither so numerous nor so blatant as is implied in the Carlos Baker biography. New research would appear to bear out my opinion.

I can, however, sympathize with the enormity of Baker's task since I have recently been presented evidence that there are glaring blanks and possible errors in my personal recollections of events in my own "misadventures." I expect I shall come across even more such evidence as old friends read this book and react each in their own way. I hope it will turn up some of those facts I have been unable to find.

Everyone's view of a great man is colored by what they wish to see. In Cuba, for example, Papa is viewed as a supporter of the revolution. The fishermen of Cojímar chipped in and paid for a bust of him to be erected in the plaza between the Terraza Cafe and the old Spanish fort. It is quite handsome and they all say it looks much like him. When I saw it, I was struck by its obvious resemblance to Lenin, on one of whose mass-produced busts I believe the beard was slightly altered to try to make it resemble Papa's.

One of the most frequent questions I have been asked in the

years since my father's death has to do with my opinion regarding the merits of the various books which have been written about him. Usually the question is in the form of, "What do you think of Hotchner's book, *Papa Hemingway?* Or, "Why does Baker seem to have such a hard-on for Hemingway?

Whatever the form, the questions have usually elicited a quick and not-thoroughly-thought-out response from me. A good interviewer, like Denis Brian, can get the ball rolling like that and then go on to draw out further comments which I have given, almost subconsciously, and which tend to reflect my gut reaction at the time. Such reactions, however, have never been the result of deep or searching thought. If anything, I have avoided that for a good many years and, thus, kept my life simple and aimed at survival and enjoyment of the things and people I love most deeply.

I think this is, however, a place to treat the subject from my point of view in more than a cursory manner. Also, it may be my only opportunity to do so.

First, I would like to explain why I feel as I do about Carlos Baker's biography of my father. My objections to it are to what I perceive as his attitudes toward my father. His book is an absolute necessity to anyone doing anything in research about Hemingway because it is so full of detail. It is not all accurate, but it is very close and is accurate according to the sources available to Baker at the time.

Once, while using it to check out something brought up by a friend of mine, Denne Petitclerc, I noted something of interest and then started going through the book with a marker highlighting all the adverbs Baker used to describe the manner in which Papa did, said, or reacted to anything. What was revealing was that the vast majority of adverbs were negative in their implications and yet were the paint Baker used to color Papa in the book. I believe this was probably subconscious and I believe it was the result of his not having had the opportunity to meet his subject and thus having to rely most heavily on those he came to believe knew him best.

In particular, I think Baker relied heavily on the person to whom (along with his wife) he had dedicated the book: Buck Lanham. Certainly Buck was a man Papa would have approved of as a witness in his behalf. He represented many of the qualities Papa most admired: a man of action, a military man of some stature yet a combat soldier, a man who had been with Papa during some moments of which Papa was inordinately proud, a witness to his correct and even courageous behaviour under combat stress.

But I believe Papa made a mistake in believing that Buck Lanham was, indeed, his best friend. I think it becomes clear as one reads Baker that Buck changed his view of my father with the passage of time and with the onset of changes in my father's personality which occurred as he approached his last few years. Furthermore, I believe that Buck's wife, whom Papa considered a bitch of the first water and said so to me, never forgave Papa for not taking her seriously and, being a tough lady, her view of Papa was sure to wear down Buck's resistance after a time.

In any case, it is hard for any one individual to see the many facets of another man's personality or character, or to be patient with the changes for the worse which may occur. Buck Lanham's view of Papa changed with time and it was surely a big factor in coloring Baker's overall representation of my father. When I first read *Ernest Hemingway: A Life Story,* my initial reaction was, "Who the hell is he writing about? It sure isn't anyone I know!"

Of course, I was wrong in a way, for the man Baker wrote about did exist for those people who viewed him that way. The tragedy is that Papa thought he had actually joined Buck Lanham's club, something you could never really do without a service academy ring.

Hotchner's book is a whole different story. It is a very complicated story as well. I was around some of the time while Papa and Hotch were good frinds and, let me assure you that they were good friends, despite any efforts on Mary Hemingway's part to erase that fact. His book, for all its faults, gives the best account of what it was like to be around Papa during the period of time Hotch knew him. Mary calls it totally inaccurate, but the parts where I was around are true, and my own harshest criticism of the book lies in the way it leans over backward to portray Mary Hemingway in the best possible light. She objected to it legally on the basis that Hotchner used letters from Papa for much of his material and that, further, Papa had specifically forbidden the publication of any of his letters. She continued to insist on this principle despite using many of Papa's letters in her own work.

I cannot help but believe that her real objection to Hotchner was that he was infringing on what she considered her own personal territory, one on which she intended to write, herself, and one in which she would brook no interference, particularly from Hotch, whom she considered an opportunist.

I have to state right here that one thing I am not is a scholar. Especially am I not a Hemingway scholar, and for that reason I have not read most of the scholarly books written about him, except a few cursorily. Those I have read were interesting, but most had the fault of having a thesis of some sort, or a whole series of them. I find it amusing to recall that Papa said, on learning that a course was being offered at Princeton with him as the subject: "If I could disguise myself as a student and attend that course incognito, I'd bet anything I couldn't pass."

About five or six years ago I started talking regularly on the telephone, and then on one or two occasions in person, with Peter Griffin who had obtained Mary's permission to do a biography of Papa with access to all of the material which has become available to scholars: the material Baker used and more. Having more time available than I had had before, I tried to be as helpful as possible and, following my mother's death, I made available to him (and to the Kennedy Library) those letters of my mother's which she had previously withheld, which covered the period when she and my father were courting. I was struck by Griffin's insight into my father's personality and by some of the things he had dug out for himself which should have been recognized before but weren't. His first volume about my father's early years (published in 1985 by Oxford University Press) portrays a person who seems to be very much alive with all of the strengths and weaknesses one might expect. I was so impressed I wrote a foreword to it.

As the result of an encounter with Professor James Nagel of Northeastern University, I have come to learn about an organization called the Hemingway Society. Of course, I should have known about it long before, but I was pleased to learn that one of its purposes is to elicit cooperation between all its members in the sharing of information, new discoveries or findings, or whatever may add further knowledge of their subject. One thing about which I believe all these scholars would agree is that the subject of their research would have been totally shocked to find himself thus institutionalized.

While all of this is interesting, and even fascinating to some, and while I must admit I have enjoyed a bit of fanning of the flames of controversy, I think it often leads us to lose sight of the main point: Ernest Hemingway was, above all else, a writer, and, although his life was exciting, it is his work which is truly important.

Much of his posthumous work would have been rejected out of hand by his own critical faculty without extensive rewriting — cutting and pruning he would have refused to have anyone do but himself. All of his posthumous work should be viewed in this light, as different people have participated in the "editing" process.

Over the twenty five years since his death much of his posthumous work has been published with varying results and acceptance. My brothers and I have only recently participated in the decisions of whether or not to publish. Our influence was first felt in the decision finally to publish *The Dangerous Summer* with the insistence that the comic and very human sequences in which A.E. Hotchner played a role not be deleted as had first been proposed to us.

I believe Scribner's was surprised at the success of the book and were fortunate in obtaining the services of a fine new young editor they put to work on the much-examined work known as *The Garden of Eden*. Tom Jencks, correctly I believe, saw the true thread of the story, and did the sort of pruning job I surmise Papa would have done. I have read it as edited and find it to be of exceptional quality, giving me a spooky sense of the return of the master. Its publication date, May 1986, is the same as for this book. Although very few have read it, there is a fantastic amount of gossip about it, based on little more than opinions by "experts" who had made previous pronouncements on the unpublishability of the material. The book is fascinating and will shake up more than a few literati. It is deceptive and not at all necessarily what it appears to be. It goes far to illustrate that, while a writer like Papa makes use of actual people, incidents and places he has known or heard about, what he writes he creates and it is always a mistake to try to put the name of a real person to a character in his fiction.

Publicity attendant on the first presentation of the Paris-Ritz Hemingway Prize brought me two voices from the past. One was Jean de Marcilly, with whom I once spent a long evening driving from where he had exfiltrated German territory on a tragic night when several of his resistance comrades were shot through the stupidity of a bunch of overzealous GIs. The other was in the form of a letter from a lady who had been a young girl in Le Bousquet d'Orb at the time of its liberation. She wrote me about her family, the Greniers, and included some snapshots they had taken of Jim Russell and me with two Frenchmen and an American whom I now remember as a shot-down flyer who attached himself to the local resistance. One of those photographs is included in the picture section of this book.

When Dan Callaghan and I traveled to the Cévènnes to retrace some of my steps in those days, I discovered that the French Maquisard, Robert, was really René Ribaud. When we found him in 1977 he told us that the local Communist Party decided to repay him for having helped us and the FFI by putting him in "quarantine," forcing him out of the restaurant business, and making him work in the mine under the bullying domination of their union until retirement age. Then, after retirement, he became chef at the Hotel du Nord in Le Bousquet. We shed some tears together, then he showed us the drop zone where we had landed that night, along with several other memorable places. Many of the old gang were still around and they hosted a party to end all parties for us in the bar next to his kitchen at the hotel. Dan and I both had the flu and almost died of the hospitality, but after all those difficult years, we were glad to see that things were now going well for Robert.

In his book, *Wild Bill Donovan: The Last Hero,* Anthony Cave Brown describes my mission according to the record and attributes the code name *Étoile* to it. I had forgotten that. The names of people in other parts of the mission are only vaguely familiar to me now, though one, E. Ernouf, rings a bell. I think I must have met him either after or during training. Perhaps it's like Colonel LeSouef was wont to say: "I say, chaps. You do realize, don't you, that the lack of phosphorus in our diet affects our memory? Phosphorus is most important for one's memory and the lack of it may cause you to be forgetful."

Fish, I'm told, are a good source of phosphorus. I think I may have to start eating more of them.

INDEX